The Rose and the Pomegranate

By

Leah Toole

The Rose and the Pomegranate

Copyright © 2024 Leah Toole. All rights reserved.

All rights reserved. No part of this publication may be reproduced, stored, or transmitted in any form or by any means, whether electronic, mechanical, or photocopying, recording, scanning, or otherwise without written permission from the author.
It is illegal to copy this book or any parts of it, post it to a website, or distribute it by any other means without permission.

Also by Leah Toole

The Tudor Heirs Series

I – The Saddest Princess
...
II – The Haunted Queen
...
III – The Puppet King
...
IV – The Forgotten Prince

To Bella.
For making me feel accomplished, and for looking at me with the purest regard. Knowing that I make you proud with my writing is reason enough never to stop.

Your Mummy

Part I

Sometimes, the slowest burn
forges the strongest fire.

Chapter I

14th November 1501
St. Paul's Cathedral, London

Fifteen-year-old Catalina de Aragon was getting married.
According to the contract arranged over a decade ago, she was to marry the English King and Queen's heir, their eldest son Prince Arthur, to finalise the alliance between their two countries of Spain and England.
Catalina had arrived in the wet and grey country just ten days earlier and had had very little time to adjust to the new weather, language, and customs, before being prepared for the wedding ceremony.
She would never have admitted to it, but she was frightened and anxious of this new life, so far away from all that was familiar. But Catalina knew what was expected of her, for she was the portrait of a well-bred princess. Any untoward emotions were to be concealed, borne in silence.
As the daughter of the great Isabella de Castille and Ferdinand de Aragon – the two co-ruling Catholic monarchs of the most powerful regions of Spain – Catalina had known from a very young age what it meant to be a woman of high birth: they were married off to broker alliances.
But Prince Arthur, whom she had only officially met upon her arrival on the muddy shores of England, appeared to be good-natured; his many letters over the years having given her a glimpse of the young man she had been promised to since the age of three.
But on the morning of her wedding, despite the rigorous sense of propriety that had been instilled in her, she could not stop her hands from shaking.

*

By mid-morning, Catalina and her entourage of Spanish ladies made their way to St Paul's Cathedral where the ceremony was to take place.

The city and the holy building were grey and dreary, so vastly different to the vibrant and colourful life she had left behind, where different shades of blue and terracotta tiles made up the walls of the Alhambra.

She was met at the entrance of the Cathedral by a young boy with bright orange curls, who would soon be her brother-in-law. He flashed her an excited grin and bounced from one foot to the other, for it was he who would walk her down the aisle to her betrothed.

"My lady," Prince Harry said as he offered her his arm.

Catalina smiled and took Prince Harry's arm, having to lean into him slightly as they walked, for at the age of just ten-years-old, the prince was a fair bit shorter than Catalina.

Trumpets sounded as they took their first step down the walkway, which was covered with dark red carpet that had been tacked down for this special occasion.

Catalina felt the murmurs of the English and Spanish nobility as she was escorted towards the altar, and for a moment she wondered if they were mumbles of approval for her, or for the charismatic prince that led her, grinning brightly, as they walked through the great crowd.

The Spanish Princess was wearing a dress of white satin embroidered with pearls and stitched with gold thread, pleated in the Spanish style. She wore a white silk veil bordered with gold and precious stones, almost as long as her waist-length hair, which hung loose down her back and over her shoulders – a symbol of her virginity.

Her round cheeks were flushed, giving her pale skin a rosy glow, and her full lips were slightly curved upwards in a nervous smile.

She was a sight to behold.

And her betrothed, Prince Arthur, made that quite clear when he turned to watch her approach, his eyes wide in awe, his mouth hanging slightly open in appreciation.

Catalina dropped her gaze at his reaction, her small smile widening at his approval.

At the high altar where the ceremony was to take place, Prince Harry unlocked their arms and delivered the bride to his older brother, but not before grinning brazenly and winking at the couple.

The nuptial mass lasted for three hours, the Archbishop of Canterbury uniting England and Spain with much ceremony and tradition.

Throughout the ceremony, Catalina had noticed Arthur cautiously stealing sidelong glances at her, the princess sometimes catching his eye and smiling shyly at him from under her veil. It was all the communication they were allowed during the grandiose service, but it was enough to put Catalina at ease, realising that he, too, was nervous of the life of matrimony that lay ahead of them.

Baynard's Castle, London

Due to the couples' young age – both of them fifteen-years-old – they were not expected to consummate their marriage during the bedding ceremony, which took place on the eve of their wedding day.

Instead, the bishop merely blessed the marriage bed while the couple lay as stiff as two boards underneath the blankets, the crowd of noble lords and ladies surrounding them as witnesses.

Later, after the royal chambers had emptied out, Catalina was hoping to engage in small talk with her new husband, in an effort to get to know each other better.

She lay on her back, her hands interlocked over her chest, the fingers picking and pulling at each other in her awkwardness. She wondered if he would say the first thing, or if she should turn to him and smile, but her nerves kept her frozen, staring up at the ceiling.

She could see Arthur in her peripheral vision, laying beside her just as petrified as she, his arms on either side of him, tucked underneath the blanket.

She felt something nudge her side then, one tiny, cold graze of his pinkie finger as he had tentatively crossed the gap between them underneath the covers. Instinctively, Catalina flinched at the cold touch and immediately wished she hadn't.

Quite abruptly, Prince Arthur turned on his side then and shuffled as close to the edge of the mattress as he dared without falling off, his back to his new wife.

Catalina bit her lip at her imprudence and covered her face with her hands. She lay there for a few moments, listening to his quick, shallow breathing until it became more rhythmic, and she believed him to have fallen asleep. Only then did she allow herself to move, turning her back on her husband and closing her eyes, her final thought before sleep took her being that tomorrow would be another day.

The following day however, Catalina awoke to an empty bed – his side of the bedsheet having been tucked in neatly and his pillow plumped, though the servants had not yet entered the chambers.

She frowned, not completely surprised by his absence but certainly by his ability and resolve to make the bed. It evoked a strange feeling in her.

It was odd: a prince making his own bed…

The princess sat up and stretched as her ladies entered the rooms then, one of them carrying a silver tray.

"Good morning, Your Grace," her Moorish lady, Lina, said with a bright smile on her face, her small teeth looking exceptionally white against the contrast of her dark skin, "So…how was it?"

She set the tray down on the table by the fireplace and walked over to the princess while her other ladies busied about the rooms lighting the fire and opening the shutters.

Lina sat down on the bed and searched her mistress' face, "Did…"

Catalina met her lady's intense gaze and lightly shook her head. Lina had been in the princess' service for three years, shortly after her Muslim family had converted to Catholicism during the conquest of Granada. Lina was not her real name but the name she had adopted upon entering the princess' royal service, as proof of loyalty: Catalina, after the princess herself, Lina to avoid confusion.

Since her appointment into Catalina's household, the two young women had bonded beyond the boundaries of obligation, a friendship having blossomed despite their vastly differing backgrounds and pasts.

Lina sighed then, a reassuring smile spreading her plump lips, "You were not expected to, on any account," she said, "There's plenty of time for all that."

Catalina nodded and rose from the bed, heading towards the breakfast tray. She peered at the English food – so different from what she was used to in Spain where everything grew fresh and colourful – and a pang of homesickness clenched her stomach.

With an exasperated sigh, the princess sat down and nibbled at the cold cuts of meat and sipped at the warm small ale.

"I have decided to anglicise my name," Catalina said after she had finished her meal, Lina having appeared at her side to remove the tray.

"Katherine," the princess continued, looking up at her lady, "It is only right that I be known henceforth as Katherine, as I am now a Princess of England."

Lina smiled and nodded approvingly, "An excellent idea, Your Grace."

Catalina nodded once, a curt jut of the head, and then she stood, "Well then ladies," she said, "Get me dressed and ready so that I may announce my decision to my lord husband and the English court."

The foreign princess made her way through the grey castle and to the great hall, where she knew the king and queen would be at this time.
Upon entering the vast room, its ceilings so tall one could get lost in it, Catalina immediately felt more at ease, the fires on either side of the great hall warming the place to a temperature she was more accustomed to.
The courtiers all watched as the Spanish Princess made her way towards the king and queen, her new parents-in-law. Her hands were clasped elegantly before her, a rosary bead hanging from them – the very image of piety – and as she and her ladies approached, Catalina was touched to see Queen Elizabeth of York rising from her throne and walking towards her with open arms.

"Welcome, Princess," the queen said, and she embraced her quickly, "I trust you are being taken good care of?"
Catalina smiled and nodded before curtsying to the queen, "Your Grace," she said in friendly greeting.
Queen Elizabeth took Catalina's arm in hers and led her towards the thrones.
Elizabeth of York, Catalina had learned years ago, was the White Rose of York to King Henry Tudor's Red Rose of Lancaster – as symbolised on the Tudor crest itself, the Red and White Roses merged together in unity. She was the daughter of the Yorkist King Edward IV, and her marriage to the Lancastrian Henry Tudor sixteen years prior had brought an end to the thirty-year war that England had been burdened by, the Cousins' War.

And upon Catalina's arrival in England, Queen Elizabeth had been nothing but kind to her, which the young princess had been extremely grateful for.

As they approached the thrones, the queen left Catalina to stand before them as she resumed her seat beside her husband the king, and Elizabeth smiled encouragingly at her new daughter-in-law.

Catalina curtsied elegantly before the monarchs of England, her dress of green velvet ballooning at the sides.

"Your Highnesses," she said, her Spanish accent strong and her English slow and pensive, "I am come to bid that I be known henceforth as 'Katherine'. I wish to immerse myself into my new life here as the Princess of Wales, starting with the anglicisation of my name 'Catalina'. I want the people of England to know that I am theirs, and no longer Spain's, for that life is behind me, and before me, only England."

She met her father-in-law's gaze, his eyes – one slightly lower than the other – reflecting respect and regard back at her.

"So be it," the king replied clearly with a nod of his head, his crown glinting as the sunlight shone through the large stained-glass windows.

Later that day, Prince Arthur, who had snuck out of bed that morning to avoid his new wife, continued to sneak around in the hopes of avoiding her further.

He had steered clear of the great hall where he knew most of the court would be – following their king around, as ever – and instead chose to spend the morning holed up in his royal apartments, his nose deep in his Bible.

But he was not left to his own devices for long, for shortly after noon, his mother entered unannounced, as though she knew he would be hiding away. Which, as his mother, she likely did.

"Oh, Arthur," Queen Elizabeth said before *tutting* in gentle disapproval, "Why do I find you here and not in the hall getting to know your new wife?"

Arthur dropped the book onto his lap and lifted his gaze to meet his mother's, and Elizabeth smiled at her precious boy.

As her firstborn, Arthur had always held a special place in Elizabeth's heart. Though she loved all four of her surviving children equally, she and Arthur had always had a special bond, one that was never addressed aloud but was very much present, nonetheless. He had been the one to turn her into a mother, the one who had brought hope of a bright future for England after decades of civil unrest and war. Arthur was the light at the end of the dark and dismal tunnel of their past, and he would be the one to keep the country at peace after she and her husband were dead and buried.

He was their legacy.

But for now, he was still her little boy – though he had only the day before gotten married – and he clearly needed his mother's guidance on how to overcome this awkward first stage of what it meant to marry for political gains.

"We have nothing in common," Arthur told his mother now, his blue eyes expressing worry, "It was easier to talk to her through letters when she was miles away in Spain."

Elizabeth gently cupped her son's pale cheek with her hand, "You will stumble over conversation to begin with, as is natural," she said, "Your father and I went through the same. But look at us now, completely devoted to one another and with four incredible children to show for it."

Arthur breathed an embarrassed laugh and looked away. Elizabeth removed her hand from his face.

"You must be the one to make the effort, my son," the queen continued, "She has left behind her entire life, left all she has ever known and just this morning given up her birth name, for this union."

Arthur frowned up at his mother.

Elizabeth nodded, "She is to be known as Katherine from now on."

Arthur swung his legs off the bed and inhaled as he looked thoughtfully at the stone floor, "I quite liked her name. Catalina."

Elizabeth laughed, a sweet sound like birdsong, and Arthur rose and offered his mother his arm. She took it, and together they walked out the rooms.

"You and Princess Katherine will be just fine," Queen Elizabeth predicted, "I am sure of it."

Chapter 2

December 1501
Richmond Palace, Surrey

Two weeks later, however, the couple had not yet shared so much as a dance, nevermind a conversation past the pleasantries, and much less a private moment.
Catalina – now to be styled Katherine – did not know what she could have possibly done to incite such indifference from her husband, but she tried not to let it provoke her, choosing instead to spend her days in the presence of those who cared for her company.
Margaret Beaufort – Arthur's grandmother and mother to King Henry VII – was one such person. Katherine had learned almost as soon as she had arrived on the English shores that Margaret Beaufort was an exceptionally pious woman. That much was clear from her attire alone: her headdress appearing like that of a nun, and a heavy, bejewelled cross hanging from her neck at all times. Over the past two weeks, Katherine had enjoyed many hours in companionable silence with the older lady as the two of them prayed quietly together in the royal chapel, some friendships being made without so much as a single spoken word.
Katherine had also grown to enjoy the young Prince Harry's company. At the age of just ten-years-old, Prince Harry had proven himself a very lively boy, never too shy to spend the morning playing backgammon with his new sister-in-law or inviting her to observe him at archery. Katherine had shared many laughs with the young boy in the weeks since her arrival, and she was glad to see that not all seemed to want to distance themselves from her.
Only her husband.
Katherine sighed now as she thought about Arthur and how cold he had been to her since their wedding.

She did not know what she had done to cause him to want to avoid her, and she could only imagine it was some kind of personal turmoil he was dealing with that was the cause of his coldness. Nevertheless, Katherine would not be the first to broach the subject. That was his responsibility.

And Katherine was too much her father's daughter to give in first – stubbornness and pride being at the very heart of the Spanish temperament.

"What is the matter?" one of her new sisters-in-law, Princess Margaret Tudor, asked as the two of them walked the beautiful palace gardens bordered by neatly trimmed oval hedges.

It was winter and it had snowed in the night, but Margaret had invited Katherine for a leisurely stroll – which Katherine had briefly believed to have been a joke, for who would want to walk about in this awfully cold weather?

But upon meeting Margaret's serious gaze and detecting not a hint of humour in the invitation, Katherine had nodded in agreement and wrapped herself in furs before heading out the door, inwardly groaning to be leaving the fireplace's warmth.

Katherine looked at Margaret now, "It is nothing," she said, tightening her furs around her.

Margaret, though she was but twelve-years-old, was not fooled, "It is Arthur."

It was not a question, and yet Katherine had nodded, one corner of her mouth twitching.

"He avoids me still," she admitted, "I do not know what I have done, Maggie."

Margaret exhaled, her breath creating a white mist before them as they walked, "You have not done anything," she said, "Arthur, he –"

Then she shook her head, unsure if it was her place to discuss her older brother's shortcomings.

Katherine turned her gaze to Margaret, her eyes questioning.

The Tudor Princess sighed, "My two brothers are very different, complete opposites almost," she said, her pale cheeks blushing at the statement, "Arthur, though he is older, he is not as comfortable in himself as Harry is. Arthur is uneasy, he is shy. You have not done anything. It is he who has to battle through this."

Katherine swallowed and nodded, glad to have gauged a little perspective into *who* her husband was.

"As long as I have not spoken out of turn..." Katherine mumbled in response as she looked longingly back at the palace, wondering when they could return to the warmth. She sniffed, the cold giving her a runny nose.

Margaret followed her gaze and laughed, "You have not been built for this weather, have you my dearest Katherine?"

The Spanish Princess smiled and hung her head, "One day I hope to be accustomed to it. But it is not this day."

Margaret took her sister-in-law by the arm and steered her back up the path to the palace, the two young women giggling at the differences between them.

Arthur and his younger brother Harry were sitting opposite one another at a stone chess table in the great hall, one of the great fires of the hall warming them from the December frost outside.

Prince Harry the Duke of York was hunched over the chess board, his chin in his hand as he perused the sixty-four squares with a heavy frown between his light red eyebrows, while his brother Arthur sat back in his seat with his fingers intertwined as they rested casually on his belly. Arthur was absentmindedly gazing up at the great hall's high ceilings, admiring the intricate stonemasonry of it as he patiently awaited his younger brother's move.

Harry raised his hand and put a finger down on one of the pieces, snapping Arthur's attention back to the game, but Harry swiftly removed his finger from his piece with a frustrated groan.

"You have to move that rook now, brother," Arthur reminded Harry gently, "You touched it."
The young prince clicked his tongue and gave Arthur an exasperated look, "Barely!"
Arthur shrugged, "Rules are rules."
Harry shook his head and, while making a face, begrudgingly moved his rook.
"One day I will beat you at this damned game, Arthur," Harry said as he watched Arthur sit forward to peruse the board, "If it is the last thing I do."
"Keep trying, Harry," Arthur chuckled and swiftly moved his bishop, mumbling, "Checkmate."
Harry opened his mouth to throw insults at his older brother then, when suddenly a man's voice interrupted his thoughts.
"Your Graces," their father's messenger said with a bow of his head, then turned to address Arthur, "Your father the king requests an audience in his chambers."

"What is the issue, son?"
King Henry VII had requested that Arthur meet him for a private discussion in the king's chambers, having heard – as well as noticed with his own eyes, both the bad one and the good one – that his son was not acting as a young man ought to upon marrying a beautiful and exotic princess.
"What's so wrong with her that you cannot be around her?" the king continued, "Is she dull? Does she not pique your interests?"
Arthur hung his head in shame, his jaw-length auburn hair hiding his face slightly. He did not respond.
His father exhaled loudly and ran a hand through his own greying hair. Then he took a step towards his heir and put a hand on his shoulder, "Look, my boy, women are mysterious creatures. Even I, after many years of marriage to your mother, have moments where I would prefer to be alone or merely in the company of men."

Arthur looked up to meet his father's eyes, glad to have found some common ground on this topic.

"But your wife," the king went on, "We have picked you a good one. She is intelligent *and* beautiful. What more could you have wanted?"

At that, Arthur shook his head, "Nothing, Father."

Henry stepped back, let his hand drop away from his son's shoulder, "Is she unappealing to you? Is that it?"

The prince frowned, fearful that his virility would come into question, "No, Father!"

Henry Tudor shook his head, exhausted with the matter, "Then, goddammit boy, conclude the marriage already! There cannot be any slip-ups with this, our alliance with Spain is imperative to our future, Arthur, to *your* future as king!"

Arthur pushed his shoulders back, straightened his back, "I understand," he said, meeting his father's eyes.

"Good!" the king said before taking a seat by the fire, "Your mother and I have made arrangements for you and the princess to spend some time in Ludlow, to reside there as is custom for the Prince and Princess of Wales. Hopefully some time away from prying eyes will give the two of you the time you need to establish some common ground."

January 1502
On the way to Ludlow, Wales

The journey to Wales was a long and cold one, the roads being covered in thick snow and ice.

Several wagons had been prepared for the journey, the prince and princess' households following behind the royal carriage in which Katherine and her ladies travelled in, the prince choosing to ride ahead the carriage on horseback, with his guards and his close friend, Griffith Rhys.

Griffith was a Welsh nobleman and the son of one of the most powerful men in all of Wales. He sported a mop of thick, dark blond hair on his head and wore a slight yet constant frown between his brows, as though every thought weighed heavily upon his mind. He was eight years older than Arthur, and yet the two of them had been good friends since childhood, Henry VII having appointed Griffith within Arthur's household upon the prince's birth, with the aim that Arthur grow up surrounded by influential young men with powerful fathers. He had been one of many such influential young men, but throughout the years Griffith had been the only one to which Arthur had gravitated to for true fellowship, and it was he that he went to for genuine conversation, as well as his most private concerns.

What if someone recognises me? Arthur had protested the week before, standing huddled outside the brothel Griffith had dragged him to after he'd expressed his uncertainties about how to lay with a woman.

Keep your hood over your head, Griffith had offered with a smirk, before disappearing into the hovel.

Arthur had begrudgingly followed his friend inside, his jaw clenched the entire time as he moved through the poorly lit chambers, the moaning and groaning of women and men filling his ears.

This, Griffith had said a moment later, presenting Arthur with a beautiful, red-headed and bare-breasted young woman, *Is Margery.*

From Griffith's grin Arthur could tell that he had had her, that he had selected her for Arthur from his own experience. The thought of this woman's naked body being repeatedly used for the pleasures of men, had churned Arthur's stomach; and he had pathetically excused himself before fleeing from the establishment. Taking in deep breaths of the cold night air, he had felt ashamed and pitiful at the time, for what kind of young man was unwilling – or unable – to do what any other man did so easily: bedding women for sport.

He shook his head clear of those memories now, for the journey ahead to Ludlow was a long one, and he wished not to be taunted by his own self-doubt for the remainder of it.

The first day of the trip had been a quiet and sullen one, the princess shivering fiercely in the carriage though she was wrapped in several furs and blankets, the cold English weather continuing to disagree with her Spanish blood.

But on the second day, after a night spent in royal lodgings, Prince Arthur had been forced to forfeit travelling by horseback in favour of the carriage, the snow falling too heavily to risk the Tudor heir's health.

Katherine, her ladies Lina and Agnes, and now Prince Arthur, sat as still as statues in the carriage as it rocked them to-and-fro on the icy path, hours going by without so much as a quiet murmur being spoken by any of them.

But as each hour passed, the tension – as well as the snow – grew thicker, and then, to everyone's relief and surprise, the prince turned his blue-eyed gaze to Katherine and opened his mouth, breaking the silence and the ice.

"Ludlow Castle has been the principal seat of the Prince's Council since my grandfather Edward IV's reign began in 1461."

The statement was so filled with information that, for a moment, Katherine was lost for words, having only understood about half of what he had said.

She blinked her wide eyes at him slowly, then nodded once and offered him a smile.

Arthur frowned slightly, unsure as to whether he should continue.

"I was sent there at the age of seven with my own council, to learn how to rule. I resided there for several years until..."

Katherine watched him intently, encouraging him to continue with her silence.

"Well, until I was called home to marry," he concluded.

Katherine noticed a slight twitch of his thin lips and she wondered if it had been a small smile or a tick of resentment.

She decided to believe it to have been the former and leaned forward, "Tell me more," she said eagerly, glad to hang onto any thread of conversation he might offer her, in hopes of building a rapport with her husband.

But Arthur flinched at her sudden proximity and Katherine realised immediately that she had been too forward.

"There is nothing more to tell," Arthur said, turning his head to look out the window again, though there was nothing to see other than white, white, and more white.

Katherine leaned back once again and cleared her throat self-consciously before looking at Lina for comfort.

Her lady reached under her furs and took Katherine's hand in hers, squeezed it once.

The princess sighed and attempted another look at her timid husband.

It appeared she would have to move as delicately around him as she would do near a little bird.

Ludlow Castle, Ludlow, Wales

Upon arriving at Ludlow Castle later that day, the princess was disappointed – but not surprised – to see how grey it looked.

Perched on a rocky cliffside overlooking the river Teme, the castle occupied an area of almost four acres and was surrounded by a great curtain wall. Once through the outer gate, Katherine saw that it was large enough to house stables, storehouses, and workshops in its outer bailey.

It was magnificent, but utterly lacking in colour.

The royal couple and their household exited the cramped carriages gingerly, careful not to slip on the icy path, and were led into the warmth of the castle.

The principal rooms used by the most high-status residents were in the upper storey of the three-storey castle, and as Katherine and Arthur were escorted up the spiral staircase to the upper level, Katherine realised that Arthur was being led one way and she the other.

She pressed her lips together and raised her chin, trying not to take it personally that Arthur had quite clearly requested that she did not share his space.

The following morning, as Katherine was breaking her fast by the fireplace, there was a knock at the door and her husband entered the room.

The princess rose from her seat and, along with her ladies, curtsied to the Prince of Wales.

"Husband," Katherine mumbled, the word still feeling strange on her lips.

Arthur stood awkwardly by the door's threshold, his eyes roaming the chamber as though he'd never seen it before – though, of course, he had.

He cleared his throat then as his gaze rested on Katherine, and he took a tentative step forward.

"My father ordered that I make more of an effort."

The statement was monotonous, emotionless. And yet the confession that he *hadn't* been making much of an effort was a relief to Katherine.

She hadn't been imagining his standoffishness.

He had reached the fireplace now, and he stood awkwardly before her.

He looked down at her unfinished plate of bread and cheese.

"Please," he said with a motion of his hand, "Eat."

He took a seat on the opposite side of the table, the furthest seat from where Katherine had been sitting. She took her seat, understanding that while he was willing to be here, he needed a little distance to feel at ease.

Arthur watched the flames in the hearth licking hungrily around the logs, its colours of red, orange, and blue dancing wildly as they consumed the wood.

Once Katherine had finished her meal in silence, Lina stepped forward and removed the silver tray.

Arthur met his wife's gaze, "Are you enjoying it here?"

The princess blinked, "I have not had the chance to explore much in the short time we have been here…"

Arthur shook his head, "No, no," he said, frowning, "Here, as in, England."

"Oh…" Katherine breathed, then licked her lips as she organized her thoughts, "Yes, very much so," she lied.

Arthur nodded, not recognising the mistruth.

They fell silent, Arthur having returned his gaze to the fireplace. As he looked away, Katherine took the opportunity to observe him.

He had inherited his mother's facial features – much like his younger brother Prince Harry – both of them having thin lips, a straight nose, and pale blue eyes. Though also tinged with red, Arthur had his father's hair: straight, and darker than his mother's, which was the colour of the early dawn.

Katherine realised as she watched him that her husband had all the appropriate characteristics of a handsome young man, but sadly his lack of confidence dulled his good looks, making them appear faded, washed out. So much so that it had taken Katherine several weeks of marriage to even notice his physical appeal.

She wondered if he knew. Or, indeed, if he cared.

As the quiet dragged on, Katherine decided that it was foolish of her to expect him to fill all the silences, her own characteristics perhaps being measured in that very moment by him; and she opened her mouth to speak.

"Does Your Grace –"

But Arthur had turned to her in that very moment, "Do you miss –" his own words crashing with hers.

The pair smiled at one another from across the long, wood table.

"You go," Arthur offered with a nod of his head.

Katherine smiled thinly, "Does Your Grace enjoy jousting?"

She had hoped to begin an excited discourse of the popular entertainment enjoyed so widely among the male population, but to her surprise, Arthur pulled a face.

"Not really," he said, "I do not see the point of it."

Katherine nodded, scrambling to think of another question to ask him. That one having miserably failed to launch.

"Hunting?" she asked, her hands clasped together tightly on her lap.

Arthur shrugged one shoulder, "It is necessary. But not my preferred form of entertainment."

"What is your preferred form of entertainment?" the princess pressed.

At that – *finally* – Arthur's eyes lit up, and he leaned forward, his elbows now resting on the table.

"I do enjoy playing chess!" he said, a wide grin exposing his white teeth, and Katherine noticed that one of his incisors jutted slightly further forward than the others, "But nothing brings me greater joy than sitting at my desk with a quill and ink and composing music."

Katherine raised her eyebrows and smiled warmly, glad to finally have some more insight into who she was married to.

"You compose music?" she said, hoping to keep him talking.

But a shadow flickered over Arthur's expression then, as though he had remembered something unpleasant, and he retracted into himself again, sitting back against his chair, the eye contact broken.

"I know," he said with a wan smile, "It is not what you had expected from a husband. Not very 'masculine'."

The princess' light eyebrows twitched together in confusion. Had she said something wrong? Misunderstood?

She shook her head, "No, Your Grace –"

But Arthur had already risen from his seat, his body language stiff as he addressed her, "Forgive the intrusion this morning, it won't happen again."
And with that, the prince quit the room, leaving Katherine dazed in his wake.

March 1502

Katherine had not spent a private moment with Arthur or shared a conversation with him past pleasantries since that first morning at Ludlow Castle over a month earlier, and Katherine's confusion had quickly turned into frustration.
She had expressed her frustration by writing letters to her sister-in-law, the Princess Margaret Tudor, who Katherine realised she was missing desperately despite only having known her for a few months.
Margaret's replies were always understanding and soothing, though they never spoke ill of her brother. And that in turn would remind Katherine that she, too, should not.
He was her husband. But above even that, he would one day be her king.
Katherine, however, would not be made for a fool, and she busied herself each day with needlework, learning of the English dances, and spending many hours at prayer. And she would go to bed at night content, knowing that she had done her duty to the extent of her ability.
Katherine was totally unaware, however, that while her days were fuelled by her frustration and her mellowed sense of duty, Arthur's were a concoction of anxiety, nervousness, and fear.
The truth was: he did not know how to woo a woman...
As a prince, Arthur had grown up hearing tales of chivalric knights, brave kings, and honourable soldiers. Stories of men who had all achieved greatness and concluded their tales with the claiming of a fair maiden's heart.
But Arthur was not like those men.

Unlike his younger brother Harry, even as a young boy, Arthur had never been enticed by the legends of bloodshed and the glory of battle. The bedtime stories their mother would tell them of their father's great victory at the Battle of Bosworth field – when Henry Tudor had killed the usurper King Richard III and claimed the throne of England – had not incited awe in Arthur. His brother however, had bounced ecstatically on his bed, a wooden sword in his hand, attacking imaginary soldiers as their mother told them the tale.

But Arthur had only listened intently, the sound of his mother's voice soothing him despite the gory words of battle that were being spoken.

It had put an end to the Cousins' War, your father's victory, Queen Elizabeth would always say in conclusion, *And though it had been a violent ending to the thirty-year war, it is a hauntingly beautiful reminder of how light will always come after an extended period of darkness.*

She had always caressed young Arthur's cheek as she had said those final words, and they had remained in his mind to this day, many years later.

The Lancastrian Henry Tudor had gone on to marry the Yorkist Elizabeth of York, the eldest daughter of Edward IV, and the warring houses of Lancaster and York had been unified. A splendidly romantic finale to their tale.

And it was what Arthur had hoped to achieve with his bride… if only he could get past the nervousness in the pit of his stomach. The exotic Katherine of Aragon had come from a place of wonder and delight. A country where colour, warmth, art, and beauty were in abundance. No doubt she felt smothered and dulled here in grey, rainy England. No doubt she felt suffocated by her husband's lack of humour, confidence, or presence.

Arthur was just Arthur.

He was a lover of the smaller things in life: the lull of a well-versed poem, the tune of a gently played harp, or even the smell of the early morning breeze.

Great battles, conquest, and glory were not what spurred Arthur on. And it was this very fault in his character that he knew would be his biggest burden in life.

His father had never said anything against it, never spoken a word, whether good or bad, about it. But Arthur knew that he was not as manly as Henry Tudor had hoped his heir to be. And it was that self-doubt that made Arthur falter in his connection with his wife.

Surely, she wished for someone better than he. Someone with better looks, better charm, better charisma. Someone more like… Harry.

Arthur sighed heavily, thoughts consuming him as they so often did, his mind being a miasma of troubled notions from morning until dusk.

He pushed his wandering thoughts aside as he made his way towards the window in his chambers, his hands clasped loosely behind his back as he walked.

He peered down into the garden, which was finally beginning to show signs of Spring, spots of colour being visible among some of the rose bushes even from this great height.

He observed the trees and shrubs blowing gently in the breeze, the little birds hopping about on the pebbled path between the hedges, picking at the ground in search of worms. Only after several moments did he allow his gaze to wander towards the group of people that were strolling leisurely in the garden. Long enough so that he could continue to tell himself that he had come to observe the beauty of nature, and not *who* was walking among it. The people wandering within the garden's confines being but a mere coincidence…

Katherine and her ladies walked slowly through the beautiful gardens, grateful for the break from the constant downpour of rain that had befallen the land for the past two weeks.

It was not yet warm however, and they continued wrapped in furs to keep the chill at bay. But the clearer sky and the promise of sunshine was enough to urge the princess outside.

"The roses are budding," Katherine noticed, smiling as they approached the thorny bushes.

"The worst of the year is certainly behind us," Agnes said, turning her face towards the weak rays of sun peeking through the wispy clouds.

Katherine sighed, "Hopefully the change in weather will thaw the mood between Arthur and I."

She had intended to sound hopeful but had faltered, her doubt clouding her ability to think positively.

"For now, just enjoy the sun on your face, princess," Lina said, closing her dark eyes and raising her chin.

Katherine smiled and followed suit, turning her pale face up towards the sky, her eyes closed for a moment as she breathed in the dewy air. Then her eyelids fluttered open lazily, her mind soothed for a moment, and as her vision slowly focused on the grey castle before them, she caught sight of a figure at a window looking down at her. Their eyes locked for a fleeting moment, a moment in which Katherine felt the beginning of a smile taking shape. But then Arthur broke free of her gaze and urgently stepped back into the shadows of his confinements, and Katherine's smile evaporated into thin air.

Chapter 3

The following morning, Prince Arthur awoke from a dream which had seen him and Katherine in ten, twenty years' time, surrounded by young children as they enjoyed the summer air on a leisurely stroll in the palace gardens.

The dream had been as brief as a whisper, nothing following him into consciousness apart from the echoing laughter of children and the warmth of Katherine's hand in his.

It had been no more than a fleeting illusion in his subconscious state, but the feeling of profound achievement the dream had left behind in his chest had been enough to spur Arthur out of bed that morning with a joyful leap.

This would be the day. Arthur was ready.

The dream had, ironically, been a wakeup call for Arthur to push aside his childish fears of rejection and to quash his gnawing anxiety. It had opened his eyes to the reality that was his situation: that he and his wife would not even have the *hope* of achieving such a future if he did not act.

He dressed quickly, his groom aiding him with the more finicky parts of the attire, and without even making the bed – which Arthur enjoyed doing each morning – he strolled eagerly out of his chambers.

He found Katherine and her ladies playing cards in the hall, the darker of her ladies, Lina, laughing candidly as Katherine told her something, their cards held close to their chests to keep them secret.

The hall was almost empty save for the princess, her ladies, and a handful of courtiers and servants passing through on their way somewhere else. Agnes Tilney spotted him first and curtsied, causing the other two to raise their heads and put down their cards at Arthur's approach.

Once all were standing, Katherine and Lina, too, curtsied.

"My lord," Katherine mumbled, though the smile she had worn before his arrival had faded, and for a moment Arthur's nervousness returned. But he swallowed it down and allowed the dream's lingering warmth in his chest to take over. He offered Katherine a smile.

"My lady," he replied, maintaining eye contact for a moment longer than he would have ever normally dared.

"May I join you for a game?" he asked, waving his hand toward the table behind her.

Katherine blinked and followed his gaze over her shoulder, "Of—of course, Your Grace."

They took their seats opposite one another, Lina and Agnes retreating to the window in the far corner of the hall to give them some privacy, and Katherine realised this was the closest she and Arthur had been since their journey to Ludlow nearly two months prior.

"How do you fair at *primero*?" Arthur asked as he dealt out the cards.

Katherine smiled, pleasantly surprised to see a different side to the usually timid and closed-off Arthur.

She shrugged casually, playing coy, aware that too much of a reaction might frighten him away, "You will have to find out."

Arthur grinned, flashing his teeth, his slightly protruding incisor catching Katherine's attention as it had done the first time she saw it. It was, Katherine realised, the one physical flaw he appeared to have, his face being otherwise perfectly well proportioned, almost handsome.

They began their game, the two of them watching the other from over the top of their cards, searching for a hint to the quality of their hand in the other's expressions.

A silence ensued while they arranged their cards and took their turns, Katherine feeling a welcome sense of comfort descending on them, and she found herself smiling.

"I saw you yesterday," she said then, unable to keep the moment unspoken any longer, "By the window."

Arthur did not reply, continuing to look down at his cards and swapping one with another in his hand.

"I think you saw me too," the princess continued carefully, knowing that to utter the wrong thing might spook him, but equally aware that at some point they would have to learn how to converse.

Arthur laid down his cards, "I win."

Katherine looked down and sighed through her nose before laying her losing hand face-up on the table.

When she looked up, Arthur was watching her, his blue eyes containing a warmth that was foreign to her.

It was when his gaze dropped to her lips that she knew what he was about to do, and her heart skipped to think she would finally get to kiss her husband after three months of rocky marriage.

She held her breath, willing him to lean forward and take what was rightfully his, and then suddenly he closed the space between them, the table digging into their stomachs as the two of them pressed themselves forward to reach the other.

It was not what she had expected.

Toothy, awkward, and wet, Katherine had pulled away first, her nose red from their uncomfortable merger.

Arthur's cheeks burned brightly when they pulled apart, just as aware as Katherine that their first kiss had been a blunder.

Katherine willed the frown between her eyebrows to melt away, but Arthur had noticed her dissatisfaction, and with that one look, his earlier enthusiasm was squashed.

"Forgive me," he mumbled as he stood hastily, "I have – somewhere I need to be."

And with that he fled, leaving Katherine behind feeling like she had failed a vital test.

April 1502

Disaster had struck.

Though the couple hadn't spent time together since they had shared their clumsy kiss two days earlier, the Prince and

Princess of Wales had been complaining of chills and light-headedness throughout the morning of the 1st of April.

And by the afternoon of that same day, the princess had collapsed on her way to chapel, and been taken to bed.

The Prince of Wales had held on for only an hour longer than his bride before, too, fainting during a meeting with his small council.

Both now lay abed in their separate apartments, physicians hovering over them as they examined the shivering, clammy youths.

"What is it?" Lina whispered to Agnes as they stood by the princess' doorway, a respectable distance from their mistress as they had been advised by the physician.

Agnes swallowed hard, her hand pressed to the base of her throat as she stared at their ashen mistress, "It's the sweat."

Lina frowned, "Sweat? *Que es?* A fever?"

Agnes shook her head, "English sweat. *Sudor Anglicus.* It is a mystery even to our physicians."

Lina turned back to watch the bearded old man peering at the princess without touching her.

"Is it…dangerous?"

Agnes breathed in slowly, then nodded, "Death is common," she whispered.

Just then, Katherine moaned uncomfortably and thrashed her legs under the blankets, though her eyes remained tightly closed.

"The princess is strong," the physician mumbled to the ladies then as he hurried past them and away from the princess, "There is nothing to be done but keep our distance and pray for her recovery."

And with that he was out the door, his heavy robes trailing behind him.

Across the castle, Prince Arthur was abandoned just as quickly by his physician, the man hastily informing the prince's good friend Griffith that only prayer could save him, and the frown between Griffith's brows grew deeper at the morbid news.

Only the prince's groom remained by Arthur's side to wipe his clammy forehead and cover him with furs when he would kick them off in a fit of shaking or vomiting.

The couple remained unconscious all night, sometimes calling out in their restless sleep or groaning in pain but otherwise silent. They shivered and thrashed uncomfortably for hours; their minds blunted in a hazy state of sleep but their bodies writhing as though fully awake. Their sheets and covers were completely soaked in sweat, their hair matted and moist against their skin, their teeth chattering uncontrollably.

And when neither of them had awoken the following morning, riders were sent out to inform the king and queen of their son and daughter-in-law's ailments, so that they may prepare for the worst.

Richmond Palace, Surrey

Queen Elizabeth of York stared at the messenger in horror before pressing a shaky hand to her mouth.

She felt as though she had been winded, her breaths failing to go in or out as the news of her eldest son's fragile condition was broken.

The sweating sickness.

Her first born...the Prince of Wales and future King of England, was likely already dead...

Her husband, King Henry Tudor, who stood beside her just as stunned at the terrifying news, was the one to break the silence.

"What of Arthur's bride, the *infanta* of Spain?" he stuttered, "Is she...?"

"Princess Katherine of Aragon, too, is affected by the illness," the messenger informed them, "But there is still hope."

Queen Elizabeth's vision blurred with tears and her head felt heavy. She swallowed hard to stop herself from being sick.

There was no hope. The sweating sickness was fatal, everyone knew that. Their chance of survival was slim to none; and suddenly she couldn't help but imagine the worst.

Arthur had been the most beautiful of babies. From the moment he had been born fifteen years ago, Elizabeth had known that he would have made an incredible King of England.

Her love for her firstborn child had, of course, fuelled these feelings initially. But as the years had gone by, Arthur had proven himself to be as gentle, kind, and selfless as Elizabeth had predicted he would be.

Queen Elizabeth had borne her husband many more children after Arthur's birth – three of which had been lucky enough to survive the dangerous years of infancy – and all of which she loved more than life itself.

But Arthur had always been special.

Perhaps it had been due to him being her first child, the one who had turned her into a mother.

Or perhaps it was that he would have been Henry's heir, the one to take over as King and to one day rule England in his father's stead. She did not know.

But one thing Queen Elizabeth did know for certain: that she would not survive if Arthur were to die.

The queen inhaled a shaky breath then and blinked away the tears in her eyes. She needed to know what had become of her son.

"Return to Ludlow as quickly as you can," she ordered, "We expect fresh news to arrive with the dawn."

King Henry and Queen Elizabeth stayed awake all night, frantically pacing up and down the length of their shared bedchambers or sitting still as statues before the fire, staring unblinkingly into the flames.

When no news had come by four in the morning, the King of England looked over to his ashen-faced wife and broke their heavy silence.

"What will we do if Arthur—?"

"Don't say it!" the queen interrupted harshly, a tone she would never normally have taken with her lord husband, "Don't even say it…"

Henry Tudor opened his mouth to speak but closed it again, he hung his head in shame.

But his fears would not stop tormenting his mind, and Henry went on to consider just *what* the death of his heir would mean. The reality hit him instantly, like an arrow to the heart: If Arthur were to die, the Tudor dynasty might fall.

King Henry had always known that any popularity he'd had, had come from *who* was by his side to rule: the pure-blooded daughter of Edward IV, the White Flower to his Red, and the promise that their union would lead to heirs that would continue his legacy of peace.

The birth of their first-born son Arthur had led to public rejoicing throughout the country. He had been truly loved by the people from the moment he had been born, for he was the living, breathing guarantee of a continued future without bloodshed; and Henry Tudor had made sure to evoke this knowledge in his heir. That his role for the future was to ensure harmony. Peace before glory. Always.

And the truth was: if Arthur were to perish, Henry's other son, Harry, would not be ready to replace his brother, for he had not been prepared to rule the way Arthur had been.

Harry's path as the spare had meant an entirely different upbringing to one a future king ought to have had. He had been spoiled with the freedom to pursue his own desires, and it had allowed him to become selfish, immature, and, frankly, entirely ill-equipped to ever be King of England.

No, Harry would not be ready to take on this task, to step into his brother's boots. But if Arthur were to succumb to his illness, Harry would have to…

A cold chill ran over Henry Tudor's spine as he considered the bleak future which would follow if news came that Arthur had not survived the sweat.

Another hour passed before Henry or his queen spoke again, the king having slowly convinced himself into accepting the only other option they had if the worst were to happen.

"We have Harry…" Henry VII whispered hoarsely, his eyes shining bright with unshed tears.

Queen Elizabeth looked over at her husband and, after a long pause, nodded.

"We have Harry," she agreed, sounding as uncertain as Henry felt.

And they both fell back into their gloomy silence.

News came with the first light of dawn, just as the queen had commanded.

At the sound of galloping horse hooves thundering closer, the royal couple leapt from their seats and hurried out the doors, down the wide staircase, and into the courtyard to meet the messenger.

The messenger practically fell from his horse in an effort to convey the information as quickly as possible, his steed not even having fully stopped before the young man's boots had hit the ground.

He handed his king a note as he panted heavily before them, exhausted from the hours of riding at a dangerous speed.

As the king tore the wax seal from the letter, Elizabeth stared at the messenger, hoping to read his face for a hint of what was to come.

But the man appeared to know nothing.

It must not be good news.

Henry urgently unfolded the note and squinted down at it, his heart beating hard in the base of his throat.

"What is it?" Elizabeth pleaded, "What does it say?"

Henry looked up from the note, his face a blank slate Elizabeth could not decipher. She realised her ears were burning and her breathing was coming in short and too quickly. She was getting light-headed from the anticipation.

Henry handed the letter to his wife, who snatched it without a beat of hesitation.

She looked down at the words scrawled weakly on the paper, her tears blurring her vision slightly.

I am survived.

Elizabeth half exhaled, half exclaimed with relief and raised her face to the early morning sky, thanking God for this miracle.

She could vaguely hear her husband beside her as he breathed an elated laugh, then slapped the young messenger heartily on the shoulder and pressed a pouch of coins into his hand.

But no other sounds registered, for Elizabeth had become fixated on the lazy oranges and pinks of the sunrise as it peaked over the horizon, the colours more vibrant than she had ever seen them before.

And the Queen of England smiled, knowing in her heart that she would never forget the beauty of that morning sky, alive with hope and promise.

Their future was secured.

Chapter 4

The only cure for the terrible disease, it seemed, was to survive its symptoms for the first twenty-four hours.

"You are lucky to be alive!" Griffith Rhys said some weeks later as he squeezed Arthur's shoulder, "The sweating sickness you and Princess Katherine contracted has consumed countless lives since it mysteriously appeared in England in 1485," he continued as they sat companionably by the fire, "No one knows of its origin or how to treat it. Your physician was a bumbling fool when it came down to it!"

Arthur nodded unenthusiastically, aware of his good fortune and feeling guilty for it. Not everyone had been so lucky, Arthur's groom, as well as two of Katherine's servants, having died just hours upon becoming infected.

Arthur would be sure to pay for a respectable funeral for them; it was the least he could do for their loyalty and devotion.

"God was watching over us," Arthur finally said, feeling his friend's eyes on him, awaiting a response, "Surely He has bigger plans for me than to succumb to disease."

Griffith nodded approvingly, "It would appear so."

May 1502
Ludlow Castle, Ludlow, Wales

It had been a month since Katherine and Arthur's brush with death, and the pair had fully recovered.

It was a bright morning, the warmest Katherine had yet experienced in England, and she was glad to see the end of her first English winter.

Her ladies were flitting around the room excitedly, readying their mistress to take her breakfast outside in the gardens, the promise of sunshine on her blanched skin being too wonderful to pass up.

Once they were seated at a hexagonal stone table in the gardens surrounded by delicious smells and sounds of nature, and the servants had placed their trays before them, Katherine was so engrossed in the beauty of it all that she hardly noticed her ladies rising from their seats.

She squinted against the sun as she looked up to identify the cause of their interrupted meal and saw her husband standing beside her.

"My lady," he said in greeting with a bob of his head.

Katherine rose and curtsied quickly, "Forgive me, I did not notice your approach."

Arthur dismissed her apology with a wave of his hand, then he turned to her ladies and offered for them to retake their seats.

"I do not wish to disturb," he said, "Only to invite you to supper with me this evening in my chambers. I do believe it's high time we got to know each other better."

Katherine stared dumbfounded at her husband, who she had been co-existing with for several months like two ghosts confined to their separate parts of the castle.

"You wish to supper with me?" she asked slowly, making sure she had understood.

Arthur nodded, "The prospect of death has opened my eyes to my foolishness. Life is for the living. And I for one wish to know my wife before death chooses to take me."

He spoke so fluidly, without hesitating or overthinking like she had noticed he often did, as if he were weighing up each word before he spoke it.

Katherine opened her mouth to respond but no words came out, so surprised was she at this change in character. Who was this young man, and what had he done with the timid Arthur she had known?

"My lady will be there," Lina interjected shamelessly when Katherine did not reply, and Katherine threw a horrified look her way.

But Arthur took no offence to the intrusion, and instead bowed his head in thanks at Lina before reaching to take Katherine's hand and bringing it to his lips.

"Until then," he said with a smile.

Then he turned on his heels and left.

That evening, as Katherine's ladies buzzed about her like bees on a flower, dabbing lavender water along her jawline and choosing which gable hood would look more beautiful with her dark red velvet dress, Agnes and Lina could not stop chattering and giggling excitedly.

"Do you think tonight?"

"I don't see why not."

"He was like a totally different Arthur."

"The fear of dying a virgin must have frightened him into action."

And their giggles would mushroom once again.

But Katherine paid them no attention. She was simply glad to have seen a glimpse of the man Arthur could be if he managed to overcome his self-doubt. A man who was comfortable in his own body and who spoke without fear of misstep.

Though they were both still young, Katherine knew that she was ready. She was ready to do her duty. She *wanted* to do her duty.

As a princess, it had been instilled in her from a very young age that a woman's greatest honour in life was to bear her husband children. And as the daughter of the greatest monarchs in all of Europe, Katherine had prayed for as long as she could remember that she would be blessed with a fruitful marriage. Tonight would surely be the night. The night where she would conclude the alliance between England and Spain and achieve the goal she had been charged with.

*

Upon entering Arthur's chambers later that evening, Katherine felt butterflies of eagerness and nervousness in her stomach, and a ready smile was tugging on her lips.

Arthur stood by the fireplace when she entered, its embers glowing in the hearth, the warmer weather calling for fewer logs to be burned throughout the day.

Half of his face glowed orange as he turned to welcome her with a friendly smile.

He looked taller than Katherine remembered, as though his newfound confidence had added more height to his slender frame – his back straighter, more composed. And she realised she found this new version of him very attractive.

Katherine felt her cheeks blushing, "My lord," she said in greeting as she bobbed a quick curtsy.

Arthur stepped towards her, "There's no more need for that here," he said, "When it is just us, we are equals."

Us.

She liked the way that word had sounded.

Arthur dropped his gaze, "Do…do you like pheasant?"

Katherine nodded, though it wasn't her favourite.

She would've agreed to eat anything if it meant she would be able to complete her task.

"Come," Arthur said then, turned away from her and towards the table.

Before her were many dishes of delicious looking foods: sugared grapes and almonds, pastries in all kinds of shapes, mostly in the Tudor rose, and of course the promised pheasant.

Katherine and Arthur took their seats, and the servants began to dish out servings of all the delicacies.

The couple ate in silence, and for a moment Katherine feared that perhaps she had imagined Arthur's new self-confidence.

She risked quick glimpses in his direction on more than one occasion while they dined, but each time he was casually eating his supper, as though it were no different from any other day.

But then, once the servants had cleared their plates, Arthur leaned forward with a ready smile.

"Katherine," he said, and it occurred to her that it was the first time he had addressed her by her name. And she liked hearing him utter it.

She hesitated for a moment, "Arthur," she replied, an undertone of doubt in her voice as she addressed him so informally.

Arthur inhaled as if to speak but then frowned slightly and looked away, suddenly unable to utter the words he was so eager to say but moments before.

"Um..." he mumbled instead, looking down at the table, an unsure smile tugging at his lips. Then he shook his head.

Katherine sat back in her seat slowly, touched the prayer beads tucked in her sleeve, waited.

After a moment of awkward silence, the prince rose from his seat and called to his new groom, "Bring in the musicians."

The boy fled the room and returned moments later with three men in tow carrying their assorted instruments.

Katherine looked up at Arthur who now stood beside her, his arms hanging stiffly at his sides.

"Do you wish to dance?" he asked with fervour, though his eyes did not meet hers.

It seemed the timid young man was still in there after all.

And to her surprise, Katherine was a little glad for it.

She nodded, stood from her seat, and as the music began playing joyfully behind them – the two of them standing face-to-face for a moment, waiting for the other to make the first move – Katherine suddenly took her husband's hand in hers and planted it firmly on her lower back before taking the other in hers and taking the lead.

Arthur chuckled in surprise but did not attempt to take control of the dance, the young pair jumping and turning in each other's arms without rehearsal or routine, but simply by feeling.

They enjoyed each other's company for the remainder of the evening, dancing and laughing as the music filled the air.

They did not consummate their marriage that night. They did not even share a goodnight kiss.

But that evening, Katherine and Arthur had succeeded in laying the foundation for a marriage built on friendship.

June 1502

As it turned out, Katherine enjoyed Arthur's company greatly. He was soft-spoken, patient, and kind, precisely the kind of man one would hope to have for a husband.

But she was not in love with him, and she often wondered if she ever would be.

Since that first dinner, where they had danced and laughed and broken the ice between them, they had spent almost every day together, sometimes meeting up for supper, other times for a leisurely walk in the gardens, in an effort to make progress in their relationship.

But so far nothing more than lingering glances had taken place, Arthur's burst of courage having dried up quicker than either of them had expected or hoped.

Katherine was becoming anxious, her patience being tested again and again as each day ended in another non-consummation. And judging by the weekly letters she received from her mother and father back in Spain, they too were becoming perturbed with the lack of progression with this alliance. For without a consummation, the marriage – and the Anglo-Imperial treaty – was not fully finalised.

But on this day, when the couple had decided to picnic in the small field behind the castle, Katherine had had enough of waiting for Arthur to make his move. And she made it her personal mission to take matters into her own hands, once and for all.

The weather had grown stiflingly hot, much to the princess' surprise, who hadn't believed England to even be capable of producing such heat. But this day had brought with it a refreshing breeze, and Katherine had taken it as an invitation from God Himself to use nature's splendour to Katherine's advantage.

And so, with the permission from the Lord Almighty – and the insistence from her Catholic parents – Katherine would turn the tables on her husband and woo *him*, since he seemed completely lost as how to woo *her*.

"Such a great idea, Katherine," Arthur approved once they had settled themselves on the many blankets and cushions Katherine had ordered to be set up in the field beneath the shade of a tree.

"A beautiful day for it," Arthur went on, inhaling the fresh air. They were completely alone – no guards being needed within the safe confines of the castle grounds. Sitting on opposite corners of the blanket, Arthur had stretched his long legs out in front of him as he leaned back, his arms extended behind him. He was smiling that pleasant smile Katherine had learned meant that he was genuinely at ease, and she was glad to see him so relaxed.

Katherine sat facing him, her own legs tucked underneath herself in the only position that felt marginally comfortable in her many layered dress and corset.

There was food set up before them, but Katherine couldn't care less about the many delicious dishes, for her stomach was in knots of anticipation.

Arthur was enjoying the summer air and the sound of the bees and birds around them with his eyes closed, that easy smile tugging on the corners of his lips.

This was the moment, Katherine thought, the moment she could lean forward and plant a kiss on him without the awkward build-up of watching each other approach.

Should she do it? Now? Before they'd even had a chance to enjoy the food?

Before she could talk herself out of it, Katherine suddenly pounced on Arthur, knocking him backwards so that she was lying on top of him, and pressed her lips to his in a quick but firm peck.

Lying on his back with Katherine on his chest, Arthur stared up at her wide-eyed. He had never noticed before, but up close he could see she had one little freckle on the end of her small nose. In that moment, Arthur forgot about his self-doubt and frets, and as the pair stared at each other, their faces so close he could taste her breath, Arthur tentatively brushed his lips against hers, like an unspoken confession that he, too, had been ready for the next step but been too afraid to be the first to take it.

And just like that, their bodies relaxed, and they allowed themselves to melt into each other, their kisses becoming slowly more daring, their hands exploring the other's body over their clothing.

And later, much later, when they came up for air, Arthur stood up, took Katherine gently by the hand and led her back to his bedchambers, leaving the picnic behind, completely forgotten.

Chapter 5

December 1502
Richmond Palace, Surrey

The court was overjoyed to see the return of their Prince and Princess of Wales for the Christmastide, but no other was more overjoyed than Queen Elizabeth herself, who had been desperate to hold her eldest son in her arms.

"My darling boy!" Elizabeth exclaimed, her arms open wide and her smile wider still as Arthur and his guards entered the Palace courtyard on horseback.

"Lady Mother," Arthur said in greeting before he swung from his horse and allowed himself to be folded into his mother's tight embrace.

"Oh, how I have missed you," the queen professed as she kissed her son's cheek and breathed in his scent, "You gave us quite the scare. Your father and I feared we might never see you again."

Arthur grinned ruefully at his mother, remembering his and Katherine's close call with death earlier in the year, "We are well, Mother, truly."

At the royal carriage's arrival just a moment later, Arthur withdrew himself from his mother's hold and headed towards it to open the carriage door for Katherine.

He offered her his hand to aid her exit, which Katherine took without hesitation while flashing Arthur a grateful smile.

Queen Elizabeth watched as her beautiful boy assisted his bride down the steps of the wagon, the princess looking up at Arthur with a pretty smile, and Elizabeth's chest ached with pride to see that they had clearly developed some mutual respect and fondness for one another despite their political union.

Remembering the beginning of her own love story which had begun, like Arthur's, as a diplomatic match, Elizabeth looked fondly at her own husband, who stood watching their son's arrival under the archway of the palace entrance. She turned and resumed her place beside her king.

"Your Graces," Katherine greeted the two monarchs with a curtsy upon her emergence from the carriage.

"Welcome back," King Henry VII replied warmly, "I trust your journey has been without difficulty?"

"We met no trouble on the road," Arthur replied eagerly, "other than the rocking of the carriage causing the princess some queasiness."

The queen shot her husband a knowing look, but the young couple did not notice.

Henry Tudor nodded his head, a quick jerk to signify the end to the pleasantries, "Come," he said, offering his queen his arm and turning to head inside, "Let us celebrate your return. Your mother and I have organised a splendid banquet and dancing in your honour."

"I am thrilled that you are back!" Princess Margaret said giddily as she and Katherine danced the galliard, Margaret having pulled her new sister and friend to the dancefloor as soon as the plates had been cleared.

Katherine had learned various English dances during her time at Ludlow, her excellent musical education having made it easy to perfect the dances of her new homeland, and the galliard was one of her favourites.

"I am glad to be back," Katherine replied as the two of them hopped and twirled in time with the other dancers.

"I dare say the two of you are getting on well?" Margaret teased, smirking.

Katherine returned the smile, "It took some time," she admitted, "But we have succeeded in becoming friends."

"Friends?" Margaret replied mischievously, "*Just* friends?"

Katherine breathed a laugh and allowed herself to be spun around by one of the other dancers before gravitating back to Margaret.

"For now," she offered her husband's sister, grinning playfully.

Margaret giggled, "I am to be wed soon," she said then, a mixture of thrill and fear flashing in her eyes, "To the King of Scotland, James IV."

Katherine frowned, "When? You are too young to marry yet."

"I was married by proxy last year to seal the Treaty of Perpetual Peace with Scotland. I'll be sent to Scotland soon to officially wed the king when I reach my fourteenth year."

Katherine nodded approvingly, having worried for a moment that Margaret would be sent to be married before the customary age of fourteen. She took her sister-in-law by the hand and proceeded to hop in unison to the music.

"Fear not, dear sister," Katherine said, "It may prove difficult in the beginning. But I promise you, all will be well."

They shared a private smile, one which said they would always have one another to look to in times of difficulty, the two young princesses sharing the similar destiny of leaving behind all that they knew, to make a life in a country they had never inhabited, with a man they had not previously met.

January 1503

Following his brother and sister-in-law's return from Wales for the Christmastide the month before, twelve-year-old Prince Harry was glad to have been able to spend time with them before he himself would be sent away to fulfil his duty.

Harry, as the second-born son to the King and Queen of England, had had a completely different education to that of his older brother.

While Arthur, as the heir to the throne, had been taught of languages, ethics, history and politics – all the makings of a King – Harry's education had been laxer, the spare heir being educated not by scholars and poets like Arthur, but for the most part by their grandmother, Margaret Beaufort. It was perhaps because of this that Harry could never quite manage to beat his brother at chess; Arthur having been taught strategy while Harry had been taught the holy Scriptures of the Bible.

Margaret Beaufort was their father's mother, and the matriarch of the Tudor House. As a descendant of John of Gaunt and King Edward III, Margaret Beaufort held a claim to the throne of England through her Lancastrian bloodline. But having been born a female had of course stripped her of any right to inherit the throne for herself, which had, during her youth, led to others hoping to claim her right through marriage on their own quest for power.

At the age of just twelve, Margaret had been married off – for the *second* time in her young life – to a cousin of the former King Henry VI, a noble Welshman named Edmund Tudor.

Her marriage at such a young age to a gentleman in his mid-twenties had risen many eyebrows, for it was a whole two years younger than the customary minimum age to marry. Despite that, it had simply been assumed that Edmund Tudor would wait the two years to consummate their marriage; but to many people's astonishment, the young Margaret Beaufort had become pregnant swiftly after their wedding and gone on to birth her first and only child, Henry Tudor, at the tender age of just thirteen.

Traumatised from barely having survived the ordeal of childbirth at such a young age, the already-pious young girl had turned her love to God; for He would be the only one who would surely never hurt her. And in the decades that followed, though Margaret went on to marry three more times, her final husband gave her permission to take a vow of chastity, her devotion to God having remained the one constant in her life.

Catholicism and God were Margaret's one true love, and as Prince Harry's tutor, she had made sure to instil her passions into her young grandson.

"At Oxford you will learn far more than I and Bishop Fisher could ever have taught you," Margaret Beaufort was telling

Prince Harry on the eve before his departure, "Their studies of philosophy and theology are unmatched."
Harry grinned excitedly at the mention of his other tutor, Bishop Fisher having been who had inspired the young prince to pursue the path of priesthood.

"Perhaps one day I shall be as knowledgeable as Archbishop Warham himself."
Margaret Beaufort smiled, her crooked teeth flashing briefly, "My dear boy," she said, "With a passion for Catholicism such as yours, you should reach even higher still. A Cardinal!"
Harry grinned as he wriggled further underneath his blankets. Margaret stood from her seat on the edge of the prince's bed and leaned over to peck his forehead.

"Tomorrow, your path to greatness will begin, my dear Harry."

February 1503

With Prince Harry Duke of York gone to Magdalen College in Oxford, the youngest of the Tudor princesses, Mary Tudor, became Katherine's shadow.
At the age of just seven, Mary had readily accepted Katherine as her new sister, her mother and older sister Maggie's approval of her having made the little Mary's decision to like Katherine that much easier.
But with her closest companion now gone from court, Mary had grown that much more interested in Katherine, her days of playing and exploring with her brother Harry having come to a screeching halt with his departure.

"My lady mother says Maggie is marrying the old King of Scotland soon," Princess Mary was telling Katherine on their way to chapel, "She says he is *thirty*!"
Katherine smiled down at her little sister-in-law, "That's what I heard."

"And he has dozens of children already!" Mary went on, "Illegitimate ones too."

Katherine nodded, only half listening. Katherine had been suffering with a dull ache in her lower belly since the night before, and it had continued to pester her throughout the night and this morning. She had hoped to alleviate some of the pain through prayer, but now wished she had instead stayed abed and avoided Mary's irksome jabbering.

"Do you think Maggie will visit us when she lives in Scotland?" Mary continued, her voice having taken a more sombre quality, "I will miss her."

"I am sure that she will," Katherine replied, forcing a cheerful tone, remembering that it was not Mary's fault she felt so rotten. But just then, as the little Mary opened her mouth to continue her ramblings, Katherine doubled over, a sharp pain shooting through her belly.

"Your Grace!" her ladies called frantically from behind Katherine and Mary as they approached their mistress, then, "Fetch the physician!" to the guard standing sentry nearby.

"What is it?" Lina whispered to Katherine as she moaned in pain, leaning against the wall of the stone hallway.

Katherine gritted her teeth as the pain continued to pierce through her, her face a pale shade of grey.

"I think it is the baby…"

"The princess has suffered a miscarriage," the physician informed the king, the queen, and Arthur just hours later.

The sun outside had begun to set, the sky a dark and solemn shade of orange.

"A miscarriage…?" Arthur breathed, "She was with child?"

Henry Tudor and his wife shared a sombre look.

"She may not even have known herself, Arthur," Queen Elizabeth said.

"You knew?" the prince asked, his eyes shining with sorrow.

Elizabeth reached over and touched her son's arm, "We had presumed as much when you mentioned she had felt queasy on the journey."

Arthur hung his head, "I had no idea."

"You are young, Arthur," Henry Tudor said then, hoping to assuage some of his son's guilt, "And it is not for us men to understand the workings of a woman's body."

Arthur nodded but remained silent.

Elizabeth smiled a thin-lipped smile at her son, "It is not uncommon," she soothed, "Do not blame her."

"Blame her?" Arthur echoed, suddenly dumbfounded, "Why would I blame her?"

Elizabeth shook her head, her eyes wide, "I did not think you would. I only meant that –" the queen sighed, started again, "Do not be too disheartened over this. You are both still very young and I have no doubt the two of you will have many children in the future."

Arthur nodded gravely, "I think I should go to her."

He had said it like a question, unsure on how to approach this topic, this first experience of grief in his marriage.

Elizabeth pecked her son's cheek, heartbroken for his loss, "I am sure she would like that very much."

When Arthur entered Katherine's bedchamber, the room, and the world, was almost completely dark.

"Katherine?" he said, his voice barely above a whisper.

He heard the rustling of fabric then as her ladies hurriedly approached him.

"Her Grace is sleeping, my lord," he heard her lady Lina say, her Spanish accent still strong, much like Katherine's.

He began to retreat, "Oh, I did not –"

"Arthur?" Katherine's weak voice called from the other room.

Arthur blinked, his eyes adjusting to the darkness.

At the sound of her mistress' stirring, Lina lit a candle and led Arthur to Katherine's bedside. She placed the candle by the bedside table and curtsied before giving the couple their privacy.

"Arthur…" Katherine breathed weakly as she searched for his hand in the dim light.

The prince sat down gingerly at the edge of the bed and allowed her to take his hand, "I am here," he said, though he did not know what else he could offer her except his pointless presence. Whether he was there or not, their child would not return to them.

"Did you know…?" Arthur asked quietly then, not an accusation, but a question of wonderment, for he could not understand how he hadn't even known of his own child's existence an hour ago, and yet somehow its passing felt like the loss of a vital organ.

Katherine's face scrunched up then, her pale face looking ghoulish in the flickering light of the candle, "I was not certain," she confessed, "I did not want to tell you in case –"

In case the worst were to happen.

He did not know what to say or do as Katherine cried silently into the pillow.

"I am so sorry," Katherine blubbered then, taking Arthur's silence as an accusation.

Arthur shook his head and stroked her hair from her face, an action that had come so easily in that moment that Arthur surprised even himself.

Since the day of their picnic, when Katherine and Arthur had finally consummated their marriage, they had only been intimate one other time. Both times had been swift, pragmatical transactions, both parties being as inexperienced as the other allowing for little emotion to take over, embarrassment and discomfort still being a key element between them. And kissing and touching still did not come naturally to the pair even after over a year of marriage.

For Arthur to so effortlessly console Katherine now in this most vulnerable of settings, proved to both of them that there was something there. Something stronger than either of them had noticed until now.

A lump formed in Arthur's throat as he allowed his emotions to lead him, entirely disregarding the voice in his head that called for order, rules, and control.

This was not a moment for perfection. This was raw.

And Arthur wished to feel all of it, no matter how ugly and broken it made him feel inside.

As Katherine continued to look up at him and weep, Arthur slowly crawled into bed beside her. Fully clothed, he wrapped his arms around his wife and stroked her hair reassuringly. He kissed her wet cheeks, and she laid her head on his chest and sobbed into his shirt and jacket.

And there they laid. No words, no rehearsed actions. Just feelings.

Deep, dark, painful feelings.

Part II

The slow burn is far more enduring
than that of the fleeting flame.

Chapter 6

6 years later

February 1509
Richmond Palace, Surrey

Six years had passed in which Katherine and Arthur had embraced their marriage for what it was: a diplomatic merger. There was no passion present in their union, no burning desire to tear each other's clothes off, and certainly no desperate need to copulate whenever possible.

The couple went about their own individual lives as much as possible, the two of them content in the knowledge that they were, perhaps, destined simply to be friends.

But good friends they were, that much was certain. And in times of crisis, they had a manner of finding their way to each other.

Since the loss of their baby, Arthur had become Katherine's rock in times of need, his stoic aura never failing to hold Katherine together, or to build her back up when she was defeated. When tragic news had come from Katherine's homeland in 1504 that her mother Isabella de Castille had died, Katherine had been inconsolable, her mother's loss having hurt her soul almost beyond repair. She had holed herself up in her chambers and done little more than sleep and pray for weeks, even going so far as to refuse to eat for days on end. But Arthur had aided her out of her desolation, praying with her each morning and coaxing her to have even just a small bite of food each day. He had been serene and gentle, reminding her that those that were lost from the world would always have a way of staying with us. It had taken much patience and tenderness. But after several weeks, Arthur had managed to get through to her, and with much prayer and healing, Katherine had begun to overcome her grief.

They were each other's pillar of strength. Each other's valued companion. They were a good match in everything.
Except in passion.
It might come yet, the thirteen-year-old Princess Mary had said on Katherine and Arthur's latest return to London.
Mary, who would soon be at the age to be married for herself, continued to maintain a fierce hope that love could grow anywhere, like a flower eager to bloom even in a dry and desolate desert.
But Katherine, now a young woman of twenty-three, had much less hope of a delayed burst of intimacy, having long ago resigned herself to a life of tedium – at least when it came to the prospect of being coveted.
Even Margaret, who had departed England five years prior, to fulfil her duty in Scotland, had already discovered what it was like to be cherished. Due to Margaret's young age in comparison to her husband's when they were wed, King James IV had been decent enough to defer consummating their marriage until his young bride had reached her seventeenth year. It had meant waiting three years since her arrival in Scotland, but it had allowed for Margaret to develop respect and regard for her husband; and not soon thereafter, news had reached England that Margaret had borne her first child.
I pray only that Arthur and I may have an heir of our own soon, Katherine had admitted to Mary then, and the young princess had squeezed Katherine's hand, hoping to reassure.
You have not been lucky, she'd said, acknowledging Katherine's losses throughout the years.
Since her first miscarriage, Katherine had suffered two more, the young couple – and the rest of England – beginning to fear that providing an heir for the Tudor dynasty may not be in the royal couple's capacity.
King Henry Tudor had made his disappointment of Katherine's failings over the years perfectly clear, often ignoring her at banquets, and even going so far as to snubbing her at events.

And it had made for a tense atmosphere whenever she and Arthur visited London, which – to Katherine's displeasure – was at least three times a year.

But when it came to the king's exasperation over their lack of heir, Arthur had always stood by her, never allowing his father to lay all the blame on Katherine. And for that, at least, Katherine was grateful.

For the remainder of the year when they were not summoned to attend court, she and Arthur resided in Ludlow, away from the scrutiny of Henry Tudor and his council, and where they could return to the carefully laid out routine that had become their daily lives – a perfected, careful dance of co-existing under the same roof without invading too much of each other's space.

But despite all of Katherine's heartache – her unsuccessful pregnancies, and her unfulfilled marital passions – she had faith in God's plan for her, and that His divine intervention would soon come to light.

And truth be told, given her failings to produce a child after seven years of marriage, Katherine was grateful to have a husband as understanding as Arthur. Despite his limitations, Arthur *was* a good man.

He had grown to be tall and broad-shouldered, with a smile that always touched his eyes, and a laugh that brightened even the gloomiest of days. He listened intently when she spoke and respected her in the rare occasions when they had differing opinions. He had held her through all her losses and never given even an inkling of reproach, even calming her when she herself sobbed and raged at her own body's failings.

For all intents and purposes, Arthur was – *almost* – the perfect husband.

But deep down he was still that same timid boy that Katherine had met all those years ago, his uncertainty and insecurity overshadowing every of his achievements, no matter how big or small.

Except now, after many years of careful observation, Katherine had come to understand that Arthur's insecurities were not of his own doing, not self-inflicted scars of an unknown, reasonless hatred for himself.

No. Arthur's insecurities had come from the weight of too-heavy expectations. Expectations that originated from none other than his own father. Katherine had learned over the years that Henry Tudor was himself riddled with infirmities – paranoias birthed from the knowledge that others had a greater right to the throne than he. And he had unwittingly succeeded in transmitting this lack of self-worth onto his own son and heir. The irony of it all had not escaped the princess, and it pained Katherine to watch the growing anxiety in her husband's eyes whenever they made their slow approach to London.

This visit, however, was not just the mere thrice-annual gathering for the festive seasons. This time there was something new to be celebrated – something which Katherine and Arthur both hoped would deflect from their continued childlessness.

"Can you believe Harry has graduated from Magdalene College a deacon?" Arthur stated proudly as he and Katherine travelled together in the royal carriage.

Katherine smiled, knowing the question to have been rhetorical. Arthur grinned excitedly, turning his head to look out the window as they made their way through the palace gates, "I am looking forward to seeing how he has changed."

"Yes," Katherine agreed half-heartedly, barely remembering what the little Prince Harry looked like before they had all gone their separate ways.

"I do hope he hasn't changed too much," Arthur continued after some thought, "I have missed his mischievous nature, much as it irritated me when we were boys. I could do with some light-hearted fun."

Katherine smiled warmly at her husband, glad to see Arthur excited to return to court for once.

When their carriage came to a halt in the palace courtyard, Arthur was so eager to see his younger brother that he shot out of the carriage without offering Katherine his hand, something he had always usually done. But Katherine did not begrudge him and was simply pleased to see Arthur so giddy to reconnect with Harry.

"Brother!"

Katherine heard the voice call out and for a moment could not place where it had come from, for surely it had not been the little Prince Harry from her memory to boast such a deep, gruff voice.

But before she could shake her confusion, a tall, slender young man with hair as bright as the evening sun was embracing her husband and slapping him warmly on the back.

"Look at you!" the young man was saying, "Look at those shoulders!" and he gripped Arthur by the shoulders with hands that Katherine noticed were surprisingly veiny.

Arthur was laughing the laugh Katherine knew meant he was at ease, and in that laugh was her confirmation that this was indeed the little Prince Harry, returned from Oxford.

Except he wasn't so 'little' anymore.

At her approach, the two brothers turned to her, and Arthur held out his hand for her to take. She did, but her eyes remained fixed on Harry.

"Princess Katherine," her brother-in-law said with a grin, his voice curling around her like smoke.

"Harry," she replied simply, fully aware that her throat felt too dry.

March 1509

Though King Henry Tudor had been taken ill twice since their return to London, the king would not be deterred from celebrating Harry's return to court.

The royal couple had organized a splendid Spring Tournament for their youngest son's arrival, with many events taking place such as jousting and archery, both of which were Harry's favourite pastimes.

During one such archery tournament in the field behind the palace, Katherine, Princess Mary, and Queen Elizabeth were watching from their cushioned seats underneath the canopy as Harry and his good friend, Charles Brandon – who had grown up alongside Arthur and Harry within Henry Tudor's court – took their turns; Arthur and the king standing on the sidelines to observe and talk.

It was Harry's turn to shoot his arrow, and Katherine watched intently as he pulled his bowstring tautly, the muscles in his slender arms flexing. He let loose his arrow and a slow, lopsided smirk crept over his face to see it embedded in the target's centre. Katherine could feel her cheeks flushing as she watched him, her breathing becoming uneven, her mouth dry. She forced herself to look away then, terrified that someone might have seen her gawking at her brother-in-law. She focused her attention on Arthur and King Henry instead, the father and son now appearing to be frustrated with one another, Henry gesticulating wildly. It made Katherine sit straighter in her seat, suddenly nervous to think her father-in-law might be badmouthing her to Arthur yet again for her failure to produce any children. She could not hear what the men were discussing, the distance and the audiences' collective murmur between them, drowning out the men's conversation. Beside her, the queen and her daughter spoke of the weather and of suitors for Mary, but Katherine could not bring herself to care, and she found herself focusing on the men's lips, desperate to know what was being said.

But all she could make out clearly were the sporadic hacking coughs that regularly arose from the king, making Katherine wish that Arthur would not stand so close to his father.

As Charles Brandon took his turn at archery, Katherine noticed Harry had sauntered over to join his father and brother at the sidelines, leaning casually against the wooden fence. His presence interrupted Arthur and Henry's discussion, for which Katherine was grateful. She smiled at Harry's easy stance – so unlike Arthur's own stiff posture.

As Harry stood beside his brother then, Katherine was surprised to see that – despite the different shades and texture of their red hair, and slightly different builds – the two brothers could easily have passed for twins.

Both had eyes as blue as the midday sky – though Arthur's pupils, Katherine knew, were rimmed with a gold outline. Both had thin lips which naturally pulled to one side first when they smiled. Both were tall and sported an athletic figure and broad shoulders.

Katherine frowned at her realisation as she watched the king and his two sons laugh at some joke Harry had quipped.

How had she not noticed the brother's similarities sooner?

But even more incomprehensible still: why did she feel no lustful desire for Arthur, when Harry, who was his carbon copy, made her breathing quicken and her heart race?

April 1509

King Henry Tudor's condition had quickly worsened, and the court was buzzing with agitation.

"We need to inform Arthur," Queen Elizabeth mumbled tearfully as she and her mother-in-law Margaret Beaufort stood by the far window of the king's bedchamber.

Two physicians were looming over the ashen-faced king, one murmuring to the other to lift the king's head so that he may spoon feed him a tonic.

Queen Elizabeth half sighed, half sobbed at the sight, pressing a trembling hand to her mouth.

"What am I to do without him, lady mother?" the queen whimpered quietly, turning to her mother-in-law.

The older lady did not reply and merely continued to stare at her son, her boy, her only child, as he fought to stay alive.

"I don't know," Margaret Beaufort whispered wearily after a moment, wrapping a frail arm around her daughter-in-law's shoulders and pulling her close as though she were a child.

"I honestly do not know."

At the age of fifty-two, King Henry VII, the first monarch of the Tudor dynasty, was dead.

He was mourned by his children, his mother, and his wife, as well as the people of England, despite their recent growing resentment of him.

And so, the sun had set on the reign of Henry Tudor, making way for it to dawn on the new reign of his son, the Prince of Wales, who, with his father's passing, would henceforth be known as King Arthur of England.

Chapter 7

May 1509

The former Queen of England Elizabeth of York – now to be styled the Dowager Queen Elizabeth – had taken the loss of her beloved husband very hard, and following his funeral the month prior, had ordered for dozens of her dresses to be recreated in only black fabric.

"I shall mourn him forever," the Dowager Queen murmured sombrely on the eve following her husband's funeral, "What is even the point of colour?"

Margaret Beaufort, who felt equally as broken as her daughter-in-law – if not more so – took her gently by the hand.

"As will I," the mother of the late king replied, "But there is much to do. Arthur and Katherine will need our guidance during this time, as well as our patience as they find their footing."

Elizabeth sniffed and shook her head without looking up, "I fear for their future, lady mother," she admitted in a rash whisper, "They have been wed nearly a decade and have no living heirs to show for it."

Margaret Beaufort swallowed. She too had, of course, been disturbed by this.

"The princess came from a fertile line," Margaret assured Elizabeth, "Her mother birthed seven children, five of which reached adulthood," she paused for a second to allow her conviction to set in, "There is still hope for heirs."

Elizabeth inhaled a shaky breath and met Margaret's gaze, "She does not love him," she said accusingly, unable to understand how this perfect match had gone so terribly wrong, "I did not wish for this life for him. A life without love *or* heirs…it is unthinkable."

She wiped at her puffy, red eyes with a handkerchief. Margaret took the Dowager Queen's hand and squeezed it, urging Elizabeth to look at her.

"God is with us," the pious lady reassured the former queen. Elizabeth met Margaret's sharp gaze and nodded weakly, "Yes," she mumbled half-heartedly, having no energy left to sustain the conversation, "God is with us."

22nd June 1509

As was custom before a coronation, Arthur and Katherine made their way to the Tower of London with a great procession, where they would stay before their joint crowning.

The streets of London were luxuriously decorated in anticipation of the ceremony, houses and shops were adorned with intricate tapestries, some even with cloth of gold.

The crowds of people that had come to observe were so vast that railings had been put up along the streets to prevent the public from disturbing the parade.

England was eager for their new monarch to ascend the throne. London was humming with excitement.

Arthur, at the head of the procession, rode gracefully on a horse adorned with gold damask, while above him a gold canopy was being carried by the Barons of the *Cinque Ports*. He wore robes of crimson velvet trimmed with ermine over a gold jacket.

Behind Arthur, his brother Prince Harry Duke of York, Griffith Rhys, and many lords, knights, and esquires followed on foot.

Katherine's procession followed Arthur's, Katherine being carried in a litter supported by two white horses adorned with white cloth of gold. She wore a gown of embroidered white satin, her wavy hair hanging loose over her shoulders and down her back, similarly to on her wedding day eight years prior.

Upon their arrival at the royal apartments in the Tower of London, they enjoyed a splendid banquet of many delicious dishes, fine music and dancing, which Arthur and Katherine only observed from their seats at the high table, too exhausted from the enormity of the day. But Katherine was secretly glad to be overlooking the festivities, for this way she was able to watch as Harry merrily whirled one lady after another around on the dancefloor.

The merriment was concluded in the late afternoon to allow time for prayer at St. Stephen's Chapel, where the pious couple spent the next few hours praying to God in silence, followed by an even quieter night in separate bedchambers.

24th June 1509
Westminster Abbey, London

The day of their coronation was a Sunday and also Midsummer's Day, and Katherine only wished that she felt more fulfilled.

This – right here – *this* was her destiny, a destiny she had been promised since the age of three: to become the Queen of England. And yet, now that the day had finally come, Katherine felt nothing but deflated, her continued sorry state of childlessness clouding the otherwise bright and sunny day. And as her ladies dressed her in preparation for the most important day of her life, Katherine couldn't help but wonder just how different her life would've been, had she married the *other* Tudor Prince instead.

As soon as the thought burst into her head like an unwelcome guest, Katherine's stomach dropped with shame.

What a hateful, sinful thing to think!

Harry was undeniably charming and charismatic – attributes she clearly appreciated in a man, for why else would she feel so lured in by him – but Arthur was her husband. And Arthur was a good man.

If only he were more like Harry.

She frowned at her reflection in the mirror and shook her head, disbelief over her wicked thoughts causing a churning of

disgust to develop in her stomach as her ladies continued to flit about her none the wiser, preparing her for the grand ceremony ahead.
Was God testing her?

Later, Arthur and Katherine made their way to Westminster Abbey with the Barons of *Cinque Ports* carrying a canopy over the royal couple as they walked along the path towards the abbey, the bright sunshine above illuminating their way.
Once inside the abbey, the noble couple was ceremoniously met by the Archbishop of Canterbury William Warham, who led them down the aisle to their thrones.
The abbey was filled with clerics of the realm, members of the nobility and many lords and ladies, all of which were delighted to be witnessing such a momentous occasion. Among them was the Dowager Queen Elizabeth of York and the late king's mother Margaret Beaufort, both of which, too – despite their continued worry for their future – could not help but beam proudly as they observed the couple's ascent.
As Arthur and Katherine were anointed according to sacred tradition and ancient custom by the archbishop – the crown of Edward the Confessor resting on Arthur's head, while Katherine received the smaller crown of the Queen Consorts of England – Elizabeth of York wiped a tear from her flushed face. As her son and daughter-in-law were crowned, a burst of pride eclipsed the grief she had been consumed by of late, hope being planted in its wake. And Elizabeth allowed this seed of hope to guide her, clasping her prayer beads in her hands and silently praying to God that He would yet grant her son an heir of his own to continue the Tudor dynasty.

29th June 1509

Just five days after Arthur and Katherine had been crowned, the Lady Margaret Beaufort Countess of Richmond and Derby, and the mother of the Tudor dynasty, died at the age of sixty-six, following her beloved son into the afterlife.

A grand funeral was organised in Westminster Abbey, one with all the rights and respects of a would-be queen, Arthur wanting to acknowledge his grandmother's own connections to the throne of England.

Her good friend and Harry's former tutor, Bishop Fisher, preached the funeral oration, praising her marvellous gentleness unto all and expressing the great pain all of England would feel at her loss.

"She is with your father now," Elizabeth consoled her children after the funeral; her youngest, the Princess Mary, openly weeping at their grandmother's loss, so swiftly after their father's.

Elizabeth embraced her daughter, noting as she looked over her shoulder that Harry, too, was trying to hold back tears.

The news of their grandmother's death hit Harry hard, for not only had he been her favourite, but she had always been his biggest supporter and influence. With her inspiration, Harry had been encouraged to pursue his passion to become a man of the church, had graduated in theology, in part, because of her guidance; and he would be eternally indebted to his beloved grandmother. He thanked God that she had at least lived long enough to see him become a deacon. And Harry thought then, as his mother took hold of his hand and squeezed it, that if she were to continue to watch over him in the afterlife, Margaret Beaufort would hopefully witness him one day becoming a Cardinal, just as she had wanted.

July 1509

Unlike his predecessor Henry VII, the new King Arthur was widely beloved by his people.

Henry VII – or Henry Tudor as many had continued to call him throughout his reign – had been no more than tolerated by the people of England; but never beloved, for the paranoid king had resorted to many underhanded measures to keep the people in check: passing illegal taxations and increasing the cost of bread being but some of the many sly processes he had allowed to enrich the crown at the expense of his people.

And so, when his son Arthur inherited the throne and declared that he would put an end to his father's illegal practices, the nobles and the poor folk alike had expressed their sincere gratitude.

His council, however, had not.

"By becoming lax on the nobles, Your Grace is allowing them to acquire more riches and power," the late king's financial agent, Edmund Dudley, said.

As a new king, Arthur had inherited his father's Privy Council, men of various educational backgrounds, titles, and responsibilities, who had aided the previous monarch in running the country. And since his coronation, Arthur was beginning to note which of them he would wish to eliminate.

"Riches and power which were their right until my father took them from them?" Arthur countered without making eye contact. He was slowly tapping a rolled-up document against the edge of the table, trying to act nonchalant though he still felt apprehensive during these meetings with the much older, much wiser men.

But his statement had worked, and Edmund Dudley squirmed in his seat.

Arthur continued, willing himself to fix his gaze on Dudley, "Riches and power which, as his financial agent, you aided my father in obtaining, Sir Dudley."

Dudley licked his lips and averted his gaze from the young king, "I only ever did what your father asked of me."

Arthur raised one eyebrow, laid the rolled-up document on the table before him, "Of course," he offered insincerely, then, "Nevertheless, it is done. But I will not reign as my father reigned. Until my people give me just cause to clamp down on them, they may live as they please as long as they remain within their legal rights."

The Privy Council nodded, eager to agree with their new king, none more so in that moment than Dudley, who was nodding so vigorously it looked almost painful. But Arthur did not trust the former king's favourite, the man having been allowed to reach far too high under Henry VII's reign. And if Arthur were to take on board anything from the shambles which was Edmund Dudley's apparent abuse of power in recent years, it was that a king should never have a favourite from among his Privy Council.

"Furthermore," Arthur said, casting his gaze over the group of men before him, eager to go on with the meeting, "I wish to put the crown's money to good use. My father was a tight-fisted man. A miser. He enjoyed hoarding the crown's riches for a rainy day," many men before him nodded. Arthur continued, "I cannot say I'm not grateful for the monies I have inherited from his penny-pinching ways. But I wish to further England's development with it, not hoard it uselessly as he did."

"Was there anything specific you had in mind, sire?" one of the late Henry VII's oldest and most loyal advisors, the Bishop of Winchester and Lord Chancellor Richard Fox, asked.

Arthur graced him with his full attention, believing that Fox would likely continue to show his loyalty to the crown. He was one advisor Arthur wished to keep within his council.

"I have no desire for warfare, unless it be absolutely necessary, gentlemen," Arthur declared, hoping to make himself clear from the very start of his reign, "Glory attained upon the battlefield is not something I would willingly seek out," he picked up the rolled-up document before him once more and allowed his announcement to settle before he continued.

"That being said, I am not a naïve man. I know that, though England has peace treaties and alliances with Spain and Scotland, we are not entirely safe from invasion. But I believe it is time we put our minds to strengthening England from within, rather than relying entirely on foreign allies for our protection."

The men sitting around the council table looked at one another in bemusement.

"How, Your Grace?" one asked.

Arthur sat forward in his throne with a grin – excited to make his announcement – and unrolled the document before him, revealing a large and detailed sketch, "With ships, gentlemen. With great, big, warships."

Arthur had sketched the designs for the two new warships himself, adding an entirely new design feature to them which had never been done before.

"I call them 'gun ports'," Arthur said with a grin, showing the design to Harry and Griffith later that day.

Harry perused the sketches with interest, "Gun ports," he repeated, then nodded, "I like it."

Arthur thanked his younger brother with a nod.

"These are excellent, Arthur," Griffith added, tracing the lines of the larger of the two ships with his fingers as he examined the intricate designs.

"Are you planning an invasion then, brother?" Harry asked, his pale blue eyes shining with hope of an affirmative answer.

Arthur raised his eyebrows and glanced at Griffith before replying, "Only you would hope so, Harry."

Harry chuckled, unfazed, then bent over to further inspect the drawings.

"Pomegranates?" he said, noticing the fruit displayed upon the smaller ship's badge.

Arthur nodded, "Katherine's personal emblem."

Harry raised his eyebrows before scoffing an imprudent laugh, "A bit ironic, isn't it? The pomegranate being a symbol of fertility."

Arthur flinched at the remark, "Don't be crude, Harry," he said, "She is your queen. Show some respect."
Harry held up his hands in mock defeat, "I am only jesting, brother," he said, looking to Griffith for a hint of encouragement. But the more mature man gave nothing away, his face remaining serious, almost offended, at the prince's humourless jibe. For Griffith's alliance did not rest with the Duke of York, but with the king.
Realising his blunder, Harry's smile quickly turned into a scowl before he turned to quit the room, muttering something about lack of humour, and leaving Arthur behind with his sketches and a bad taste in his mouth.

August 1509

Prince Harry and King Arthur were riding at the head of the royal household as they travelled out of London on progress following Arthur and Katherine's coronation. Progress was recognised as a vital part of maintaining a king's authority as monarch, and with Arthur only recently crowned, it was important that he present himself to his people. As England was mainly a rural kingdom with most people living and working on the land, to be seen by his subjects, the monarch was expected to venture out of London; and by visiting the localities, a monarch was presented to his subjects against a background of ceremony and ritualised splendour.
Since Harry's reckless remark regarding the new Queen of England, he had been on his best behaviour, taking special care to always bow his head in Katherine's presence, address her with the utmost respect, and to never speak ill of her. At least not out loud.
Arthur had noticed the change in him, and he was glad for it, since it would be disastrous indeed to have the royal family in disharmony so soon into his reign.

"I wish to further my understanding of theology by learning from the best, Your Grace," Harry now said, just a short while into their journey out of London.

"Archbishop Warham is a busy man, Harry," Arthur replied with a twitch of his auburn eyebrows, "But I do believe our late father's chaplain, Thomas Wolsey, would appreciate an apprentice."

"Wolsey?" Harry frowned, remembering him in his father's service during Harry's childhood, and having recently heard scandalous rumours about him.

Arthur nodded as they swayed gently upon their horses, their journey having slowed to a steady walk, "Yes, Wolsey was recently appointed Dean of Lincoln shortly before father's passing."

Harry shook his head briefly, "I hear he is not as celibate as he ought to be, brother."

Arthur breathed a laugh at Harry's words, "Yes, I hear he has relations with a woman. Joan Larke, I believe is her name."

Harry had not yet taken his vow of celibacy – not yet having been mandated to do so as a deacon – and though the young man had enjoyed relations with several ladies in recent years, Harry firmly believed that when he was to make that vow before God, that he would *never* again take another woman to his bed. And the fact that Thomas Wolsey was so blatantly disrespecting God and breaking his vow; well, it didn't sit right with him.

"The edict that priests should remain celibate has not been wholeheartedly accepted, Harry," Arthur said, sensing his brother's cynicism.

Harry nodded, "I am aware," he said, though he continued to quietly judge the older man of the cloth.

But Harry knew that Wolsey, despite his obvious shortcomings, was no doubt knowledgeable and respected in his field, their own father having clearly respected his opinions enough to appoint him Dean of Lincoln in his short time in the late king's service. Harry turned a smiling face to Arthur.

"If Your Grace permits it," he said, having made his decision not to look a gift horse in the mouth, "I would very much like to further my work under the Dean of Lincoln's expert eye."

Arthur nodded proudly at his brother, "I shall see to it that it is done. As soon as we return from progress, you, Harry, will be taking that one step closer to priesthood."

Harry grinned and shifted excitedly on his horse, "And who knows, brother. Maybe one day I shall become archbishop, and you and I shall be the two pillars of England."

Arthur returned his brother's smile, though he was slightly irked by his arrogance and sense of entitlement, and he was reminded yet again of how different they really were.

For the following few days and weeks, the royal progress travelled through Hamworth, Sunninghill, Woking, Farham, Esher, Enfield, and Waltham, staying at the towns' finest royal lodgings, and in each location, dozens of their people would gather simply to catch a glimpse of their new king and queen as they passed through.

The royal couple would wave and sometimes give out coins, and women and children would come up to the queen's carriage and hold plucked flowers up to her which she accepted gratefully.

"We pray for your good health, my queen," they would say, and Katherine would nod in thanks.

But every so often they would give voice to Katherine's failings, "May God grant you many sons soon!" and she would shrink back into the shadows of her carriage.

Katherine knew they did not mean to hurt her, but her insecurity over her inability to carry a child to term was becoming more and more of a worry, especially now that she was queen.

The pressure to produce an heir had never been so great.

September 1509

Upon their return to London, a great banquet had been organised with many plays, dances, and songs, and the court was quite clearly glad to be back.

Katherine and her sister-in-law Princess Mary sat at the high table together, talking animatedly about the developing betrothal between Mary and Katherine's nephew, Prince Carlos de Castille. Though Carlos was but nine years-old and would not be of age to marry for several years, his recent inheritance of the Low Countries upon his father's death, and the fact that he would one day become King of Castille, made him an excellent match for marriage. And Katherine was proud to see that her dear sister-in-law would be the one to claim that respectable title, further uniting the royal families of England and Spain.

Later, when the banquet and plays had concluded and the musicians began their jolly tunes, Mary gasped with excitement before pulling Katherine up from her seat.

"Let's dance!" she declared excitedly at the cheerful music.

At his sister's exclamation, Arthur turned from Harry beside him and looked up at them, "You like this one, Mary?" he asked merrily.

"Is it one of your compositions, brother?" the young princess asked as she took Katherine by the hand and hurried to the dancefloor in a flurry of velvet and silk, too eager to dance to wait for his response.

Curious, Katherine looked over her shoulder to see Arthur smiling at them in confirmation. She returned his smile warmly, pleased to see him embrace and proudly boast what he had once believed to be a show of weakness.

The ladies danced and giggled merrily, holding onto each other's hands as they spun round and round with the other courtiers.

Wine had been flowing in a constant surge all evening, cups never fully emptying before a servant would emerge from the shadows to refill them, and before long, Arthur and Harry were laughing and talking loudly, smacking each other on the shoulder in brotherly regard as the court danced and frolicked on the dancefloor.

But now, as Katherine was being spun around, her stomach full of good food and her heart even fuller with great company, Katherine broke free of her dance partner and embraced her sister-in-law warmly.

"I am weary," she admitted to the younger lady with an exhausted laugh, "You carry on, Mary, I shall return to Arthur." Mary went to reply but was suddenly grabbed from behind and twirled around by Harry's close friend, Charles Brandon, before disappearing with a joyful laugh in among the crowd. A little breathless, Katherine picked up her skirts and headed back to the high table where Arthur and Harry continued to talk excitedly, their seats pushed closely together.

Too caught up in the merriment, Katherine did not notice her husband's deeply furrowed brows as she approached, nor did they notice Katherine taking her seat beside Arthur. And just as she had lowered herself into it, the queen caught the tail end of their heated conversation, and it succeeded in evaporating her cheerful flush in an instant, sending a cold chill to course through her veins.

"—until she gives you a son, royal Princess of Spain or not, Katherine is entirely useless."

In her shock, Katherine let out a sharp gasp and her shaky hand knocked over a cup of wine, a river of red spilling over the edge of the table and dripping onto the stone floor, like a puddle of blood seeping from a stab wound to the gut.

And it certainly felt like she had just been gutted.

Arthur turned in his seat to face her, his flushed face suddenly paling as he realised her presence.

"Katherine –"

But she could not tear her gaze from her husband's brother, who sat slumped in his seat beside Arthur and taking another big gulp of wine, unaware – or uncaring – that he had just utterly crushed her.

And just like that, it was as if a spell had broken.

Katherine blinked quickly to remove the film of tears that had threatened to spill over. She tore her gaze from Harry and looked at Arthur, offering him a half-smile of reassurance, before looking back at Harry who continued to simply sit there, picking at his teeth with the nail of his pinkie finger, as though no great thing had just happened.

But it had.

For in that one string of words, Katherine had come to realise that Harry Duke of York was a cad! And that beneath his charming, chivalric bravado, was a disrespectful, chauvinistic pig who had *never* deserved her regard!

She returned her attention to her husband, who was staring at her wide-eyed, fear that she had overheard his brother's disgusting remark quite clearly etched upon his face.

He did not share Harry's opinion, that much was clear. But Katherine had known as much even before this moment of clarity.

Suddenly, it was as if she could finally see Arthur clearly, as if for the past few years she had been looking at him through a misted window, and it felt as though the sun had just risen over their marriage for the very first time...

This was the man who deserved her regard. This man that had stood by her – *held* her, *soothed* her – through her losses, while even she herself had hated her body for her failures.

He who had always managed to make her feel cherished despite his own limitations at showing physical affection.

It was a minor problem all of a sudden, his coy demeanour, now that Katherine could see in ugly contrast just how Harry might have reacted had she suffered the same losses while married to him.

The fact that she had even daydreamed about the possibility of married life with Harry instead of Arthur now made her feel sick to her stomach, and she took that opportunity to dismiss herself from the festivities.

"I am tired," she told her king, before rising from her throne and reaching a hand to softly stroke Arthur's face.

In that simple touch she conveyed a secret apology for having believed for so long that he had not been enough. She had been foolish.

For quite the opposite was true: Arthur was *precisely* what she had always needed. And rather unexpectedly, after nine years of marriage, she realised he was exactly what she wanted.

Chapter 8

October 1509
Richmond Palace, Surrey

Katherine felt as though she were floating on air.
Following her epiphany the month before, Katherine was overjoyed to suddenly see Arthur in an entirely new light.
While she had always believed him to be handsome, all of a sudden she saw beauty in more than just his looks. Even his slightly misaligned incisor that she had noted as a flaw for all these years was now an endearing feature to Katherine, a tiny imperfection which made him somehow all the more interesting. And now, just the thought of her husband caused a burst of girlish excitement to flutter in her chest, and a smitten smile to creep over her face.
What she had previously seen as a fault in his character was now the very attribute she appreciated most in him; his composed, stoic stillness no longer being a lapse in strength as she previously thought, but a promise of a future of unyielding security.
Following her realisation, whenever she passed Harry in the hallways of the palace – the young man completely unaware of her altered perception of him as he followed Dean Thomas Wolsey around – Katherine no longer saw him as the charming one of the two brothers, for his insincerity and dishonour had finally come to light.
But in a way, Katherine was grateful to Harry and his artificial persona, for he had opened her eyes to what truly mattered in a marriage: mutual respect, understanding, and compassion.
Everything else was buildable on that. And with Katherine's newfound insight into her relationship, she was ready and willing to explore a deeper connection with her husband.

"Has the king received my message?" Katherine asked Lina as they made their way to the chapel for their morning prayers.

"He did, Your Grace," Lina replied with a knowing grin, "He has accepted your invitation."
Queen Katherine exhaled slowly to alleviate some of the growing anticipation in her chest, "Good," she said with a hopeful smile, "I leave it with you, Lina. Be sure to ready my bedchamber for a romantic evening with the king."

Later, when the sun was beginning to set over the horizon, King Arthur knocked gently on the doors to the queen's chambers and entered a short moment later with his eyebrows arched, assessing the dimly candlelit rooms.

"Katherine?" he called into the shadows, closing the door behind him.

He stepped inside tentatively and headed towards the hearth, the fire giving the dark rooms a blazing heart. Once he was standing beside it, Arthur squinted his eyes in hope of adjusting to the darkness, when a figure emerged from among the shadows.

She was wearing her wavy hair loose over her shoulders, its length trailing down like two bronze waterfalls over her chest, and as she slowly approached, Arthur noticed that Katherine was barefoot beneath the full-length, white silk nightgown she was wearing.

She stopped just inches away from him and his gaze travelled up the length of her body before meeting her eyes, which were looking up at him in a way she had never looked at him before. Her lips were slightly parted, and in their proximity, Arthur could hear that her breathing was coming in short and shallow, as though she were nervous, or perhaps...excited?

Arthur frowned briefly, unsure of what had brought this on.

In the past, Katherine had never voluntarily lain with him. He had known of her reluctance in the way she had often looked away during their couplings, or kept her arms pressed firmly at her sides throughout.

Her obvious indisposition had been the very reason why they had not shared a bed more than two or three times a year; and only then because of their sense of duty to produce an heir. When their couplings had led to miscarriage after miscarriage over the years, their marital unions had become even less frequent still. Arthur had always respected her reluctance, never pushing her to do anything she had not wanted to do.

But never had their encounters occurred such as this, with an elusive invitation, candlelight, and a lustful seduction.

This was an entirely new turn of events within their marriage. And Arthur, though he did not know of the reason behind it, was indisputably pleased for its development.

Though he had struggled with his boyish insecurities for the first few years of his marriage to Katherine, Arthur had never questioned his feelings for her: he had always loved Katherine of Aragon.

Ever since their very first meeting just days before their union before God, Arthur had felt that warm wave of infatuation taking over his body; and in the months that had followed, admiration and respect.

But it had been when she had lost their first child that he had known that he had fallen in love with her; for in that moment of utter despair and misery, Arthur had wanted for nothing more than to draw the pain and sorrow out of her, even if it had meant that he would shoulder it all himself.

Eight years had passed since his realisation that he was in love with Katherine, and in that time, Arthur had grown to accept that she might never reciprocate his feelings.

He had never voiced his feelings aloud, never forced them onto her in the hope that she might return them; for after so many years had passed, he had little hope that she ever would.

But now, for some unknown reason, Katherine was looking up at him in a way he had long dreamed she would, in a way which suggested she *did* harbour some feelings for him beyond that of marital duty and friendship.

"I…" he attempted then, falling short of the right words.

He didn't know how to respond to the look in her eyes, did not know if he was reading too much into the setting due to their desperate need for a successor…

But while Arthur struggled to sort through his barrage of thoughts, Katherine gently pressed her palms against his chest, rose up on her tiptoes, and quietened his mind with a gentle kiss. With their lips pressed together, and her hands burning on his chest, Arthur cautiously allowed his fingers to skim over her silk nightgown and down her back, and before long, their gentle kiss developed into something Arthur had never expected. With a low moan, Katherine's kiss grew deep and intimate, like she was claiming him for the first time.

And Arthur felt in that instant like he had finally been given the key to what had previously been a perpetually locked door.

November 1509

"Reparations will be completed before the Christmastide, Your Grace," Arthur was being informed the following month as he sat upon his throne in the great hall, "The final touches are being made as we speak."

"Excellent news," Arthur replied with an excited grin, "I shall make the necessary arrangements for the move."

In light of Arthur's wish to strengthen England from within, he had decided to invest in making one of his favourite residences, Greenwich Palace, much larger, ordering stables, forges, a new banqueting hall, and armouries to be built. And with the coming of a new year, he was hoping to move his court from Richmond Palace to reside there.

Arthur had always been fond of Greenwich Palace, ever since his father had elevated it from a mere manor with his own few renovations years earlier. And its convenient positioning beside the River Thames allowed for closer proximity to the royal shipyards, which Arthur was particularly interested in.

Arthur sat back in his throne, sighing contently as he cast his eyes over the many courtiers conversing or playing cards and chess within the great hall.

It all appeared to be falling into place of late: the building of his warships had begun, the renovations of Greenwich Palace were going smoothly; and when his council brought forth the renewed Anglo-Scottish Peace Treaty – which had needed Arthur's royal seal and signature as the new King of England – he had signed without ado, eager to continue at peace with their neighbouring country.

As Princes of England, Arthur and Harry had been brought up with tales of military victory in France, and of English overlordship of Scotland. And though those tales had stirred up a hankering for war in Harry, Arthur had been perceptive enough to understand that war was not something to be entered into lightly. And unless there was ever a definitive *need* for anything other than peace, the young king was happy to continue the period of tranquillity England and Scotland had enjoyed since their sister Margaret's marriage to King James IV. Arthur was not interested in risking his people's bloodshed in the pursuit of glory.

With the welcome developments occurring in the young king's life – both political and personal – Arthur allowed himself to enjoy the peace that had begun to settle within himself.

February 1510
Greenwich Palace, London

Queen Katherine of Aragon was with child, but she was too afraid to announce it, for fear of it ending in loss, as all the other times had.

"Until I am showing there is no need to tell the king."

Despite her nervousness, Katherine couldn't hide her smile at the mention of Arthur, and though the decision to not yet announce her condition came from a place of trepidation, just the thought of her husband now aided in easing the heavy anxiety in her chest.

How incredible it was, Katherine thought, the power of perception; for Arthur had *always* been Arthur. Nothing about him had changed other than how *she* saw him, and yet Katherine now felt giddy at the mere mention of him.

It was a beautiful feeling, to wake up beside her husband and to feel the warmth of his hand on her hip, as though letting go of her, even in his sleep, was unthinkable, despite having spent their first decade together sleeping apart.

In the months that had followed her enlightenment, Katherine and Arthur had opened up to one another in ways that had been completely foreign to them, presenting each other their hearts as though they were newlyweds once again, with no encumbered past, and nothing to lose.

In the dead of night, sitting in dim candlelight, they had breathed incredulous laughs at having learned about their shared mistaken beliefs that the other had not wished to share their space; lack of proper communication having served as a literal physical barrier between them for all those years.

But soon their laughter had dwindled into regret upon having realised just how much time they had lost due to something so trifling.

"I should have been more assertive," Arthur had said one night as they lay on the floor before the fireplace of his chambers, naked save for the furs draped haphazardly over their bodies. He'd shaken his head at himself, his auburn hair brushing his shoulders.

"We could have both done things differently," Katherine had countered softly, fully aware of her own failings, "I was too stubborn to see what was right in front of me."

They had fallen silent, Arthur running the tips of his fingers along Katherine's pale neck.

"I love you, Katherine," he had suddenly said, looking up at her, devotion shining in his eyes as the lazy embers in the fireplace cast an orange glow over half his face. He'd grinned. It felt good to finally be able to speak the words aloud.

"I've always loved you," he proclaimed, the words feeling freeing, "But...I'd always wondered if I would do," he'd admitted then, a frown replacing his grin, "Whether I'd be enough. For the daughter of Spain."

"Arthur –"

"No, Katherine," Arthur had interrupted gently, "Let me say it. I need to say it," he'd looked up at her in wonder, "I've loved you for years. And I had accepted your indifference. But this – I had given up hoping for this."

Katherine reached for him, "You are more than enough."

Arthur smiled meekly, shaking his head, and Katherine tightened her grip on his hand.

"Hear me when I say this, Arthur," she'd asserted, "You are more than enough. You are my strength, and I'm ashamed of how long it's taken me to see it. I would never have survived all the losses without you."

Arthur made a face, "Of course you would have –"

"Arthur," she'd said, reaching up to cup his cheek, a sad smile on her face, "Don't undervalue yourself. I am *lucky* to be yours."

Yours.

The word burst in Arthur's chest like a cannon, his crooked grin returning. Katherine noticed the surge of light in him and smiled triumphantly, repeating the word as she nestled up against him.

As they lay in each other's arms before the warming fire, Katherine watched the glow of the embers and silently chastised herself for having wasted so many years. She had looked right at Arthur, but never really seen him. And it was a tragedy, for he was everything she'd ever needed.

Like Harry, Arthur was slender and tall but broad-shouldered. With subtle yet defined muscles, possessing an athletic physique though he lacked interest in jousting and archery. But despite his physical attributes, it was his eyes which Katherine was drawn in by the most. Though a sky blue – again, like Harry's – Arthur's eyes were unlike any other, not mostly because of their gold outline, but due to the warmth and kindness they exuded.

How they crinkled when he laughed, and how he squinted them in thought; Katherine could not get enough. But it was their intensity when they were making love that had taken her heart captive; for in that look, she could see their entire future.

A future devoid of uncertainty and reservation, and filled with the knowledge that, all along, they had been meant for one another.

March 1510

The following month, Katherine stood before her king in the great hall as he sat upon his throne, her hands clasped together before her, her prayer beads hanging from between her fingers.

"I have news I wish to share."

At her words, the courtiers within the hall began to shush each other as they all turned to listen, eager to hear the queen's important announcement.

Arthur dismissed Griffith from before him and cocked his head at his wife, his eyes conveying his ignorance.

Katherine grinned excitedly, delighted to be able to utter the words. Finally!

"I am with child, Your Grace," she announced enthusiastically, "I carry your heir in my womb."

The crowd behind them erupted in cheers and calls of joy, and Arthur was up from his throne in a flash, his eyebrows raised as he made his way towards her.

"How do you feel?" he asked, taking her hands in his, though he knew she must feel confident enough to announce such a development before the entire court.

"I am further along than I have ever been," she told him elatedly, "I have missed five courses and I believe I felt the baby quicken this morning."

"Oh, that's wonderful!" Arthur breathed in amazement before kissing his queen, "*You're* wonderful."

Katherine blushed, her eyes welling up with the thrill of looming motherhood.

"I do believe it is a boy, Arthur," she whispered then, rubbing a hand over her tiny bump.

Arthur held Katherine's face in his hands, "Boy or girl, Katherine, I do not care," he whispered elatedly, "As long as they are as strong and as beautiful as their mother."

Chapter 9

1st July 1510
Greenwich Palace, London

Queen Katherine of Aragon gave birth to a robust baby boy just four months later with Elizabeth of York by her side through every step of the way.

Katherine, having previously only experienced loss when it came to childbearing, had been frantic and anxious for those last few weeks before the birth, and had requested that her mother-in-law accompany her in her period of confinement to help soothe her stormy soul.

It had been Elizabeth who had lovingly rubbed the foul-smelling ointment on Katherine's belly to aid with the pains, she who had held Katherine's hand throughout the difficult labour, and she who had cried tears of joy alongside Katherine when the midwife had announced the baby's favourable gender. Elizabeth had mothered her daughter-in-law through the testing ordeal of childbirth and led the way on Katherine's own path to achieve motherhood. And Katherine would never forget her part in it.

"He is so small," Katherine whispered later as she held her swaddled infant in her arms.

Elizabeth peered lovingly at the squished up little face, "He is bigger than either of my sons were at birth," she said, smiling proudly at Katherine, "You did well."

The words were so simple and yet they meant so much.

Katherine had completed her duty as a woman and as a queen, she had given her husband a strong and healthy son to follow in his father's footsteps to one day claim the throne of England. She had done what she, and no doubt the entire country, had believed her to be unable to do. And it felt delicious.

This moment had been worth the wait.

Her son squirmed in her arms then, his mouth opening into a little yawn before cracking open his eyes ever so slowly to assess his surroundings. He looked around himself, seeing nothing, utterly blind to everything except his mother's face so close to his.

As mother and son locked eyes for the very first time, Katherine gasped, "He has Arthur's eyes!" she whispered in amazement, suddenly realising she had hoped for it all along. Her face shone with sheer joy and wonderment at the realisation, as if the babe in her arms was all the more perfect for having inherited his father's features.

"He does," Elizabeth agreed, although she wasn't looking at her grandson.

Instead, the former Queen of England was observing her daughter-in-law in these precious first moments of motherhood, and the undeniable truth which was finally so clear to see: Katherine of Aragon was in love with Elizabeth's son.

And that, above even the birth of her first grandchild, was the greatest gift of all.

The king and queen's son was immediately titled Duke of Cornwall upon his birth and declared the heir apparent to the English throne.

"She's finally done it!" Harry declared merrily as he barged into the king's chambers unannounced, after having learned of his queen's triumph, "Your wife has done what was expected of her. At last! God be praised!"

Arthur, surrounded by Griffith and several other courtiers, inhaled deeply and let the comment roll off his back. This day was not for anger, but for celebration; and he would not let Harry ruin his good mood. Beside Arthur, however, Griffith groaned and shook his head.

Harry, unfazed, put down the two cups and silver jug of wine he had brought, then flashed Arthur his most charming smile.

"Well done, brother!" Harry said, clapping Arthur on the shoulder, hard.

Arthur nodded in thanks, "We will baptise him –"

"A toast!" Harry interrupted, which Arthur wasn't entirely surprised at, "To the wonderful Queen Katherine!" he poured wine into the two cups while the men in the room mumbled "To the queen", then he knocked back the contents of his cup in one gulp.

"May she grant you many more heirs in the near future."

Arthur raised his cup to that and as he took a sip, Harry added, "Lord knows it took her long enough to grant you this one."

At that, the room went still, and Arthur put his cup down slowly, observing his brother as he refilled his own. Someone in the small crowd cleared their throat.

"Careful, brother," Arthur said, a warning.

Harry looked up, his eyebrows raised.

"What?" he laughed.

Arthur ran his tongue over his teeth, his eyes narrowed at Harry, "She is your queen," he said.

Harry shrugged, "And you are my brother," as though it granted him protection to disrespect the noblest lady in all the realm.

Griffith sucked his tongue between his teeth, a sound that clearly conveyed his annoyance.

"Brother or no," Arthur said, "I will hear no more of your prejudice against her."

"Prejudice?" Harry scoffed and looked about the room, but none of the men offered him so much as a wary glance, "It is mere banter. Innocent chat between brothers, between men!"

Arthur was shaking his head, "It is disrespectful. Not only is she my wife and now the mother of my child, but she is also the Queen of England. And if you cannot muster the strength within you to hold your tongue when your poisonous thoughts come to you, then I can no longer allow you in hers, or in my, presence."

At that, Griffith crossed his arms over his broad chest, a smirk tugging at the corner of her lips. It was about time Arthur stood up to his crude brother.

Harry stared at Arthur with wide eyes, his chest heaving with adrenaline at the confrontation.

Then he swallowed, his Adam's apple bobbing slowly, "Very well," Harry said with a bow of his head, "My apologies, brother."

Arthur continued only to glare at Harry, making no effort to assure him that all was well now that he had apologised. For words did not promise change. Actions did.

Bonfires burned brightly throughout the city of London for five days and nights to commemorate the prince's birth. Wine flowed at the expense of the crown, and the people were overjoyed to bear witness to the beginning of a new era.

The prince was baptised on his fifth day of life, the boy having been deemed strong enough by the midwives to postpone the christening until then.

The report of the boy's promising health had been a huge relief to the new parents, a sickly child having had to have been baptised much sooner, if not straight away, in case they slipped away from this world.

But their son showed no signs of weakness, the rolls on his arms and legs indicating a well-nourished body, and the force of his cries confirming the strength of his lungs. He fed well from his wetnurses throughout the day and slept for most of the night. And Katherine was completely and utterly besotted with him.

For the first two nights after his birth she had hardly slept, watching the rise and fall of his chest as though to look away even for a moment would mean missing a vital part of his development.

But on that third night, exhaustion had taken her, and mother and child had slept the whole night through, their bond so true it may as well have been a physical thing, like a blanket keeping them safe and warm.

But now, on the morning of the fifth day, when the baby was being taken away to be christened, Katherine felt herself becoming anxious, for she was not allowed to attend the grand event, a woman's bleeding following childbirth – as well as childbirth itself – being considered sinful and unclean, and before a mother was permitted to return to society, she had to be cleansed of her sins and churched by a priest.

"I will bring him back in no time," the Dowager Queen Elizabeth promised as she held the sleeping infant in her arms, "Sleep and he will be returned to you soon."

Katherine sniffled and brushed a finger over her child's mop of auburn hair, "Hold him tightly."

Elizabeth smiled, "What kind of godmother would I be if I did not?"

6th July 1510
Chapel of the Observant Friars, Richmond, Surrey

A twenty-four-foot-wide walkway had been newly gravelled and strewn with flowers between the palace hall and the Chapel of the Observant Friars in preparation for the prince's christening. Barriers were erected on either side on the morning of the event to keep the excited public from coming too close to the monarch's precious heir. The way was hung with rich and colourful cloth of arras to keep the bright July sun from the prince's delicate skin on the procession's way to the chapel.

The French King Louis de Valois and the Archbishop of Canterbury William Warham, had been chosen for the prince's godfathers. Katherine of York the Countess of Devon and daughter of Edward IV, as well as the prince's grandmother Elizabeth of York, for his godmothers.

Vast crowds of people had gathered for a glimpse of their new prince, and an excited buzz was reverberating from the crowd as they awaited the commencement of the lavish display.

Then the little prince emerged, carried safely in Elizabeth's arms and with his other godparents following behind, the Bishop of Winchester appearing as proxy for the French King, who had remained in France but had been good enough to send fine christening gifts of a gold cup and a silver rattle.

The priest awaited them at the chapel door and upon their arrival Elizabeth of York presented the prince to him so that he may be blessed before entering the church.

Throughout the length of the aisle, on both sides towards the baptismal font, hung beautiful tapestries that had been hand stitched and decorated with pearls and precious stones.

At the silver font, the old priest took his place beside it, "I ask you, oh Lord," he called, "to bless this water so that this child may be cleansed of sin," he touched the water with his right hand and completed a prayer over it.

He then, ever so carefully, sprinkled the water over the prince's wispy red curls three times, "I baptize you in the name of the Father, the Son, and the Holy Spirit."

The old priest then turned to the crowd of lords and ladies within the church, and as Elizabeth held the prince up high for all to see, he called out, "This child has been reborn in baptism and is now a child of God. He has been reborn and will forever be known as Arthur, his royal Highness, Duke of Cornwall, and Prince of England!"

Greenwich Palace, London

"Arthur," Elizabeth whispered lovingly into the baby's ear before passing him to his mother as she continued to lay abed, "I approve, of course."

Katherine smiled down at her son, "Artie," she said, "For now."

Elizabeth nodded and took a seat beside Katherine's four-poster bed. She watched them for a moment, remembering when she had held her own baby Arthur in her arms almost a quarter of a century ago. *Had it really been that long?*

"Enjoy this," Elizabeth said, smiling sadly, "Before you know it, he will be a young man, marrying a foreign princess whom he has never met."

Katherine looked over at her mother-in-law. She was smiling, but underneath her smile was the pain caused by the passing of time, and a gentle warning that no matter how hard you might hold onto your children, there will come a day when they will no longer fit in the safety of your arms.

September 1510

Following their son's birth and Katherine's emergence from confinement, Arthur had made his adoration and appreciation of her endeavours clear by having organised dozens of plays, jousts, and balls to take place in her honour.

He had never been one for dancing, but on this joyful occasion Arthur himself took part in one of the plays to express his love for her through the arts, the play's finale having been a great dance where the king, of course, chose his queen from the audience for his dancing partner. And every night following her return to court life, Katherine and Arthur had snuck away from the festivities to continue the merriment in the bedchamber, leaving the court to continue celebrating without them, for no amount of dancing and music could compete with the thrilling waves of ecstasy that came from the couple's lovemaking.

"To think I used to dread our couplings," Katherine chuckled into Arthur's neck as they lay in each other's arms afterwards.

"Dread?" he laughed in horror, pulling away to look at her.

"Well, you know," she replied teasingly, running a hand down his defined chest and abdomen, "It was never as good as this."

Arthur stroked the hair from her face and ran his thumb over her lower lip, "We were so young," he reflected.

Katherine sighed blissfully as they regarded each other in intimate silence, her fingers continuing to caress his hairy chest absentmindedly.

Then Katherine slowly edged her hand lower, to his navel and further still, and when she felt him react to her touch, she climbed on top of him and lowered her mouth to his ear.

"We are still young."

Part III

Through the darkness of loss
shines the light of that which we hold most dear

Chapter 10

3 years later

June 1513
Greenwich Palace, London

England was thriving under the reign of King Arthur.

The construction of the two new warships designed by Arthur three years prior had been concluded in 1511, and England's naval capacity had been vastly strengthened because of it.

The larger of the two had been named Mary Rose; Mary, after the Virgin Mary, and Rose to signify the Tudor emblem, which was also its badge. And she was the largest ship in the entire English navy.

Her smaller sister had been named Peter Pomegranate after St Peter, and its badge was the queen's emblem of the Pomegranate.

At the beginning of his reign, Arthur had also petitioned his Parliament to pass a new law to tackle the increasing number of beggars in cities and towns in a much more effective way than his father's statute of 1495 had ordered: where vagrants were to be rounded-up, punished, and commanded to leave the town. This policy of the former king's had not remedied the problem, but merely succeeded in moving the vagrants from town to town. Nevermind the fact that it had not considered a category of people who were unable to support themselves due to illness, disability, or age. All beggars, regardless of their disability – whether it be physical or mental – had previously been punished equally. But the increasing number of vagrants on the streets was a problem which needed addressing for the people's greater good, since the homeless inadvertently spread disease.

Arthur's new law, therefore, had called for a new way of dealing with the problem of poverty, where only those who fell into the category of being undeniably unable to support themselves were allowed to continue to beg, while all that were able-bodied were ordered to find work or face imprisonment at Ludgate Prison.

Over the three years that followed since its passing, London and the surrounding towns had seen an exceptional decrease in the number of beggars – whether it be due to them having found work or having been imprisoned being of little consequence, as long as the spread of disease and death were on the decline.

"We shall have to revisit the issue in the years to come," King Arthur told his Privy Council, who by now had been narrowed down to only those he trusted, Edmund Dudley having been removed and forced into retirement just months after Arthur's crowning, "But for now it is achieving the desired goal."

The Dean of Lincoln Thomas Wolsey, who Arthur had recently granted a seat within the council, nodded his head, "Sometimes the few must suffer for the greater good."

Arthur's jaw ticked, he didn't like to think of it that way, but Wolsey was right.

"Moving on, gentlemen," the king said, "Any news from Spain?"

The king's sister, the Princess Mary, had been officially betrothed to Queen Katherine's nephew Prince Carlos de Castille the year before; and with the prince's fourteenth year approaching, England and Spain were in constant communication to conclude the alliance.

"Spain has sent a letter requesting the Princess Mary be dispatched to Castille within the year," the old Lord Chancellor Richard Fox said, "in time for a wedding to take place as soon as the boy reaches maturity."

Arthur nodded, "I shall inform her personally," he said, "With Queen Katherine with child once again, Mary will not be made to go easily."

*

As Queen of England, Katherine's responsibility went beyond that of providing heirs for her husband and king, but to also use her wealth and position to help those in need, and she would often dedicate quiet afternoons such as this to making shirts, smocks, and sheets to distribute to the poor.

Katherine, Elizabeth of York, and the Princess Mary were busying themselves with this task, sitting in a semi-circle by the window of the queen's chambers and chattering contently, when Katherine suddenly exclaimed and pressed a hand to her bulging belly.

"What is it?!" seventeen-year-old Mary asked, reaching over to place her hand over Katherine's as her lady, Lina, stepped forward to check on her mistress.

Katherine shook her head and breathed a laugh, "It is nothing," she said, rubbing at the piercing ache on her bump, "The babe is merely dancing again."

Elizabeth of York was clad in black from head to toe as she had vowed she would be following Henry VII's death. She would never come out of mourning, she had said. And even four years later, there was not a hint of colour to be found in her wardrobe.

"He has been more active lately," Elizabeth said casually, as though the pains Katherine was feeling of late were completely normal, "He must be eager to be born soon."

"Not too eager, I hope," Katherine mumbled fearfully, shifting uncomfortably in her seat, "I still have another month before I enter my confinement."

Elizabeth and Mary smiled reassuringly at her.

"The child is active. It is a sign he is happy," Elizabeth soothed, before covering her mouth to cough lightly.

"Do you wish for a girl this time, sister?" Mary asked, hoping to steer the conversation to a brighter mood.

But Katherine was riddled with trauma, "With as much loss as I've had I only wish for it to be healthy."

Following little Artie's successful birth, Katherine had suffered two more early miscarriages, both pregnancies having been so short-lived that she had not even been sure of them until her missed courses had made a bitter appearance four weeks too late.

But the royal couple had never given up hope of a full nursery, Artie's birth and thriving health being proof enough that Katherine *was* able to bear live children.

"With the kicks this one gives you, I have no doubt it will be another strong boy," Elizabeth predicted, then cleared her throat as though a tickle was troubling her.

Katherine smiled, and the babe within her landed another kick straight into her ribs.

"*Oof*," she exhaled in pain, dropping the shirt she had been stitching as she pressed her hand onto her side, and forced a strangled laugh, "Either that," she said, "or he's trying to kill me."

The following week, all Hell broke loose when the Queen of England was taken to her bedchambers, screaming and crying hysterically.

Her brow and cheeks were damp with sweat and tears as she thrashed uncontrollably in her bed one minute, then lay limp and motionless the next, the only sign of life being her chattering teeth.

"What is wrong with her?" King Arthur asked the physicians frantically as they hovered over their queen.

One of them shook his head, giving Arthur no better idea as to what the problem was.

He set his jaw and took some paces back, giving the doctors space to observe his wife properly.

As he stood back and watched, Arthur stared at Katherine's face in fear, willing her to look at him. But her gaze was glassy-eyed and unblinking as she stared blindly up at the ceiling.

The king wished to summon his mother, to ask her for her wisdom or even just for her company during this strange and frightening situation. But the former queen had been laying abed for the past two days, a rattly cough having taken hold of her completely out of the blue. She needed her rest. And Arthur would not call her out of bed simply to alleviate his own anxieties.

"*Baby...*"

The weak voice came suddenly from Katherine as her eyes continued to stare eerily at the ceiling, and Arthur was beside her in an instant.

He took her limp hand, "What? What is it, Katherine?" he whispered frantically, his eyebrows bunched together in panic.

"The...the baby..." Katherine's thin voice managed.

"She says it is the baby," Arthur told the physicians, who had retreated and were talking quietly among themselves.

"Did you hear me!?" Arthur called, anger overriding his other senses, "The queen says –"

"My lord," one of the bearded old men interrupted, though his voice was low and calming, "The queen is miscarrying."

"Miscarrying?" Arthur breathed the word as though it had been gut-punched out of him.

The old men nodded, "There is blood."

At the mention of blood, Arthur returned his attention to the bed, where he only then noticed drops of the dark red liquid.

"But..."

No other words came out, for there was no arguing with what he saw. Katherine was losing another of their babies.

Only this time, she would have to go through labour, and watch it die before it had even had a chance to live.

The queen had snapped out of her delirium shortly after the contractions had started, and her cries and screams had echoed throughout the castle walls for hours since.

Arthur had wanted to stay with her, had wanted to hold her hand and wipe her brow and whisper words of encouragement. But king or not, a man was not permitted within the female-dominated world of childbirth, and the midwives had quickly shooed him and the physicians out before closing the door to the queen's bedchamber firmly behind them.

He had stood by the queen's closed door for what had felt like mere minutes as she screamed and screamed from the other side of it, but when he'd finally turned away, the sun had been swallowed by darkness, hours having passed without Arthur noticing.

In his uselessness to aid his beloved, Arthur had allowed his feet to take him to his mother, where he hoped he would find some solace.

"Lady Mother?" he called gently into the darkness of Elizabeth's royal apartments. He heard a rustling of bedsheets before a candle was lit by one of Elizabeth's ladies.

A young girl hurried towards the king with the candle in her hand and curtsied, "Her Grace has only just fallen asleep, my lord," she whispered.

A ragged, wet cough burst from the shadows like a warning, "I am not asleep, Margy. Come in, Arthur."

At the invitation, Arthur moved through the gloom and towards his mother's voice. He took a seat by Elizabeth's bed and waited patiently while her lady helped to prop her up into a sitting position, his mother wheezing heavily at the exertion.

Arthur frowned to see her looking and sounding so frail, and for a moment he didn't know which of the two most important women in his life he was more afraid for.

"Katherine –" Elizabeth wheezed.

"She is having the baby," Arthur interrupted, before covering his face with his hands.

Elizabeth nodded slowly, licked her cracked lips with effort, "You will get through this."

Arthur looked up at his mother with tears in his eyes. He reached over and took her hand in his and almost flinched at how cold it felt.

Mother and son locked eyes then, and Arthur saw a look in her eyes that he had not been prepared for.

"Do you fear it?" Arthur whispered, realising suddenly that rest would not cure his mother's ailment, for Death had come knocking on these castle doors. And it was only a matter of time before It would collect.

Elizabeth smiled and Arthur was reminded of her sitting at the edge of his bed over fifteen years ago, as she'd told a young Arthur and Harry the stories of their father's victory on the battlefield.

"I only fear that my death will bring pain to my children," the Dowager Queen of England admitted humbly.

"The entire realm will feel your loss, Mother," Arthur muttered, his voice cracking under the heavy strain of heartache.

Elizabeth reached up a hand and stroked her grown son's stubbly cheek, "Do not hold in the sorrow, my boy. It will eat you up inside if you do."

At that, Arthur allowed the tears he had been holding in to fall, taking in this last piece of motherly advice that she had to offer. The door to the chambers suddenly burst open then as a wide-eyed messenger boy stood panting in the doorway, "Your Highness, it is the queen!"

Arthur was up from his mother's side in a flash, his legs driving him forward to be with his wife in this hour of need, while knowing that in doing so, he was leaving his mother behind to die alone.

Completely disregarding protocol, King Arthur surged through the doors of Katherine's chambers and hurried towards her.

He was stunned at what he saw, but he forced his face not to convey his alarm. The bedsheets of the queen's four-poster bed were stained and splattered with dark blood, his wife laying among it, panting heavily with her long hair wet with sweat and tears as it stuck to her forehead and neck. The air was thick with the distinct smell of iron.

He'd never seen a horror quite like it, and he realised then that childbirth and combat were one and the same.

This right here was a woman's very own battlefield.

He skidded to a halt beside the bed and bent down on one knee, taking his wife's hand in both of his, thanking God that she had made it through.

"You're alright," he mumbled against her knuckles as he kissed them.

"The baby…" Katherine rasped as she lifted one weak hand and pointed to the midwives in the corner of the room, where a baptismal font had been brought in to quickly baptise the little soul if it had been born alive.

Arthur looked up and followed her indication, a lump forming in his throat as he spotted a limp little arm through the crowd of midwives.

He squeezed his eyes shut and turned back to Katherine.

"He wasn't meant for this world, my love," he soothed quietly, stroking her wet hair from her brow, "He is with God now," though he and Katherine knew that to be untrue, for an unbaptised child did not enter Heaven, its little soul being forever lost in limbo instead.

Tears rolled down her cheeks then, and Katherine turned away from Arthur, heartbroken, before whispering one single word.

"She…"

July 1513

Following Arthur's swift departure from his mother's chambers on the night of Katherine's stillbirth, one of Elizabeth's ladies had hurried to fetch the Princess Mary to her, so that the former Queen of England would not die alone.

It was the only comfort Arthur had to hold onto in the weeks that followed his mother's and daughter's deaths, for the thought of his most gentle lady Mother dying without at least one of her children present would have been too terrible to bear.

But grief hung in the air like a black cloud of late, the king and queen's losses being felt all over the country.

They had named their daughter Elizabeth, in honour of Arthur's mother, and had had one much-too-short moment to hold her before she had been taken away forever.

Katherine would have held her until the end of time if she had had the chance, but Arthur had ordered for the midwives to take baby Elizabeth away when Katherine had begun to sob so uncontrollably that she'd struggled to breathe. And the memory of his broken wife as she had been separated from their lifeless child would eternally haunt his subconscious.

But it had been the right thing to do. For the body would have begun to decay quickly in the summer heat, and no amount of time would have erased that kind of image from their minds.

According to the laws of God, stillborn babies were not allowed to have a grave on consecrated ground and were to be buried in an unmarked plot instead. Arthur, however, was not about to simply toss their daughter into an anonymous hole to be forgotten for eternity, the strength of his guilt being too great to ignore. He knew it was irrational, for nothing could have stopped their child from being born too soon. But he was the *king*. And he had been utterly powerless to prevent it…

And so, to alleviate some of the guilt that was eating away at him, Arthur chose to disregard God's laws – just this once – and used his authority to persuade Bishop Fisher to allow for baby Elizabeth to be enclosed in the same coffin with her grandmother and namesake.

"No one will have to know," the king had assured, handing the bishop a purse of gold coins.

Fisher had taken it reluctantly, "God will know."

Arthur had not replied to that, his heartache overruling his conscience. Let God punish him when it was his time to meet Him.

They had held a grand funeral for Elizabeth of York.

Upon hers and baby Elizabeth's deaths, the bells of St Paul's Cathedral rang out to signify the death of a royal, and soon all the other churches followed suit, the city of London going both deathly silent and alive with sound all at once.

Brought through London on the way to Westminster Abbey, Elizabeth of York's coffin was transported on a beautiful hearse drawn by six horses.

The entire city of London was in mourning, dozens of ambassadors, lords, and ladies riding in single file behind the hearse, followed by hundreds of poor folk walking behind, carrying torches and candles.

Harry Duke of York, who had been ordained a priest and taken his vow of celibacy the year before, held mass at Westminster Abbey during the coffin's entry. He remained calm and professional throughout, but underneath the façade, the young man was devastated over his beloved mother's loss.

Bishop Fisher officiated the requiem for the final mass, and after the sermon, the coffin was placed in the Tudor tomb beside Elizabeth's adored husband, Henry VII, the two former monarchs reunited once more.

And unbeknownst to anyone except Bishop Fisher and the king and queen themselves, baby Elizabeth, too, was being buried; to be held in the safety of her grandmother's arms for eternity.

Chapter 11

September 1513
Greenwich Palace, London

Since Elizabeth of York and baby Elizabeth's deaths, Katherine had requested that their son visit court more often, her recent loss having awoken a need within her to keep her only child close.

On one such visit, the two of them were facing each other at a games table in the palace garden beside the fountain, the spray of the water cooling their faces every so often when the wind breezed by in the right direction.

Katherine was watching Artie as he stared at his cards with an intense focus, his tongue sticking out the side of his mouth as he thought of his next move, and Katherine couldn't help but smile at her beautiful boy.

At the age of three, there were not many card games the young prince was old enough to understand, but upon his visit to court he had begged his mother to teach him to play Cent after observing Griffith Rhys and another courtier playing it one evening after a banquet. And Katherine had not hesitated to meet Artie's request, teaching him the simple card game the very next day and playing it every day thereafter.

"*Quart*," Artie announced as he sat forward to display his cards, his chubby cheeks flushed with childish joy.

"A run of four?" Katherine asked proudly, leaning forward, "Good!"

Artie grinned and kicked his little legs, "Does that mean I win?" Katherine did not have the heart to tell him that he'd lost three rounds ago and instead nodded and rose from her seat.

"You defeated your poor mother most victoriously," Katherine said, holding out her hand for Artie to take.

He hopped down from the seat with a giggle and together they headed towards the fountain.

"Look!" Artie exclaimed, pointing at their distorted reflection in the water, "It's me and you, mama."
Katherine chuckled, her heart aching with love for him, "It is, my darling," she agreed without looking to where he was pointing. While Artie excitedly observed his surroundings, giggling and squealing as the water from the fountain splashed him, Katherine watched him intently, in the hope of engraving this moment into her memory forever. For if he were to be their only child, Katherine would cherish every single second God were to grant her with him.

October 1513

"Don't you wish for glory?" Harry was asking his king the following month, as the brothers shared a private dinner together in the king's chambers.
Harry was chewing loudly, seemingly unaware of his brother's distaste of it.
"No," Arthur replied, "I wish for peace."
"Heh," Harry scoffed mockingly, "Peace," he shook his head, "If I were king, I'd have taken the opportunity to invade France while they continue distracted by their own troubles with Spain."
The countries of Spain and France had been at each other's throats since April, the two powerful nations continuing to bicker over who held the right over the neutral part of Navarre in the Iberian Peninsula.
Arthur raised an eyebrow, "If *you* were king?" he asked disparagingly.
Harry shrugged one shoulder, then took a gulp of his wine.
"I just mean: if England seizes this time while France is distracted and weakened, we could claim France!"
Arthur suppressed his desire to laugh in his younger brother's face, and instead inhaled deeply before explaining the situation as he would do to his three-year-old son.

"I have sent monetary aid to Spain to settle our contractual obligation to them as their allies, that is all I am prepared to do. This is not our war."

Harry pulled a face, quite openly showing his disagreement.

Arthur narrowed his eyes at Harry's disrespect, "If I march an army to France," he said, as coldly as he dared to without causing a greater rift between them, "not only would I be breaking our peace treaty, but no doubt Scotland – who have their Auld Alliance with France – would take *that* opportunity to attempt to invade England in reconciliation. England would be at war simultaneously with France *and* Scotland, nevermind the fact I could only be in one place at once to defend my country, leaving my wife and son, as well as my people, vulnerable."

Arthur shook his head and frowned at Harry across the table, "Are you so blinded by 'honour' claimed on the battlefield that you cannot see what might follow such enormous decisions?"

Harry wiped his mouth with the back of his hand, indifferent to his brother's tone, "I guess this is why you are the king, and I a priest. I do not have the mind for tactics. Chess was always your game."

Arthur couldn't help but breathe a laugh, and a silence befell the two men.

After their plates were cleared and they both sat back in their seats with their hands folded over their full bellies, Arthur cast an eye over his brother.

Harry wore a long-sleeved, hoodless robe made of black material, and a heavy gold cross around his neck. His coppery hair was cropped, his curls cut short to appear only wavy, and his cheeks and chin were clean shaven, unlike Arthur's, who found little enthusiasm to shave these days.

He appeared well in himself, too well almost, given the fact their mother had just died.

"How are you coping?" Arthur asked then, to which Harry turned a smiling face at him.

The younger brother waved his hand in the air, dismissing the king's question as only a brother could, "God keeps me sane."
Arthur nodded his head, "You always did find comfort in God."
"Don't you?" Harry asked, his eyebrows furrowed.
"Of course," Arthur replied, "But you are different. God was always your special calling. And you are rising quickly."
Harry grinned, "I have you to thank for that."
Arthur picked up his wine, "No," he said warmly, though Harry was of course right, "No, only you deserve credit for what you have achieved."
Harry raised his cup at that, "To the Tudor brothers' achievements!"

February 1515

Over the following year and a half, with the country continuing at peace, Arthur was able to focus on the further strengthening of England.
Arthur was of the belief that Spain and France were countries of the future, their culture, architecture, and passion for the arts being of great interest to the young king; and he wished to be the one to guide England into becoming a powerhouse of equal cultural influence. And investing in the education of the future generations to come was paramount in order to achieve that.
Arthur therefore commissioned for many schools, colleges, and universities to be built in all the largest cities within the coming decade, to allow for a wider range of higher educated people, with the ideal that literature, Latin grammar, and mathematics to be every person's basic education.
But of course, not everyone would be able to attend, many poor folks being unable to give up their work in the countryside, harvesting food and making money for their family, in exchange for an education they would likely never use.
But many in the cities awaited in anticipation for their construction, and the hope for a better life in the near future.

The navy and military force had also continued to thrive, the king ordering for yet another large warship to be built not long after the Mary Rose and Peter Pomegranate. At this growing rate, the English navy would be one to be reckoned with, soon matching Spain's own naval capacity.

Arthur's reign was proving to be a successful one.

But in his domestic life, Arthur and Katherine were struggling.

"Perhaps God is punishing us!"

The king and queen were sitting side by side by the fireplace in the king's chambers. The room behind them was engulfed in shadow, no candles or torches having been lit within it, the only light being that of the roaring fire before them.

Arthur looked bewilderedly at his wife. At the age of thirty, she continued as beautiful as ever, but there was no denying that she had aged much in the last eighteen months, their daughter's stillbirth having carved deep lines of grief on the sides of her mouth.

"Punishing us?" he asked.

Katherine stared into the flickering fire, picking nervously at the cuticles of her fingers, a new habit, "For burying Elizabeth with your mother."

She had whispered it, though they remained alone. But God heard everything, as she knew, and whispered or not, He was aware of their sin.

Arthur leaned over and took one of her hands in his, interrupting her nervous picking, "God is not punishing us."

Katherine looked into Arthur's pale blue eyes, the gold outline of his pupils glinting in the fire light.

"Why else have I not conceived since?" Katherine asked for the hundredth time. It never hurt any less to say it.

It was unusual, that much was true, for a married, fertile woman to be without child for so long. Women of such classification were commonly with child for more months of their youth than not.

But Katherine had experienced undeniable suffering, both physical and mental, and Arthur was not unaware of the pressures she was putting on herself.

Since baby Elizabeth's death, Katherine had become – if possible – even more devout. She would rise early and spend hours each morning at chapel, followed by more hours each evening at her private *prie-deux* in her chambers. She would fast two days per week, to cleanse her body and soul, she had said.

Arthur did not feel comfortable with the amount of blame she was putting on herself, and he often reminded her to think of their son for strength, that they were blessed to have a healthy male heir.

It would help her to see clearly sometimes, but soon the glassy-eyed look in her eyes would return, as well as the nervous picking of her fingers.

"We will have another child," Arthur said reassuringly then, his rumbling voice soothing Katherine for a moment, "Or we won't. It does not matter to me. Artie is strong and wise beyond his years. He will fill our hearts with enough love and pride as though there were twenty of him."

Katherine smiled at that, the image of their beautiful son appearing in her mind, with his wispy red hair and his eyes as brilliant and gentle as his father's. She allowed the image to consume her for a moment, the weight in her chest lifting just a little as she relaxed.

"The days that he visits are the happiest of my life," Katherine admitted, knowing that they were Arthur's too.

At that, Arthur raised her hand and pressed a kiss to her knuckles, "Then we shall send for him again. Anything to see you happy, my love."

March 1515

Upon his birth, Prince Artie had been set up with his own household, to reside separately from his parents and court life to ensure his health and safety; as was custom for all royal children.

His governess, the Lady Margaret Bryan, had been entrusted to oversee all of the little prince's daily routines, making sure that he had fed and slept well during infancy, and teaching him the essentials of language, reading, and writing in the years that had followed. His household, as the future King of England, was made up of dozens of servants, cooks, guards, ladies, and of course, the Lady Bryan.

But it was his mother's arms he sought out most of all, the sweet sound of her voice, and the warmth of her kisses on his neck bringing a burst of joy to the young prince whenever he was allowed to pay a visit to court.

At the age of five, Artie understood his position well. As the son of the King of England, Artie would be expected to follow in his father's footsteps. It was widely known throughout the country that his father, King Arthur, was a wise and generous king. One who did not enter into anything lightly, and who preferred to focus his attention on bettering England as a nation, rather than extending his reach in the claiming of other countries through war. He was a good king, Good King Arthur people called him. And Artie hoped to be as beloved as his father one day.

"My darling Artie!" the prince heard his mother's voice call as he exited his carriage.

"Mama!" he yelled enthusiastically as he raced towards her, knowing that he would be chastised by his governess later for disregarding her teachings of composure and decorum.

But it would be worth the telling-off, for in an instant his mother had wrapped him into her arms and was kissing his neck.

"You grow more handsome every day!" Katherine said in between smooches to her son's soft skin.

Artie giggled and squirmed out of her loving embrace before taking a step back. He looked up at his royal parents with a playful smile on his face, excited to be standing before them.

"Lady Mother," he said with a bow, "my lord Father."

Arthur and Katherine shared a look of adoration for what their love had created, then they each took one of Artie's hands in theirs and headed into the warmth of the castle, hope burning within the royal couple that a few days with their child would quash the concern in the pits of their stomachs that he would be their only one.

June 1515

Perhaps it had been the constant praying, or the fasting, or the joy Artie's brief return to court had brought, but three months after his visit, Katherine miraculously found herself feeling the familiar nausea that signified the conception of a baby.

The smell of meat made her feel queasy during banquets, and all she cared to eat was apples. They were all signs she knew very well, and yet she could not tell her husband the good news, for too many of their conceptions had ended in grief for her to believe this one to be any different.

"How many courses have you missed?" Princess Mary asked her sister-in-law one day when the nausea was too intense to suppress, Katherine never having been able to keep much hidden from the observant young woman.

"I have missed only two courses," the queen admitted, "I cannot tell Arthur until I have missed at least five. I do not want to get his hopes up, or the country's."

Mary's betrothal to Katherine's nephew, Carlos de Castille, had not gone ahead as planned for so many years. Delays in the princess' dispatchment to Spain due to Katherine's stillbirth and Elizabeth of York's death, as well as the fact that Arthur had been informed of Spain's secret dealings with France and the Holy Roman Empire, had led to the withdrawal of their betrothal. Spain was no longer a viable option for a new alliance.

"We will make you a better match, Mary," Katherine had promised upon the scandalous development the year before.

"Truthfully, sister, I had not been especially keen to marry someone four years younger than I," Mary had admitted, dropping her gaze to hide that she was blushing.

Katherine had laughed and taken the nineteen-year-old Mary by the arm as they'd continued walking through the gardens, "Oh Mary," the queen had said, thinking back to her own awkward first few months of marriage, "Marrying a young man of fifteen...I must admit I cannot blame you for your lack of enthusiasm."

And now, a year on, Katherine was nothing but glad to have her beloved sister-in-law by her side during this worrying time.

Mary nodded, "No doubt Arthur and his council won't even notice. They have been rather occupied over who to betroth me to next."

Katherine couldn't be sure, but she thought she'd noticed a hint of something in the young woman's voice, and she flashed a quick, knowing glance at her ladies Lina and Agnes before narrowing her eyes at Mary.

"Mary," the queen said, smiling slightly, "Do you have a suitor in mind?"

Mary blushed fiercely all of a sudden, her almond shaped eyes growing wide, "No, Katherine!" she exclaimed, "Of course not. I am the sister of the king. And I have a duty to fulfil. Whoever Arthur might choose, I will do what is expected of me."

July 1515

"There is continued trouble on the Scottish border, Your Grace," Arthur was informed during a meeting of the Privy

Council, "Despite our signed Treaty of Perpetual Peace, the Scottish borderers are persistent with their raids."

"But March Law is in p-place," another council member countered, Arthur knowing immediately who had spoken due to his slight stutter: a man named Sir Henry Wyatt, who was a politician and courtier loyal to the Tudor House since before Henry VII's victory at Bosworth, "The W-Wardens of the Marches are charged with keeping the peace."

"The people residing near the borders have always been reluctant to agree on a truce between the two countries," Lord Chancellor Richard Fox said, his tone indicating that his wisdom surpassed that of his younger council members, though Wyatt was not much younger than Fox, "raids are to be expected."

"But the increase in occasions, as well as brutality in recent months has been exp-ponential," Wyatt countered.

"What has Scotland got to say about this?" Arthur interrupted his advisors' bickering.

"King James IV turns a blind eye to it, as ever," Richard Fox said.

Arthur nodded pensively, flicking through the letters from his ambassador in Scotland, "Increase the penalties for now," he said, "And inform the Wardens of the Marches that I wish for a monthly report of the raids. We mustn't let them get out of control. It could cost us our peace."

3rd August 1515

Arthur may have been preoccupied of late, but he knew his wife's tells, and he had known that she was with child perhaps even before she did.

The earliest sign, Arthur had learned over the years, was her sudden inability to rise with the dawn, tiredness causing her to sleep through his own morning ritual of making his side of the bed, dressing, and praying at his private *prie-deux* for an hour.

At first, Arthur had thought her merely to be taking a break from her strict four-hourly morning prayer at the chapel – as had become her norm since the stillbirth – but after a week of sleeping in, Arthur had allowed himself to believe what he knew to be true – that God had granted them another chance at hope.

As the weeks went by and he noticed Katherine scrunching up her face when rich meats were served at banquets, Arthur secretly ordered for the kitchens to serve meats only in pies so that the smell would be contained, and to place them as far from Katherine's seat at the high table as possible. He would have ordered for no meat to be served at all, but Arthur knew that it would only have raised Katherine's suspicions that he knew of her condition, and he did not wish to put undue pressure on her in case this child, too, did not remain in her womb.

It wasn't until months had passed of Katherine hiding her nausea and fatigue, and Arthur secretly making sure apples were available at every mealtime, that Katherine finally managed to wake up at her usual time with that first ray of sunlight over the horizon.

Arthur had already gotten up and was finishing tucking his side of the bedsheet neatly under the pillows when Katherine stretched and turned to face him. He watched for a moment as her long-sleeved silk nightgown slid off her white shoulder, and her loose, wavy hair silhouetted her beautiful face.

"Why do you do that every morning?" Katherine asked, her voice groggy from sleep.

Arthur blinked, "Do what?"

"Make your side of the bed. You are the king. You have more important things to do."

Arthur's lips twitched slightly into a lopsided smile, then he sat down on the edge of the bed, one leg folded up on the mattress. He shrugged, "It's just a habit."

"But why?" Katherine asked, stretching over to place a hand on his bare leg.

He was still in his nightshirt and knee-length hose, and Katherine appreciated his defined calf for a moment as she ran her fingers up and down it.

Her body had already begun to change, her belly becoming slightly rounded and her breasts beginning to swell, and Arthur wondered how much longer she would think to hide her condition from him. He watched her as she continued to stroke his leg, her wavy hair plaited loosely over her shoulder, cheeks flushed from the early morning chill. He loved the sight of her with child, pomegranate-ripe and luscious, and it was all he could do to refrain from laying hands on her.

"Katherine," Arthur said quietly then, ignoring her question about his trivial little rituals, his asinine need for order being of no real import, "You know I am here for you, don't you?"

She raised her gaze to meet his, "I know."

"Then let's stop pretending like we don't both know that you are with child."

Immediately, Katherine withdrew her hand from his leg, "You knew?"

"The entire time."

"Why did you not say anything?"

Arthur only looked at his wife, the two of them falling silent as the memory of each miscarriage and the stillbirth flashed between them.

"Whatever happens," Arthur said then as Katherine began chewing on her lip, "We will be alright."

"How can you say that?" *After the last time almost killed me.* She hadn't needed to say the words, but Arthur knew what she was thinking. Katherine would likely never be the same again after Elizabeth's death. To lose another...it would be too much to bear.

"Whatever happens," Arthur said again, with more certainty this time, to make sure Katherine took heed, "We *will* be alright."

6th August 1515

"A new report from the Scottish border, Your Grace," Thomas Wolsey said as he handed Arthur a note.

The king tore it open, a frown etched between his eyes as he read it by candlelight.

His frown deepened, and Wolsey mirrored his expression, "I take it, it is not good news?"

Arthur exhaled loudly, held the paper to the light of the candle and watched as it turned to ash on the stone floor between them.

"A Warden of the Scottish Marches was murdered by an Englishman," he said monotonously, his mind racing. Then he looked up to meet Wolsey's gaze, "The Scots will want to retaliate."

Chapter 12

4th September 1515

"You did *what?!*"

Arthur's voice echoed through the great hall with a rage never before witnessed by Katherine, the court, or indeed his younger sister, who stood pale-faced and wide-eyed before him.

"Say it again, Mary, I am not quite sure I heard you right!"

He narrowed his eyes at Princess Mary and the man beside her, the two of them visibly shaking at the king's unexpected reaction of anger to their news.

"We…are married – before God, Your Highness," Mary stammered.

Queen Katherine shook her head in disbelief as she sat on her throne, her husband standing beside her, stiff with fury. She knew Mary had been hiding something, even all those months ago.

"Consummated?!" King Arthur barked, the high ceilings reverberating the delicate question back at them again and again before disappearing into the air.

Mary hung her head in shame, she should have known that following her heart would not go unpunished.

"Yes, Your Grace," she whispered.

"If I might, Your Grace," the bearded man beside the princess said suddenly, taking a step towards the king, "We did not wish to insult –"

"You dare speak to me, Brandon?!" Arthur roared, his eyes blazing like fire, "You are a nobody! A mere friend of the Duke of York. No title, no land, *nothing!* And you dare to marry and bed a princess of the realm without your king's permission? And then you stand before me and say you did not wish to insult?!"

"Please, my lord, we are in love," Charles Brandon pleaded.

"Enough!" Arthur bellowed, "I could have you executed for this treason!"

"Arthur…" Katherine's voice interjected softly, hoping to dampen his rage.

But it did little to soften the blow of their betrayal, and Arthur's jaw ticked as the fury continued to rumble within him.

"Guards!" the king called suddenly, to which four armoured men stepped forward, "Seize him! Throw him in the Tower until I have decided what shall become of him."

"No, brother, please…" Mary begged as two of the guards took Charles Brandon forcefully by the arms.

"And you, my dear sister. You are lucky I do not throw you in there alongside your reckless lover. You have cost England dearly with this useless marriage. If you weren't my sister, I'd be sending you to a nunnery for the rest of your days!"

Mary watched tearfully as her husband was led through the crowd and out the great hall, then turned a tear-stained, red face to Arthur.

"If I weren't your sister," she hissed spitefully, her loyalties now lying with her new husband above her brother and king, "I would be free to marry whoever I pleased."

Arthur scoffed, "Do not disregard the hand you were born with so easily. It has served you well until you chose to squander it for the love of a nobody."

"Please Arthur," Mary said now, feeling defeated as Arthur turned his back on her and resumed his seat beside his queen, "Do not execute him…"

Arthur raised his chin and inhaled deeply, staring his younger sister down for what felt like an age.

"Traitors to the crown do not deserve mercy."

"Please, Katherine, you must speak with him," Mary wept desperately as she knelt before her sister-in-law in the queen's chambers just moments later, "Have him understand we did not seek to betray his authority."

Katherine did not know what to do.

Ever since Mary's failed union with Katherine's nephew, Arthur and his council had been inundated with potential suitors for the princess. Not only was she young, beautiful, and well educated, but Mary was known throughout Europe as the king's loyal sister. A perfect woman, and an excellent catch. And yet, as it turned out, she was not so loyal after all.

"The king has been made to look a fool by his own flesh and blood," the queen said, "You must understand that even a tolerant king such as he would have trouble accepting this treachery. A lady of high birth cannot simply marry without the monarch's permission, much less a king's *sister!*"

Mary cried harder then, hanging her head in shame and fear for Charles Brandon's fate.

"I love him, Katherine," the young princess admitted as she wiped her nose with the back of her hand, quite unladylike, "I have loved him for years. What's more important than being with the one you love?"

Katherine recoiled at the question, so surprised was she to hear Mary ask it, for surely, she of all people knew what it meant to be a woman of noble birth.

Katherine took Mary's hands in hers and squeezed them, made Mary look her in the eyes.

"Duty," she said, as though that were obvious.

"Is it?" Mary countered helplessly, "I am no longer sure."

The princess shook her head. She looked so forlorn, and Katherine felt for the young lady.

"What did you two think would be the outcome of this?" the queen asked then, hoping to understand.

Mary shook her head, "We *didn't* think."

Katherine pursed her lips as though she had known Mary's answer.

"But when Harry offered to marry us –"

"Harry married you?" Katherine interrupted, hoping she had misheard.

Mary blinked and met Katherine's gaze, "Yes," she said, frowning, "Forgive me, I thought you knew? It was he who convinced us that Arthur would be accepting of our union."

When Arthur learned of his brother's underhanded involvement in this scandal, he could suddenly understand their father's paranoia, and his mind ran wild as he stalked angrily through the palace in search of his younger brother.

How could Harry betray him like this? After everything he had done for him: recommended him to Wolsey, watched him reach high and allowed him to believe it was all his own doing? An ordained priest at just twenty-four years old...does he really think it just *happened* to him? That who he is, who his father was, and who his brother now is, hadn't allowed him to achieve it so quickly? If at all?

Did he forget that if Arthur was that way inclined, he could destroy his entire life with one word?

Compared to this, Arthur could almost forgive his sister's betrayal, for on her part it was nothing more than a thoughtless, love-induced, error in judgement. But *Harry*? What had he gained from this other than his king's dissatisfaction?

Arthur stopped to scan the great hall for his brother's coppery head then turned sharply when he failed to locate him in the crowd, heading back down the dark hallway towards the chapel, neither stopping nor slowing down when he heard Katherine calling after him.

For years Arthur had been witness to Harry disparaging his queen, had ignored his seemingly innocent comments about how Arthur chose to reign...but perhaps there *was* something lurking underneath Harry's display of credence? Perhaps there had been all along?

What other reason could there be for Harry to feel confident enough to assume he could speak for the king and marry their sister – a *princess* – off without the king's consent?

Arthur widened his strides upon finding the chapel empty and hearing Katherine's hurried footsteps coming closer. He shook his head in frustration, he could not allow this kind of deception to take place from within his own family.

No one spoke for the king, no matter how close to the throne they were. Arthur could not allow them to get away with this. He would have to make an example of his siblings.

Upon reaching Harry's chambers and knowing him to be within them due to having failed to find him anywhere else, Arthur swung open his wooden door and allowed it to bang loudly against the wall.

"Brother," he grumbled, before entering the room, meeting Harry's shocked expression.

He heard Katherine still hurrying down the hallway after him, no doubt to try and mediate. But it was time Arthur made his authority clear to his little brother. And, for once, Good King Arthur acted on impulse.

Katherine heard the crack of Harry's jaw before her mind had been able to register that Arthur had thrown a punch.

"*Arthur!*" she called instinctively as she watched her normally tranquil husband holding an alarmed Harry up against a wall by his throat.

"You think I don't know what you're planning, brother?!" Arthur growled at Harry through clenched teeth, "You think me a fool?"

Harry, clad in his robes and bejewelled cross around his neck, his pale blue eyes wide in fear, looked the very image of innocence. But Arthur knew better.

"Please, Arthur, it's not what you think," Harry croaked.

"No?" Arthur asked cynically, "It wasn't you and my sister, my own *blood*, going behind my back and making a mockery of the monarchy? *My own family?!*"

He shoved Harry hard against the wall then before letting him go and stepping away from him like a lion who had asserted his dominance.

Katherine caught a glimpse of Arthur's face as he paced up and down before Harry, his expression dark with fury. Arthur was, perhaps for the first time, not in control. The best thing for Harry to do now, was to beg for forgiveness.

Instead – in true Harry fashion – he squared up to the king, "I had believed you would be benevolent."

Katherine groaned inwardly and raised her eyebrows in disbelief.

Arthur pressed his angry face a mere inch from Harry's, his broad shoulders stiff and rounded, his fists clenching and unclenching as though he were battling within himself whether or not to beat Harry's head against the wall.

"GUARDS!" Arthur screamed into Harry's face – to which Harry at least had the good grace to flinch – and several guards appeared, grabbing Harry by his arms.

"Take him to the Tower," Arthur ordered with a dismissive flick of his wrist as he turned his back on Harry, and Katherine wondered if he would ever forgive his brother for this.

"Let him rot in there."

Harry didn't stay in the Tower of London for long.

Not only was he a Prince of England, but until Katherine gave Arthur a spare male heir, Harry was still, by all rights, in Arthur's line of succession; and it made England appear weak to have the Tudor brothers so clearly at odds with one another. And yet, Arthur could not bring himself to have him anywhere near him.

"Send him to a m-monastery, my lord," Sir Henry Wyatt said as he dabbed at the sweat on his bald head with a handkerchief, the summer heat not yet having dissipated despite the month of September.

"There he will be able to c-continue on his pursuit to serve God," Wyatt continued, "as well as be out of the way – less able to c-cause trouble."

Arthur nodded, "It is a good idea, though I fear there is nowhere far enough away that he could go to bring me peace of mind."

He shook his head, he was still seeing red at the topic of his two disloyal siblings and the potential alliance for England that had been lost due to their recklessness.

"How about Bolton Abbey in N-North Yorkshire?" Wyatt offered, stuffing his handkerchief up his sleeve.

"My king," the Lord Chancellor interjected, his low voice slow and deliberate, "It might be wiser to send him to a monastery closer to London, rather than further away, if it is peace of mind you seek."

Arthur frowned and jerked his chin in Fox's direction, urging him to speak on, "How so?"

The old man licked his lips and leaned forward, "The further away he is, the longer it will take for news to reach you here should he misstep again."

"Surely he has learned his l-lesson?" Wyatt countered, "Prince or not, he is lucky to still have a head on his sh-shoulders."

All eyes turned to the king, who sat still, his eyes narrowed in thought.

"I do believe Fox is right," he said after a moment, "The further away Harry is, the more he might get the feeling like he is not being watched."

"That too," Fox agreed with a nod of his white head.

"Barking Abbey perhaps? Just outside London?" Wyatt offered in thought.

Arthur pulled a disgusted face, "*Too* close!"

"Bath Abbey in Somerset?"

At that Arthur clicked his finger and thumb together, "Yes!" he said, pointing at Fox who had suggested it, "Yes, Bath Abbey.

It is close enough to have news within mere hours but far enough away that we shall never cross paths."

Fox and Wyatt nodded at their king.

"See to it that it's done," Arthur ordered Wolsey, who picked up a quill and began to write down the king's command.

20th September 1515

With Harry taken care of, Arthur's rage over the scandal had diminished greatly.

Though Arthur had, in his initial anger, wanted to behead Charles Brandon for treason, he was glad to have tempered his rage quickly, because he would have never forgiven himself if he had acted on impulse and ordered the death of his sister's true love.

He had never seen Mary quite as desolate as he'd seen her in the days that had followed Brandon's arrest, her eyes lacking in vibrancy and her face blotched and swollen from constant crying. And though he continued perturbed by her clear disregard for his authority as king, Arthur could not bring himself to see her widowed and forced to marry another.

However, England had lost dearly for her pursuit of happiness, a new alliance with Portugal or Italy having been on the cards for them. And as king, Arthur had to punish them.

"I hereby banish you and your…husband from England," the king announced as Mary stood pale-faced before him and the court, "You are not ever to return, and while I have chosen to spare your husband a traitor's death, let it be known that if he is to set foot upon English soil in this lifetime, I will not hesitate to take his head."

Mary had crumpled to the floor upon the announcement, the court gasping with concern for her. But Katherine, who sat as still as a statue beside her husband, had known her to have buckled in relief rather than devastation, for this outcome was most preferable compared to the horror of seeing her loved one's head rotting on a spike.

October 1515

Mary and Charles Brandon were henceforth banished to Flanders as punishment for their crime, and while Katherine would miss her sister-in-law dearly, she made herself believe that it would have been no different to Mary leaving upon having married a foreign prince as she was meant to. Only in this case, she would likely never see her again.

"Will you write to me?" Mary asked her moments before being bundled onto a horse.

Katherine shook her head, "Not for a while. But give it time. You will hear from me soon."

Mary's bottom lip had trembled, and she looked down at Katherine's growing bump, "I pray he will be as strong as Artie."

And then she swallowed her tears and turned to mount her steed before being led out of the courtyard and through the palace gates alongside the man she had given up her royal title for.

Chapter 13

18th November 1515

"France has their eye on us, Your Grace," Richard Fox informed the king after weeks of troubling correspondence with their ambassadors in France, "Their new king, Francis I, is most suspicious of England's lack of military involvement in their disagreement with Spain some years prior. He also does not trust Your Highness' reasoning behind England's military and naval growth to be innocent. He fears we are planning an invasion."

Ever since Mary and Harry's betrayals to the crown, Arthur's peaceful approach to ruling had been tested. And just when he thought he had his anger over his siblings' disloyalty under control, France was now threatening to destroy everything he had worked so hard to achieve.

"King Francis is no doubt using this fragile time within your reign to his advantage," Arthur's lifelong friend, Griffith Rhys, said, his dark eyebrows bunched together in disapproval, his perpetual frown appearing deeper than ever.

Upon Harry and Mary's banishment, Arthur had turned to those closest to him to fill the void left behind by his siblings' disloyalty and granted Griffith the title of Duke of Suffolk, which had permitted him a seat within the King's Privy Council. At the age of forty-six, Griffith had never shown much interest in marriage and the production of children – not legitimate children, anyway – and had instead spent his life serving his king, his allegiance to Arthur running deeper than that to any woman he had ever met.

Don't you wish for a family? A place to come home to? Arthur had privately asked his friend on the eve of his noble advancement.

Griffith had shrugged, *If ever I meet a lady as fair as the queen, perhaps I might reconsider.*

And he had laughed. But Arthur had known him long enough to have heard the sadness in the sound, and he hoped that perhaps this elevation into Dukedom and advisor to the king would aid him in finding happiness. Whether it came from obtaining a prestigious marriage, or simply from further serving the crown.

From across the table, Thomas Wolsey nodded, "Your Highness' fractured House will be seen by our enemies as a weakness from which they can benefit."

Thomas Wolsey had been a beacon of quiet wisdom for many years now, Arthur having often found solace in his less forceful approach to making his point – unlike Fox and Wyatt who often bickered and fought for Arthur's attention and approval. Wolsey was less obvious in his display of loyalty, choosing to show his trustworthiness not in words, but in actions, and often offering his services to alleviate Arthur from some of the pressures of his kingly duties.

While he had appreciated the generosity, Arthur was not completely out of his depth, having learned from an early age how to shoulder the many responsibilities that came with being king. But above even that was the memory of his father's favourite, Edmund Dudley, and how Arthur had observed that granting someone *too much* power could lead to unfavourable outcomes.

"We cannot go to war with France," Arthur stated simply, running a hand over his short red beard, his stubble having grown unchecked in his frustrated state of late, "England would not win."

"We'd give them a good fight," Griffith said in what he must have thought was a bolstering statement but resulted merely in aggravating Arthur further.

"We *cannot* go to war with France!" the king repeated sternly, banging his fist upon the wooden table suddenly, and Griffith looked away in shame, disappointed in himself for his blunder so soon into his new position.

"A good fight is irrelevant if the end result is total destruction," Arthur clarified.

"Exactly right, Your Grace," Wolsey agreed, nodding his head at his king.

Arthur exhaled heavily as he sat back in his seat at the head of the table, the rest of his council having grown quiet following his outburst. Only the occasional clearing of a throat or the rustling of papers was to be heard.

"Prepare my household," Arthur said matter-of-factly then, breaking the silence, as though it were obvious what must be done, "I shall go to France myself to set this matter straight."

"You can't leave me now, so close to my confinement!"

By now, Katherine was into her sixth month of pregnancy, and only two months away from entering her confinement, which would have been troubling enough already, if it weren't for her traumatic past experiences of loss.

"I'll be back before then," Arthur said as he gently held her face in his hands and pressed his forehead to hers, "I promise." Katherine could not speak, the lump in her throat rendering her completely mute. She closed her eyes in the hope of settling her troubled thoughts, but it did little to quench her growing fear.

"I love you, Arthur," she whispered as she clung onto his wrists like a lifeline, silently praying that he would stay true to his word.

2nd December 1515

Before his departure to France, Arthur had drawn up grants, giving Queen Katherine complete power as Regent of England during his absence.

The mandate gave her advice of a small council, some of Arthur's Privy Council having stayed behind in England to be at the queen's disposal and to aid her to run the country in the king's stead. He warranted her the ability to wage war against any enemies if the need were to arise, and full access to the treasury to pay however much would be necessary for the defence of the kingdom.

And while she revelled in the fact that Arthur had placed such ultimate trust in her to guard and manage the realm, clearly recognizing her loyalties by giving her an extraordinary amount of authority, it *had* all seemed rather excessive to Katherine, who had yet to see the country be invaded in the fourteen years she had resided in England.

But just a week after Arthur's departure, word came from the north that Scotland was planning to invade England in Arthur's absence; and suddenly, it didn't seem quite so excessive after all.

"F-France and Scotland must have planned this out exactly," the old Sir Henry Wyatt said, Katherine noticing his stutter as he spoke, "the new F-French King has been paranoid of England's increased military and naval capacity f-for months. No doubt this was a plot all along for them to both learn of our military p-power and to attempt to weaken it with S-Scotland doing France's dirty work for them. The Auld Alliance between Scotland and France compels them to unite against us, and attacking while England is without her king is the opportune moment to strike to assure v-victory."

At Wyatt's choice of words, Katherine stopped in her tracks on their way to the council chamber, her ladies almost bumping into her at her abrupt standstill.

"You fear Scottish victory, Sir Wyatt?" the queen asked, her face maintaining a neutral expression while her heart beat wildly in her chest.

Wyatt did not reply and merely clenched his jaw together, as if forcing himself to remain silent.

Katherine raised one thin eyebrow, noticeably disappointed in him, and resumed walking ahead, her ladies and the two members of the Privy Council she had been left with following swiftly behind.

"The king considered all possible consequences of his absence," Katherine assured the men as she entered the chamber and took a seat at the head of the table, "And he has left me in charge to see to it that we would prevail in the event of an attack. As your queen, I will not allow England to be overrun by those who claim to be our loyal neighbours."

Wyatt and Griffith Rhys took their seats at the long council table, its many empty seats emphasising the country's frailty.

The usher opened the doors then to allow for a man with a shock of white hair and a short-cropped white beard to enter. The council members turned confused faces to see who had joined them, since the rest of the council had left to France with the king.

"Your Grace," the older man said as he entered the chambers and bowed his head before making towards them.

He stood just a mere foot from the council table and bowed his head again, his back as straight and confident as that of a man half his age, "Your orders?"

Griffith and Wyatt's heads snapped back to look at their queen, a question on their faces.

"Thomas Howard," the queen said in greeting as she stood from her seat, ignoring the council members' confused expressions.

"There is no time to lose," Katherine declared, "Are you prepared to serve your queen?"

The older man nodded once, then rested his hand upon the hilt of his sword.

"I await your instruction, my queen," he said, his gruff voice sounding sure.

Katherine inhaled deeply, "My instruction is that you lead our troops against the invasion from the north."

Griffith Rhys rose to his feet, "Howard?!" he called in disgusted disbelief, "He is over seventy! What good is a leader of our army if he's dead of old age before the fighting begins?"

To Katherine's disappointment, there was a light chuckle from Sir Henry Wyatt.

She cast her eyes on old Thomas Howard. For a man in his seventies, he did not *look* like someone who had seen too many winters. Though his hair was white, and his face creased, his back was as straight as an arrow. He was fit and ready for battle, and he exuded an aura of a man whose life's goal had been to serve his country in combat; and Katherine felt strangely safe around him.

She turned to Griffith, "The Earl of Surrey is an experienced and invaluable soldier!" the queen replied fiercely, her chin raised as she perused the men before her with a scornful glare, "He will head north with our army and through our people's respect of him he will rally many more throughout the country who are brave enough to join the fight."

"Your Grace," Henry Wyatt said, his eyes downturned with dread and his bald head shining with perspiration, "The p-people of England will not feel much compelled to partake in a battle led by an old m-man."

Katherine tore her gaze from the two councillors around the table and looked to the old veteran before her, whose jaw was set tightly against the barrage of disparagement thrown at him by men of words.

She inhaled and straightened her back, hoping to hide her bump in doing so, though the entire country knew that she was heavy with child, "You are right, Sir Wyatt," she said, to which Wyatt exhaled with relief.

But Katherine was not finished, "Which is precisely why *I* shall accompany Thomas Howard in leading the soldiers to battle."

3rd December 1515

  Katherine soon received news from her informants that King James IV of Scotland was planning to position his army at Flodden Edge – a hill on the south of Branxton on the English-Scottish border – on the 13th of December, giving Katherine little time to prepare.

Immediately upon having heard of this underhanded invasion, Katherine had dispatched a messenger to Arthur in France, but having since learned of Scotland's plans to invade in mere days, Katherine was aware that her message would not make it to Arthur in time for him to return before Scotland crossed the border. She really was alone in defending England.

For a brief moment, she had considered writing to her sister-in-law Margaret to intervene on her behalf, to hopefully make her Scottish husband see reason. But Katherine knew it would only be in vain, for no man – no *king* – would lay down their arms for the sake of a pleading woman.

But being a woman herself, – as well as being seven months pregnant – Katherine knew she was entirely out of her depth. And yet she would not let it show, for though her council continued to protest against her decision to rally the troops and to be in among the battlefield, Katherine would not be deterred; she must lead by example and be a beacon of strength for her people. After all, she was the daughter of the great warrior queen Isabella de Castille, who herself had gone against traditional standards of warfare and been hugely involved in the plotting of war campaigns during her reign. This was in Katherine's blood! And to show how serious she was to stand with her people, Queen Katherine ordered for an entirely unique suit of gold-plated armour to be tailor made for her, one that would accommodate her heavily pregnant body.

11th December 1515
Alnwick, the Scottish border

The rain drops began to fall as a light drizzle at first but had soon turned into a heavy downpour, making the ground underfoot slippery and muddy.
The journey north through England had been a long and arduous one for the pregnant queen, the many hours sitting astride upon a horse in the uncomfortable armour having given Katherine second thoughts as to her body's capability.
But she had pushed on, and in each town that they had passed, she and Howard rallied many able-bodied men to join their fight, and by the time they had reached Alnwick, just sixty miles from the Scottish border, they had assembled around 26,000 men.
For days the soldiers walked behind their queen and the Earl of Surrey, their initial excited banter ebbing away the closer they got to the site of the battle, then stopping entirely when the rain had begun. And now the only sound that remained was the heavy and repetitive *ping ping ping* of the raindrops as they fell heavily upon the soldiers' helmeted heads and armoured shoulders.
And then, finally, there was their sanctuary.
"We should make camp at Alnwick Castle," Katherine called over the loud rain as she spotted it in the distance, her voice sounding sure and strong, though she felt neither, "The men need to rest before the battle."
The Earl of Surrey Thomas Howard looked at his queen, his knowing gaze mirroring to Katherine what she already knew but did not want to admit: It was not just the men who needed rest.

"You cannot head into combat, Your Grace!" Thomas Howard protested that evening once the men had set up shelter from the rain, his gruff voice pleading, "You risk too much."

"For England, I would give my own life," Katherine maintained as she continued to look over the battle tactics, her great swollen belly before her like an ugly reminder of what else she would be risking, "In the king's absence, I am your leader."

The old man's eyebrows twitched as he stared at his queen, both proud and frustrated by her determination. He opened his mouth to speak but closed it again, knowing it would lead to nothing, the queen's Spanish blood continuing to run thick with stubbornness.

Later that night, however, as Katherine was praying for God to watch over her in this time of great uncertainty, a messenger arrived carrying the king's seal.

"His Highness the king has returned to the English shores, Your Grace," the young man said, wiping the sweat from his brow with the back of his dirty hand, "I rode here as fast as I could."

He handed Katherine the letter as Lina helped her up from kneeling at the altar.

"Will he make it in time?" Lina asked, looking from the messenger to Katherine.

The queen shook her head as she tore open the king's wax seal and held the letter up to the light of a nearby candle.

After a long moment of silence, Lina could not contain her anxiety, "What news, my lady?" she half whispered, half croaked, her throat tight with worry.

Katherine dropped her arms in disbelief, her eyebrows creased, "He orders me to stand down."

Lina gasped, covering her mouth with her hand, "He does not wish to fight back? Is England to be overrun?"

Katherine shook her head, "No, Lina," she said, turning towards her Moorish lady, "He orders *me* to stand down. I am commanded by the king himself not to fight."

12th December 1515

With the news spreading throughout her army of Arthur's direct order that the queen was not to partake in the skirmish, Katherine felt a definitive shift in the attitude of the men.
Their rowdiness and banter swiftly returned, their enthusiasm about the coming fight having been restored, and Katherine realised then that it hadn't been the growing proximity to the battle that had dampened their moods. As it turned out, for Katherine to have been willing to fight side by side with them had been enough for the people of England; but they did not *actually* want her to lay down her life for them.
After all, as soldiers of the English crown, that was *their* job in this unfortunate turn of events.
And so, on the eve before the battle, Katherine entrusted Thomas Howard with leading the army, knowing that he, too, was relieved to be doing so without her.

13th December 1515

News soon came, just hours after the break of dawn, that King James IV's greatly advantageous strategy of using high ground at Flodden Edge had backfired when the terrain had proved too slippery from the downpour of rain the day before.
Katherine and her ladies all breathed a sigh of relief to have received such positive news, and though England saw a loss of nearly two-thousand men during the fighting, more news followed that evening that England had been victorious.
"The Scottish artillery guns did not perform as they had hoped, no doubt due to them having been poorly sited and shooting downhill," the messenger was telling his queen proudly, giving the message from Thomas Howard word for word, "At your order, no prisoners were taken, and King James IV himself was killed in the fighting."

Katherine's eyes widened briefly at the information, and for a moment she thought of her sister-in-law, Margaret, who would soon be told the awful news that she had been made a widow.

But she straightened her back. Such was the outcome of war. King James had known of the risks, and would certainly have done the same to her given the chance.

Margaret might never forgive her. But, by the grace of God, she would understand.

"Bring me King James' bloodied cloak," Katherine ordered, "It will be our only consolation prize from this terrible event, and a reminder that England was victorious over its enemies. Send it to my husband in London, to inform him that we have defeated Scotland in his honour."

Chapter 14

20th December 1515

Queen Katherine was hailed throughout London upon her return from the north, the people's calls for their beloved queen being heard for miles.
On horseback, she made her way through the city alongside Thomas Howard, who sported a new, red raw scar on his forehead. She waved to the cheering crowds with a forced smile upon her tired face as she tried to hide the fact that her body was screaming out in pain, the continuous riding in her condition at eight-months gestation having taken a toll on her.
And the babe in her belly had begun kicking furiously, much like baby Elizabeth had done just days before her untimely death…
Arthur and the entire court met them in the courtyard upon their entrance through the palace gates, a fanfare erupting around them as Arthur stepped forward and carefully aided Katherine down from her horse, then pulled her into his safe embrace.
"I can't believe you put yourself in danger like that," Arthur whispered hoarsely, as he took her face in his hands and pressed his forehead to hers, "How could you have been so stupid?"
He hadn't said it in anger or in degradation, but in distress, his tone quite clearly conveying how lost he would have been without her.
"I am safe," Katherine replied, pulling away to look him in the eyes, "England is safe."
He sighed deeply then cleared his throat, banishing the tears which were threatening to fall, and Katherine realised all of a sudden just how foolish she had been.
"Did King Francis receive you well?" she swiftly asked, eager to learn of his achievements in France.

Arthur grinned at that, "We were able to soothe France's suspicions through an alliance. Artie is to be betrothed to Francis' newborn daughter, Louise de Valois."

Katherine, as a daughter of Spain, raised her chin slightly at the new information, a natural reaction at the idea of a marital union with a French princess for her son – Spain and France having always had a strained relationship.

"Howard!" the king called then, and they both turned to the old man as he dismounted his steed, "You have proven yourself invaluable! You have my thanks, and my utmost respect."

The old man bent his knee before his king, "It was an honour to fight alongside so many brave men, and to discuss battle tactics with such a noble lady as her Highness Queen Katherine."

"Arise, Howard," the king said, to which the seventy-one-year-old stood up with admirable agility, "You have done England a great service, and your loyalty and efforts shall be recognised."

28th December 1515

Katherine had not been able to partake in the Christmastide celebrations due to having to go into confinement just two days after her return from the Scottish border; and she was secretly glad for the obligatory period of rest.

"Has the child ceased thrashing about?" Lina asked Katherine now, six days into their confinement, as she leaned over her mistress to plump her pillows, her dark eyes searching Katherine's face for a hint of discomfort.

"He has," Katherine replied, her voice heavy with relief, "Since our return I have noticed a calm. He must know we are safe once more."

Lina smiled, flashing her small white teeth, "Praise God," then turned to fetch Katherine her breakfast.

Through daily letters from Arthur as well as court gossip, Katherine had learned that Thomas Howard Earl of Surrey had been rewarded for his success on the battlefield with the conferment of the title of Duke of Norfolk – which his father had lost decades earlier for supporting Richard III in the Battle of Bosworth Field – and Thomas Howard's son became Earl of Surrey in his stead.

Katherine was glad to see the brave man so generously rewarded, and only wished she had spared a moment to thank him personally. But her mind had been occupied with flashing images of baby Elizabeth on their return home from battle, and though her babe had finally settled in the dome of her belly, it wasn't long before Katherine was faced with potential tragedy yet again.

18th January 1516

According to the physicians' calculations, Katherine's labour had – yet again – come too soon.

"Push, Your Grace, *push!*"

The birthing chambers were alive with Katherine's screams, the midwives' hurried calls to one another, and her ladies' mumblings of prayer. Like a buzzing beehive of nervous energy.

"Good! Well done, Your Highness. Now breathe. Breathe."

Katherine lay back against the sweat-soaked pillows and breathed as the plump midwife instructed her to, all the while trying desperately not to pay too close attention to the bloodied rags at the foot of the bed and the acrid smell of fear in the air. She felt her belly tighten just seconds later and the pain of another contraction gripping her lower back like a vice, and she steeled herself to push again.

On and on this cycle went for what felt like hours – no, *days,* – Katherine becoming more and more lethargic with every push, her grunts coming out hoarse and pained but knowing full well that if she were to give in, that she *and* the baby would die, and that she would never get to see Artie grow up.

And then, quite suddenly, just as the edges of her consciousness were beginning to darken, she felt her baby be born with one slithering gush.

Katherine collapsed against the pillows, too exhausted to even notice the little gasp that had escaped Lina from the corner of the room.

Her baby was dead, Katherine already knew it, for it had been born too soon to survive this cruel world without the protection of its mother. She closed her eyes to spare herself the pain of seeing its limp little limbs hanging lifelessly in the midwife's arms, for even years later, the image of Elizabeth had not ceased to haunt her, and she could not handle any more of such agony.

"Katherine," someone whispered down at her, but she covered her face with her hands, sobbing in devastation.

"Katherine," the voice called again, this time followed by a little squeal which brought back memories of when Artie was small.

Katherine slowly removed her hands from her face but kept her eyes closed, not fully trusting her ears or her mind in this state of great anguish. But then there it was again, that little squeak, followed this time by a sad little grunt, and then a wail.

Katherine's brows crumbled with tearful relief as she opened her eyes to see her tiny, *tiny*, baby in Lina's arms, its pink fists flailing about angrily as if in protest for the long wait to meet its mother. She let out a staggered breath, not yet fully believing that her child was alive.

She sat up gingerly as Lina leaned forward to gently place the bundle into the crook of Katherine's arms.

"It is a beautiful baby girl, Your Highness," the plump midwife said as she joined Lina at the queen's bedside.

"A girl," the queen repeated in a faint whisper, smiling down at the newborn as she presented Katherine with a gummy yawn.

"God is good," Katherine breathed, "He has watched over us this day and gifted us with this miracle. A beautiful and healthy baby girl."

And Katherine was so besotted with her creation that she missed it entirely when the midwife flashed Lina an anxious look.

"The princess is not as healthy as we would like," the plump midwife informed the king just hours later, "It is likely she will die in mere days."

Arthur ran his hand through his hair, which he had noticed some weeks ago had begun to grey at the sides.

"Does Katherine know?" he asked.

The midwife shook her head, "We have not had the heart to tell her yet."

Arthur nodded his head slowly, "Of course," he said, his voice thick with sadness, "I will arrange for the christening to take place tomorrow."

"The queen also begs Your Highness to consider the name she has chosen for the princess. In honour of your sister," the midwife added.

Arthur clenched his jaw but nodded in approval, sorrow overtaking any other feelings he continued to cling on to.

The midwife curtsied and turned to leave when Arthur held out his hand, "Please," he called gently, to which the midwife turned back round to face him, "When you tell the queen…"

He could not finish his thought, for even he did not know how best to break such terrible news. But the midwife nodded, her round face tight with understanding.

The little princess was swiftly christened at just one day old with as much ado as was possible in such short notice.

The procession of gentlemen, ladies, earls, and bishops in attendance at this grand ceremony paused at the door of the church underneath a small arras-covered wooden archway.

Trumpets sounded loudly at the princess' arrival within the Church of the Observant Friars, the babe squealing in protest at the loud sounds as she wriggled angrily in her godmother's arms. Her godmother, the Countess of Salisbury Margaret Pole, tightened her grip on her ward and bounced her gently to settle her, the little girl's face growing red as she screamed above the fanfare.

The baptism was completed more speedily than with Prince Artie, for not only was this child's christening more urgent due to her feebler health, but she was also just a girl, and she was not expected to ever take the throne – whether she were to live or not.

After prayers were said, the priest gently poured holy water from the baptismal font over her bald head, anointed her with holy oil and then swaddled her in her baptismal robe before turning to the crowd of lords and ladies within the church.

"God send and give good long life onto the right high, right noble and excellent Princess Mary, Princess of England and daughter of our most sovereign lord the King's Highness!"

Chapter 15

September 1516

Following the birth of a sickly daughter eight months earlier, the king and queen were of the understanding that Katherine would likely not bear any more children.

Their many losses over the years aside, the queen was now thirty-one-years-old and unlikely to be fruitful for much longer, if at all. But the couple continued to try nevertheless, if not for the sake of conceiving a spare heir, then for the sake of nurturing their connection, which had deepened considerably in recent years.

"Who would have thought we would be here after the dreadful start we had?" Katherine mused teasingly as she lay naked in Arthur's arms and pulled the sheet over herself to cover her scarred and loose middle.

"We were lucky," Arthur replied, his voice gruff with adoration for her as he reached beneath the sheet and gently placed a hand over her belly, wordlessly showing her that she had no reason to hide, "Not many political marriages blossom into one such as ours."

Katherine inhaled deeply, snuggling closer to him though she was already practically laying on top of him. They lay there for a while, the two of them wrapped in their own thoughts, when Katherine spoke again.

"I pray for another son every day. You know that, don't you?" She lifted her head from his chest to look into his blue eyes.

He nodded, though his eyebrows were creased, "And you know that I do not expect any more from you."

Katherine pushed off of him then and sighed, letting her long hair fall between them like a curtain, to hide her inexplicable shame.

"You don't understand," she muttered.

She did not know why she continued to blame herself for their struggles, especially when Arthur had always been nothing but accepting and understanding – almost to the point of frustration, since it made her feelings of inadequacy seem so much more out of place. A king *should* wish for sons.

Granted, they had Artie. But one male heir alone was not the makings of a powerful dynasty; and however much she tried to deny it, Katherine felt uneasy relying solely on Artie as their successor. And the continued lack of a spare heir brought a bout of anxiety to her chest.

Arthur sat up, covered himself with the sheet and swept her hair over her shoulder so that he could see her face.

"You have done your duty as a wife and as a queen," he said, as he had done so many times before, "And even if we had been less fortunate than we are, I would be saying the same. But God has blessed us with two children, one to succeed me and one to bring an alliance with her marriage, God willing."

Katherine met his loving gaze, a small smile tugging at her lips, "Mary has proven all the physicians wrong," she said proudly, allowing his calming words to wash over her, "She is as strong as Artie and equally as gifted. She is a Tudor."

Arthur reached up and cupped her cheek, before pressing a kiss to her lips.

"She is strong like her mother," he whispered as he skimmed her jawline with his lips and down her neck, "The best of us both. The Rose and the Pomegranate."

Katherine felt her body relax under his touch and she closed her eyes, allowing Arthur to make her forget her worries as only he could.

"They will both grow up to be strong and wise rulers," Arthur continued to mumble as he pressed kisses and caresses along her neck and down her shoulder, "And even *if* our childbearing years are behind us, there is always good reason to call you to my bed."

And with that he grabbed her by the waist and threw her down onto the mattress, a giggle escaping her as Arthur positioned himself between her legs and pulled the sheet over both their heads.

November 1516
Hunsdon House, Hertfordshire

With France having eagerly accepted England's proposal of an alliance through the betrothal of Prince Artie with their infant Princess Louise de Valois, Artie was henceforth on his path to becoming an adult.
At the age of just six, and with his infancy behind him, he was officially deemed too old for all manner of childish things. His chambers at Hunsdon House in Hertfordshire – the residence he shared with his baby sister, Mary – were completely remodelled, replacing all things for more grown-up alternatives. Toys were given to the poor or handed down to the Princess Mary, a new, four-poster bed was brought in, and tapestries were hung throughout the boy's chambers, depicting his father the king's own favourite Biblical scenes. Most of his household was also replaced, all female attendants being dismissed or – like the toys – sent to attend the Princess Mary.
But Artie didn't mind. For though he would miss many of his things, at least the Lady Margaret Bryan, who had practically raised him, would continue to reside under the same roof as he and only be on the opposite wing of the palace, taking care of his baby sister.
In the lady's stead, Prince Artie was appointed new tutors to begin his formal teachings of what it meant to rule England one day, one of which was King Arthur's own advisor, Thomas Wolsey. Wolsey, who had proven his patience and loyalty throughout the years, had recently been appointed as Bishop of Lincoln, and with the new title, his status within the court was raised that little bit higher. This had irked many of the nobles

within the court who, given Wolsey's low birth as the son of a butcher, did not believe him to be worthy of the king's regard. But Wolsey had never allowed where he had come from to stop him from reaching for his goals.

"The prince's education must follow humanist lines, of course," King Arthur had instructed the new tutors, "Artie must grow up knowing the humanist principal values that the protection and advancement of all society is the key to being a good king."

Wolsey and the two other men had nodded their heads.

"Latin, Greek, grammar and oration of course, too; though do make sure he is also taught fencing and riding," Arthur had continued, "Just because I never enjoyed the physical side of my education does not mean that it is not necessary for a well-rounded Prince of England."

And now, as Artie's lessons began bright and early each morning, he was beginning to experience an entirely unfamiliar feeling of what he could only describe as a weight pushing down on his little shoulders.

But Artie did not complain, and instead found solace in that special time of day when his tutors would pack up their things and leave his chambers, allowing him to head across the landing to visit his baby sister and the Lady Bryan.

"Ah, my prince!" the Lady Bryan greeted him with a cheerful smile, as she did every evening, "You have grown since last I saw you!"

Artie giggled as his former governess folded him into her arms, "You saw me yesterday."

"And since then, I am sure you have grown two inches," Lady Bryan teased him lovingly, taking his chin in her firm grip and squeezing it.

In the centre of the south-facing room stood a gold-painted cradle, much like what Artie assumed his had been like years ago, though he did not remember it. He headed towards it tentatively as he had done each day since his sister's birth, craning his neck to peer into it while still at a distance.

"Is she sleeping?" he asked, taking another step closer.

"She was, though your voice usually awakens her," the Lady Bryan said softly, "she knows the sound of your voice, and I'm sure she eagerly awaits your visits every day."

Artie smiled, his shoulders relaxing when he spotted his sister's bald head and seeing her big, blue eyes wide and searching.

Artie reached the cradle and gripped the edge of it, "Hi, Mary," he cooed, his voice instinctively taking on a slightly higher pitch.

The baby, who was now nine months old and not yet able to stand, rolled over to lay on her front and lifted up her head, her legs kicking happily underneath the blanket she had been tucked under. She beamed a bright, gummy smile at her brother, her head bobbing slightly with excitement as she screeched a happy greeting.

The Lady Bryan stood over the cradle then and lifted the princess out before carefully plopping her down on the furs by the fire, a solid fire-guard separating them from the flames.

Artie sat down cross-legged at some distance in front of Mary and held up a rattle, shook it and began singing a tune to entice the little princess to come to him.

Mary flopped herself forward from her sitting position, her belly flat against the floor, and kicked her arms and legs fiercely, as though she were swimming but going nowhere.

"The princess will crawl when she is ready," the Lady Bryan reflected as she sat down on the wide ledge of the window overlooking the gardens below, "There is no rush for a girl."

Artie looked up at his former governess, "I just want to be able to play with her soon. To play catch and hide-and-seek."

Lady Bryan sighed, raised her eyebrows, "She is learning slower than is expected," she admitted absentmindedly, "and the physicians continue unsure –"

She stopped herself then, not wanting to upset the young prince.

Artie scooted closer to Mary, shook the rattle again and smiled at her. Baby Mary rolled onto her back, then giggled and blew bubbles as she saw her brother upside down.

Artie reached forward and gave Mary the little silver rattle as a consolation prize for having at least tried to crawl towards him, and the baby shook it vigorously.

"Keep encouraging her, my prince," the Lady Bryan said as she observed the two royal children from across the room, saddened by the reality that baby Mary might not live to grow up to run around with Artie. But she wished to give him hope. For sometimes hope, like prayer, could be a powerful thing.

"The little princess might surprise us all yet."

Part IV

Fear of the unknown brings about the
opportunity for change

Chapter 16

2 years later

1st September 1518

"The young princess has died."
It was almost as though God had not been in favour of their betrothal, for within just days of one another, three-year-old Louise de Valois and eight-year-old Prince Artie were struck down with fevers; and news soon followed that the Princess of France had not survived her illness.
Lord Chancellor Richard Fox handed Arthur the letter from their ambassador in France, "The alliance with France is not to be."
Arthur only nodded, the words blurring on the note in his hand, his mind too worried for his own child's survival to concern himself with the dissolution of a treaty.
"Prince Artie is strong," Fox said, as though he could read the king's mind, "And the country is praying for his recovery."
Arthur met his advisor's gaze, hoping to draw assurance from him. But when he met the old man's watery eyes he did not feel comforted, and instead he wondered if they were wet due to his old age, or from fearing for their young prince's life.

3rd September 1518

"It is smallpox, my lord."
It had been two days since Artie had been taken to bed with intense back pain, fevers and chills, and the physicians were finally able to put a name to his suffering.
"The blisters have now spread from inside his mouth to his face, arms and legs," the king's personal physician, Dr William Butts, who Arthur had immediately sent to his son's bedside, was saying, "We have treated him as best we could, Your

Highness, but..." the old man licked his thin lips and pulled anxiously on his long, white beard, "The prince is likely to die..."

At that, Arthur closed his eyes and exhaled a long breath, as though he had been holding it the entire time.

"Does the queen know?" Arthur asked over his shoulder as he stood with his back towards the physician, his hands clutching the stone carved fireplace.

The physician shook his head, "No, Your Grace. I came to you first."

"Good," Arthur said, turning to face the old man, "Do not tell her. Do not tell anyone. The future of England hangs in the balance, and we cannot afford civil unrest. As far as the people know, Artie has caught a chill which he is likely to overcome, do you understand me?"

Dr Butts nodded and bowed quickly, his slightly hunched back becoming more prominent with the action, "As you command, my lord."

He turned to exit the king's chambers, Arthur watching him shuffle tiredly towards the door.

"You said you have treated my son," the king called after the physician then, who turned in the doorway, his hand on the doorframe for support.

"Yes," the old man replied.

"How?"

"He was wrapped tightly in red linens, Your Grace. Red, to draw out the poison in the body."

Arthur's eyebrows twitched.

"The colour of the linen will draw out the poison," the physician repeated in clarification, "Pray God it will be enough."

Arthur could do nothing but nod at that, his energy zapped from feeling utterly useless in this trying time.

*

"As per your order, Princess Mary was moved from Hunsdon House to Hatfield House for her safety," Lady Margaret Bryan told the king and queen later that day as they sat stiffly upon their thrones in the great hall, "The Princess is in good spirits and does not appear in any way to have been infected."

Queen Katherine exhaled raggedly and looked to Arthur, who took her hand in his and squeezed it tightly.

"We thank you for your diligence, Lady Bryan," Arthur said, "If the Princess were to develop any symptoms we expect immediate news."

"Of course, Your Grace," Margaret Bryan said, "Of course."

5th September 1518

"I need to go to him!"

It had been four days since Artie had been taken to bed, and two days since the physician had informed Arthur that their son was likely to die. But Arthur was yet to tell his wife, and her fears of the worst had been left to run wild.

It was time to inform her of the inevitable.

"No, Katherine," Arthur said gently as he sat slumped forward on the edge of their bed, his elbows resting on his knees, looking utterly broken.

"Arthur, I am his mother!" the queen thundered, her voice a terrible blend of pleading and panic, "I have to see him. I have to see my baby. Only I can make him better!"

Arthur shook his head as it hung heavily between his bent shoulders, "Nothing will make him better."

Katherine flinched and froze at Arthur's statement, her eyes suddenly wide with fresh terror.

"What is this?" she whispered hoarsely, "What do you know?"

Arthur lifted his head slowly, met his wife's terrified gaze and saw his own terror reflected back at him, then watched as realisation took over Katherine's face.

"No," she croaked, shaking her head, "No, it is not true."

"Dr Butts came to see me," Arthur said, deliberately keeping the *when* out of the confession, "He said –"

But Arthur did not need to finish the sentence, for the fact hung heavy in the air.

Katherine stared at her husband, her entire body shaking with fury that he had not told her sooner, with fear for her son's survival, with the need to storm out of the room and ride out to be with her baby as he lay dying, with the terrible knowledge that she could not risk her own life, thinking that she did not care what happened to her as long as her presence meant Artie would not suffer alone, with a rage towards God for testing her again and again and again and *again*.

Surely, one day she would break. Surely, one day her heart would no longer be able to take it. Surely, one day she would just *die* from heartbreak…

Katherine turned away from her husband then, too angry to even look at him, and pressed her hands to her chest as a sharp pain coursed through her. Perhaps today was the day her heart would give out.

It certainly felt like it.

6th September 1518

"With Artie's condition failing to improve, I have decided to recall Harry from the monastery in Somerset," the king informed his advisors on the fifth day of Prince Artie's affliction, "With our lack of spare heir…Harry will have to be returned to the line of succession should Artie die."

Griffith and Wolsey exchanged a look, too subtly for Arthur to notice even if he weren't blinded by sorrow.

"Your Grace and the queen are still young," Fox said, who at the age of seventy believed everyone younger than he to still be young, "There is still hope for another son."

Arthur shook his head slightly at that, "Nevertheless, the Tudor House needs to regroup. Send for Harry. He won't like it, but he will have to be defrocked if he is to one day become king."

It had been three years since the Tudor brothers had looked upon one another, and Harry was shocked to see that time had not been kind to Arthur.

Though he still boasted a strong physique and a full head of auburn hair, his eyes could not hide the strain of recent years. And Harry was ashamed to say that he had been one of those strains.

"Brother," Harry said with a sure voice as he bowed his head, his hands tucked inside the wide sleeves of his robes, "My king."

Since his banishment to Bath Abbey, Harry had had a lot of time to reflect upon the errors of his ways, many hours at prayer, and an entire year spent committed to a vow of silence having opened his mind to the truth: that he had acted out of jealousy and arrogance in marrying Mary to Charles Brandon without the king's consent.

Though God was Harry's master, Arthur was his king. And while Harry remained upon this Earth, he would do all in his power to serve God's anointed King of England, which in turn *would be* serving God.

He had been young and foolish three years ago when he had believed himself above the laws of the king. Had been arrogant to believe his close relationship with Arthur would allow him to do as he pleased. But during his time away from court, Harry had learned that there was nothing noble about being superior to your fellow man, and that true nobility came from being superior to your former self.

And so, no matter what his king were to ask of him from now on, Harry would certainly oblige.

"I have called you back because the Tudor dynasty is crumbling as we speak," Arthur announced sombrely as he sat stiffly upon his throne in the empty and dimly lit great hall.

Harry had wondered why the ambience upon his arrival had been less than welcoming, had dismissed it as part of his tainted reputation. But now confusion and dread flooded his senses, worried suddenly about what terrible thing had happened.

"What is it, Your Highness?" he asked, his pale blue eyes questioning.

Arthur rose from his throne and descended the three steps to stand before his younger brother, who even now in his robes and crosses looked so much like the young boy Arthur had beaten at chess countless times in their youth.

"You must give up your vocation and resume your place within this family," Arthur said, raising a hand to squeeze Harry's shoulder, "Artie is dying. I need you now, brother. To take his place in the line of succession as Heir Apparent."

Harry stared back at Arthur, frozen in shock. This was what Arthur had called him back for?

Not because he had been forgiven and welcomed back after having completed his punishment, or even selfishly because Arthur had missed him and had *wanted* him to return? But because he needed him to revert to his old position of heir due to Arthur's useless wife's failure to produce more than one son...?

Had Harry not warned Arthur of this *exact* outcome? Had he not foreshadowed this precise moment?

And now it was falling to him to fix the mess his brother and his worthless Spanish Queen had made.

Harry exhaled slowly, moving slightly so that Arthur's hand fell from his shoulder.

He had returned to court ready to plead complete loyalty to his king, to do all in his power and all that was asked of him to please his sovereign lord.

But *this*? This was asking too much.

The priesthood was not a vocation, as Arthur had called it. It was a calling for life, a gift from God to spend his life serving Him. Harry had worked his way up to a Priest, had gained respect among his community and made powerful connections. Harry had taken his vows seriously, had gone so far as to reject many mistresses throughout the years to stay true to his vow of celibacy – unlike so many other men of the cloth who disregarded their vow entirely! Wolsey himself praised Harry for his devotion and piety!

No, he could not do it. This one thing, Harry would not do. This was his *life*. And Harry would not give it up.

"No," he stated firmly after a moment.

Arthur visibly flinched, "No?"

"You heard me, brother," Harry said, his voice calm and steady, "I rejected that life long ago. I am not prepared to rule, nor do I wish to. Had you asked me three years ago I might have accepted, but my time away has taught me that my life was meant for the Church."

"As future king you would still be doing God's work!" Arthur countered, his voice rising with growing anxiety over losing both his male heirs at once, "You cannot desert me at this time of great peril. Artie is likely to die, Harry! My son! My only son!" Arthur was growing agitated, his eyes wild with fear for the future of England, "The country will fall into unrest if you do not do this, Harry. The War of the Roses will re-awaken. Cousin against cousin. It will be the end of us."

Harry continued only to stare at his older brother, "I am sorry, Arthur."

Arthur covered his face with his hands and pressed his fingers into his temples, a dull ache having begun to throb behind his eyes.

"What am I to do?" Arthur muttered, more to himself than anyone else. Then he spun round to face Harry and pointed an angry finger into his face, "I am the king. I can force you to accept this honour. I could have you defrocked like *that*!" and he clicked his fingers.

The brothers stared at each other, Arthur breathing erratically and Harry standing as still as a statue.

"You could force me, brother," Harry replied, "You could bend me to your will. But I would not make a good king. I would resent you and the throne, and England would head into ruin nonetheless."

Arthur clenched his teeth together, his face as red as the Tudor Rose. He knew Harry was right.

But then Harry stepped forward, a thought coming to him all of a sudden, as though God Himself had whispered it into his ear.

"All is not lost, brother," Harry assured him in his calming voice, "There is one other thing you could do to save the Tudor dynasty."

Arthur's brows bunched together, the skin on his forehead creasing in confusion, "What? What is it? I'd do anything."

Harry smiled, baring a row of straight teeth, "You could acquire a new wife."

8th September 1518

By some miracle, on the morning of the seventh day of his affliction, Artie awoke as if nothing had happened.

The blisters on his face and body continued to glow red and angry however, and though the young prince insisted that he felt well, the physicians and his royal mother and father ordered that he was to lay abed for another week, to ensure a full recovery.

"It is a gift from God!" Katherine wept into Arthur's shoulder when they received the news.

Arthur inhaled deeply and nodded in agreement, tightening his grip on his wife as her tears of joy turned into sobs of exhaustion, the past week having been the very worst of their lives.

"All will be well now, Katherine," Arthur soothed, rubbing her back in slow circular motions, "All will be well."

But even as he said the words, Arthur could not help but hear his brother's advice in his mind, as clearly as though he were standing beside him still, whispering them into Arthur's ear.

You could acquire a new wife.

It had played on Arthur's conscience on a constant loop for the past two days, and even though he had reacted disturbed and disgusted by Harry's remark, he had not been able to shake it from his thoughts.

If he asked it of her, he knew that Katherine would consider retiring to a nunnery to allow him to take another wife in the hope of siring a son to continue the Tudor line. It was undoubtedly a possibility which had needed to be considered when Artie's life had hung in the balance.

But by God's will, their heir had recovered, and Arthur no longer had any need to think of it.

And yet the words continued to echo in his subconscious.

If only Arthur could ensure that Artie would never again fall ill. If only he had some control over it.

Arthur would do anything to keep his son safe from illness, anything to keep his family whole. But for now, Arthur could only pray that Artie's health would not fail him again, for until Arthur came up with a solution to his lack of spare heir, the House of Tudor was not completely safe from ruin.

And it begged the question: If Artie *had* died, would Arthur have been able to give up the love of his life in the pursuit of a male heir?

Chapter 17

November 1518

With Artie's young bride having succumbed to her ailment some months prior, England and France were yet to settle their mutual distrust of one another, and a new plan for their peace treaty was made.

"We will offer Princess Mary to be betrothed to Francis' new son, the Dauphin of France," Arthur declared to his Privy Council, "And there must be no delay."

"But she is sickly, my lord," Richard Fox said, bunching his white eyebrows together, "France will not want to betroth their firstborn son to a sickly girl."

Arthur narrowed his eyes at Fox with such ferocity that Fox wished he had never opened his mouth, and he shrunk into his seat.

"The Princess was born weak," Griffith interjected then, hoping to deflect from Fox, who appeared as though he might burst into flames, "But the physicians maintain that she has a good bill of health, do they not, Your Grace?"

Arthur nodded at Griffith, grateful for his friend's resilient loyalty. It appeared not all his advisors were utter fools.

"She was believed to have been born a little too early," Arthur clarified, "but since her birth, as we can all attest, Mary has been as robust as Artie was at that age."

Fox and Henry Wyatt exchanged a look but did not dare to mention that the girl had only learned to walk at the age of one and a half – much later than would be expected.

"Send our offer to King Francis," Arthur ordered, shooting Fox another disappointed look, leading the man to fumble before him looking for his quill and ink.

"Tell France of Mary's beauty and her spirit, her gentle nature, and her strength in character. Francis won't be able to say no, and with any luck, he will send his ambassadors on a ship to England in no time."

3rd December 1518

Not even Arthur had really believed that Francis would accept their new offer, but to everyone's surprise, France replied swiftly that they would accept Arthur's daughter as a future bride for their heir to conclude the Anglo-French treaty.

"France must be quacking in their boots of our military standing to accept so eagerly!" Fox said with glee, grinning a gap-toothed smile around the council table.

He had meant it as a compliment to his king's reign, had meant to praise England's development over recent years under Arthur's rule, and yet all Arthur heard was another insult to his daughter's status.

"You cannot be *that* surprised, Fox," Arthur said, growing increasingly irate with the old advisor, though he had often been a beacon of wisdom in the past. Perhaps Arthur was outgrowing his need for old men within his council giving him archaic perspectives, "Mary is a princess of the noblest blood. Francis would have been a fool to reject this betrothal."

Fox shook his head, stuttering, "I only meant to applaud you, Your Grace, and your achievements as king! England has thrived monumentally since your ascension. The cities' death rates have vastly dropped, our navy has almost doubled in capacity since your father's reign, as has our military. The princess' indisputable worth aside, a match with England is not to be missed."

Arthur regarded Fox with a heavy-lidded gaze, suddenly bored of his brown-nosing, and Arthur wondered if it was really the old man's fault that he felt this way of late, or if Artie's close call with death had chipped away at Arthur's patience and serenity.

Wanting an end to the conversation, Arthur turned to the Bishop of Lincoln Thomas Wolsey, "Send word to the Lady Bryan that the Princess and her household is to be at court for the French Ambassador's arrival at the end of the month."

20th December 1518

Princess Mary and her household arrived in London just a day before the French ships docked on the shores of England, making it just in time to prepare for their meeting.

At the age of not yet three years old, the little princess had no clear understanding of the situation at hand, knowing only that she would be promised in marriage to someone everyone kept calling 'the Dauphin of France'.

But the little girl thought that, as long as she would get to see her beloved mother and father, she cared little as to why she had been summoned to court.

The following morning, Mary awoke early in preparation for the grand occasion. Her governess, the Lady Margaret Bryan, dressed her in a gown of cloth of gold and tucked her wispy auburn hair under a rich cap of black cloth. Around her neck and on her fingers, she placed half a dozen jewels and diamonds, Mary watching them with utter amazement as they twinkled in the sunlight from the open window.

When they entered the great hall, everyone turned to look at the little princess, the ladies curtsying and the gentlemen bowing as she made her way through the throng of people.

Despite the time of year, the sun was shining brightly through the stained-glass windows of the great hall, causing a kaleidoscope of beautiful colours to shine down over her mother and father as they sat, almost godlike, upon their thrones.

Little Mary approached the king and queen quickly, her heart soaring at the sight of them, and she offered them a cheery smile and an elegant curtsy, to which the courtiers all around her nodded and muttered in approval.

"Your Highnesses," she squeaked in greeting, and then took her place beside her mother's throne, her governess close behind her as they awaited the arrival of the French.

Trumpets soon sounded to announce the noblemen's arrival, and Griffith Rhys entered, escorting two men through the stone archway of the great hall.

Once they had approached, Griffith climbed the three steps and took his place beside Arthur's throne as the two visitors removed their caps and bowed deeply at the waist.

"Your Graces," said one of the bearded men in a heavy French accent, "I have come to ask for your consent to the marriage of our two nations."

Arthur, in one of his most exquisite outfits of a gold, broad-shouldered jacket encrusted with rubies and diamonds, rose from his throne.

"I, King Arthur and my wife Queen Katherine of Aragon, do hereby give our consent to the betrothal of our daughter, the Princess Mary, to the Dauphin of France, and thereby joining our two great nations."

Mary watched in silent awe as the Bishop of Lincoln Thomas Wolsey approached the two men then, his long robes flowing with each step, and presented the one who had not yet spoken with a diamond ring.

The man received the ring with a bow of his head and, to Mary's surprise, then turned to her. All eyes were suddenly on the little girl, hundreds of them staring up at her expectantly, and Mary could feel her cheeks beginning to burn brightly.

The man approached her and took her little hand in his – Mary noticing as he did, that his knuckles were extremely hairy – and placed the ring in the palm of her hand.

She met the man's kind gaze, "Are you the Dauphin of France?" she asked, her voice small but confident.

The man smiled and opened his mouth to speak but before he was able to, Mary continued, "If you are the Dauphin of France, then I wish to kiss you," and she rose up on her tiptoes and pecked the man on his bearded cheek.

The hundreds of courtiers before them gasped and chuckled delightedly, some clapping at the adorable incident.

"That is not your new betrothed, Mary," her mother said with laughter in her voice as she leaned forward in her throne and lovingly cupped her daughter's chin, "This is the Lord Admiral of France. The Dauphin of France is just an infant, and you won't be wed until you are both of age."

Mary tried to understand what her mother had said but the words held no meaning for her, and so instead she giggled contentedly and allowed her mother to lift her onto her lap as the crowd before them cheered excitedly for England's new union.

January 1519

A cluster of ugly pox scars on Artie's left cheek was a constant reminder that Arthur *needed* to take control of the future, or risk forfeiting it.

It had always been inside him, this need to have things in order. It made him feel safer, more secure, knowing that everything was as it should be.

But Artie's near death had shaken the foundation Arthur had laid for the past decade, and he didn't like the uncertainty that hung over him ever since. The threat of the destruction of his lineage was too great to ignore, and Arthur had decided it was not enough just to hope and pray that his only son would simply overcome his next illness.

Arthur himself had battled the Devil that was the sweating sickness nearly twenty years ago, and by some incredible act of mercy, God had spared both him and Katherine. But it was no longer enough to rely on God – not when Artie was the only successor Arthur had – and he had decided to put more faith in apothecaries, and the knowledge of medicine they could yet unlock if only they had the appropriate means to study.

"I call it the Royal College of Physicians of London," Arthur declared as he grinned down at the design laid out on the table before him.

"Its fundamental aim," Arthur explained, "will be to promote the highest standard of medical practice in order to improve health and healthcare."

The king's advisors nodded slowly down at the design, Sir Wyatt having picked up the grant beside it to peruse. The charter for the college's rights was put forth by six leading medical men – including the king's own physician, Dr Butts – to practice and further study medicine, and to prosecute those that engaged in illegal malpractice.

Arthur saw Wyatt and raised his eyebrows, "What do you think?"

The old man met his king's eager expression, "This is –"

"It's the future, my lords," Arthur interrupted excitedly, "With this focus on medicinal study, the three main branches of medicine will only progress. The practice of physic will improve, and before long, we will be able to heal ourselves from common disease."

Arthur's advisors nodded in approval, none of them willing to tarnish the king's new and animated perspective by pointing out that even with this new college's founding, it would be years before anything of significance would be discovered to prevent death from fatal illness.

March 1519

With Richard Fox growing increasingly more exasperating, Arthur decided that, after a decade since his coronation, it was time for some fresh faces to replace the old ones, and Fox, being seventy-two years old, was good enough to accept his retirement gracefully.

Fox's position as Lord Chancellor was therefore in need to be filled, and the position being of great importance – with the responsibility of supervising the king's correspondence and having access to the king's Great Seal – Arthur believed no one to be better equipped for the job than Thomas Wolsey, who nigh-on wept with gratitude at the elevation.

Following Harry's return from Bath Abbey, Arthur had been pleasantly surprised to note that it appeared he had left his arrogance behind him. Though he continued troubled over Harry's suggestion of setting Katherine aside for a younger alternative to produce more heirs, Arthur had chosen to believe that it had been a statement made in deflection, hoping to redirect Arthur's thinking down a different path from Harry's need to be defrocked to resume his place within the line of succession. Arthur believed he had suggested it not as a vindictive attack against his queen, but as an act of self-preservation. And truthfully, Arthur wished for nothing more than to forget about it, for the mere thought of putting Katherine through such a thing turned his stomach.

It was because of this hopefulness as to Harry's new, more mature, and less conceited character, that Arthur appointed his brother as the new Royal Almoner, to be in charge of the crown's charitable giving, and thereby allowing him a seat among the Privy Council.

With this new re-shuffle, Arthur began to feel more at ease during council meetings, trusting his men to give him well thought-out and wise advice for – hopefully – many more years to come.

October 1519

"Your sister Mary writes," Katherine informed Arthur from across the table as they enjoyed a private supper in the king's chambers, "She has given birth to a daughter."

Arthur looked over at Katherine, the mixture of sadness and joy in her voice giving him pause as to how to respond.

"They are both healthy," Katherine continued, recounting her latest letter from her banished sister-in-law.

Arthur nodded his head but did not reply, glad to hear his sister was doing well but too stubborn to acknowledge her existence aloud, her betrayal against the crown still irking him.

In the three years since their daughter Mary's birth, Katherine had not conceived even once, her best childbearing years now being firmly behind her at the age of thirty-three; and Arthur was now quite certain that a nursery full of sons would not be in their future. But despite Harry's remark continuing to taunt Arthur's subconscious from time to time, he had grown to accept this fate. He could not even entertain the idea of replacing Katherine for any reason. Not even for the security of England.

Since Artie's brush with death, he had been going from strength to strength, the only evidence left behind of his near-fatal illness being a handful of pox scars on his chest and that unfortunate cluster on his face. Physically, the illness had not stunted him, his tutors often expressing their astonishment at his skill in horse riding and archery. But it was not just the physical aspect of his education that Artie excelled in, Thomas Wolsey often gushing to Arthur over the prince's remarkable mind and ability to discuss topics which should have been beyond his realm of understanding at the age of nine.

And with Arthur's investment in the advancement of medicine, he felt comfortable in the knowledge that Artie would grow up to be an excellent ruler after his father.

"Our daughter is doing well in her studies," Katherine was saying now, having moved on from reporting news on Arthur's sister, "She has a thirst for knowledge, like her brother."

The evening had begun with a romantic setting, a candle-lit table filled with many extravagant dishes, including a tower of strawberries at its centre. Katherine's ladies had been dismissed in advance; Lina having mischievously winked at Katherine as she'd closed the doors behind her.

But during their meal, conversation had begun with his treacherous sister and steered to their children – as it so often did. Nevertheless, Arthur was still hopeful that the evening could be coaxed back into intimate territory, for though they saw each other throughout the days, he missed their private moments together, before life had become so hectic.

"We must educate Mary as best we can," Katherine continued, "And I would like to supervise her learning, so that she may learn Spanish as well as French."

Since Princess Mary's betrothal to the Dauphin of France, she had been undergoing daily lessons to learn the new language, and though Katherine knew that this was the way of the world, she wished for Mary to take a piece of her mother with her when the time came for her to be sent abroad to France.

Arthur nodded as he picked up his cup of wine, "As you wish." Katherine smiled from across the table, his easy, tranquil nature never failing to soothe her.

They ate in silence for a while then, Katherine feeling the tension beginning to build when she caught Arthur's gaze on her as their plates were being cleared of their respective meals. The servants left the chambers. They were finally alone.

Arthur rose from his seat then, "Strawberry?" he asked casually, raising an eyebrow at the tower.

Despite the stressors of recent years having peppered his hair with greys, to Katherine, Arthur had aged well. His auburn beard was cropped short to almost a stubble, as Katherine preferred it, and his blue eyes now held a certain wisdom within them that she loved, made even more irresistible still whenever he smiled to reveal little creases along their edges.

She had watched him grow from a shy young boy into a shrewd and powerful king, and she was glad to have been witness to every stage of his development to becoming the man she so fiercely loved today. And given the way Arthur continued to look at her throughout the years, Katherine was certain that he felt the same way about her, though she had visibly aged so much more.

Her many pregnancies had stretched the skin of her abdomen to an unrecognisable mess, and the days, weeks, and months spent in mourning had etched deep lines on either side of her mouth and between her brows. And yet Arthur had never complained, often even tracing those wretched lines which she so hated with the tip of his finger after their lovemaking, as though he would erase some of her sorrow with his gentle touch.

"I'll take a strawberry," Katherine said now, her gaze remaining fixed on him as he slowly walked towards the silver tray. He plucked a strawberry from the very top and turned towards her, his hand outstretched, an invitation for her to take it.

Katherine rose from her own seat, unable to hide her thrill any longer as her lips stretched into a knowing smile.

As she approached, he grabbed her firmly by her corseted waist, closing the small gap between them, and gently ran the tip of the fruit over her upper lip as he began to slowly pull out the pins of her gown with his free hand.

A shaky breath escaped Katherine as she took a small bite from the strawberry before Arthur ate the rest and threw the green hull over his shoulder. With both hands now free, he pressed her against him, their lips meeting impatiently as she reached behind her to help undo her gown.

He tasted like summer, Katherine thought as he kissed her. Like sunshine and life. A sweetness unlike any other. And as her dress fell from her shoulders and her long hair was freed from her gable hood to tumble down her back, Katherine thought that for as long as she lived, no other fruit would stand a chance to compare.

Chapter 18

September 1520
Greenwich Palace, London

It was as if God had taken the world in his hands and shaken it, for everything was suddenly in chaos.
Arthur's sister, Margaret Tudor, who had been serving as Regent of Scotland during her son James V's minority since her husband's death at the Battle of Flodden, had recently been stripped of her authority and replaced by John Steward, the Duke of Albany.

"What has brought this about? After five years of serving as Regent?" Arthur asked his advisors, tossing Margaret's angry letter aside.

"We have received rep-ports that your sister has re-married. Archibald Douglas, the Earl of Angus," Henry Wyatt stuttered.

"Meaning?"

"Meaning she has alienated the other noble Houses," Lord Chancellor Wolsey explained gently, "Scotland's clans are extremely paranoid of one another, and by appearing to favour one, the others have come together to take her down."

"Albany has been sent by France to replace her," Griffith Rhys said with an exasperated sigh, running a hand through his dark blond hair, "There is not much we can do to aid Her Grace, your sister, without insulting France and threatening the peace we have recently achieved with Princess Mary's betrothal to their Dauphin."

Harry nodded at Griffith from across the round wood table, "The Duke of Suffolk is right," he agreed, "The Anglo-French treaty is not yet complete until their marriage, which won't take place for a decade yet. If Margaret hopes for our support, we cannot give her it."

Arthur was resting his elbows on the table, his head in his hands as he pressed his fingers into the corners of his closed eyes in frustration. After a moment he let out an exasperated exhale, trying to release the tightness in his chest in the only way he could, the disorder of late causing him to feel overwhelmed.

"What of the summer harvest? Has there been any new reports?" the king asked.

Wyatt shook his old head, "No *good* rep-ports, my lord," he said, "It has not been a good year for the f-farmers, August has proven too wet to grow a good crop of grain. The people will have to m-make do and pray for the wheat and rye of the winter crop to be more bountiful."

Arthur shook his head, "It's a disaster," he mumbled under his breath, "How will the poorest families 'make do' if they can't afford to feed their children?"

It was a rhetorical question, Arthur already knowing that he would have to increase the charitable allowance given out to the poor this winter to aid those in need as much as possible. But he also knew the crown could not afford to give alms to everyone, and that ultimately, many would die of starvation.

"There is continued unrest in Europe, my lord," Griffith added, handing a letter to Wolsey beside him, who passed it to Arthur, "Pope Leo X now demands that Martin Luther renounce his writings or face excommunica –"

"Enough about that!" Arthur interrupted harshly, tossing the letter aside unread, his mind reeling from all the information, "I cannot spare even a moment of thought on that heretic's writings when England faces bigger issues."

Harry shifted in his seat, visibly angered at the topic of Martin Luther and his heretical, anti-papal teachings spreading through Europe, and had Arthur allowed for further discussion on the matter, Harry would have gladly shared his staunch views on it. Alas, it was an issue for another day.

Pinching the bridge of his straight nose with his thumb and forefinger, Arthur pushed forward to the next issue at hand, hoping to get to a matter that he could find a solution to.

"The match between Prince Artie and Princess Catalina de Castille," Arthur said, "has Spain sent word as to their decision?"

"Spain has been slow to reply," Wolsey said as he riffled through the papers before him, "Their *infanta* being kept in custody with her mother, Juana de Castille, is making it hard for them to come to a conclusion."

Queen Katherine's older sister, Juana de Castille – who had inherited the throne of Castille upon their mother Isabella's death in 1504 – had, two years later, been declared unfit to rule by their ambitious father Ferdinand de Aragon, due to her intense grief over her late husband's death. In her grief she had acted irrationally, and she had been kept confined ever since, the baby in her womb at the time of her imprisonment having been born and kept in captivity with her mother.

Arthur exhaled and looked about the table, "So what does it mean for us?"

"Give Spain more time," Wolsey offered, "We may receive word any day. It must be difficult for them to manage a mad queen."

Arthur's eyebrows shot up, not fully convinced of Katherine's sister's nickname of *Juana La Loca* – Juana the Mad – to be as true as Spain would make it out to be, her father Ferdinand de Aragon having always been a power-hungry man.

"Artie will be of age to marry soon," Harry said, speaking up for the first time, "Can we really wait for Spain to answer? Would it not be wiser to consider a match with another?"

"I agree with Harry," Arthur said without hesitation, as though he had been thinking it all along, "If Spain keeps us waiting for too long, we will have to look elsewhere. Hungary perhaps, or Portugal."

Wolsey nodded, took note of Arthur's instructions, "Isabella of Portugal would be an excellent match, my king."

"Is she not a good six years older than Prince Artie?!" Harry interjected, horrified.

Wolsey shrugged, looking puzzled, "In three years they will both be of age to marry. Whether he is older or she, what difference does it make?"

Harry looked away from his former mentor, feeling slightly like a schoolboy being scolded, "None."

"Write it up, Wolsey," Arthur ordered, "Send word to Portugal that a betrothal may be arranged within the year if negotiations go smoothly."

February 1521

To cement the alliance made between England and France, the two countries had organized a lavish gathering to officially sign the treaty and to celebrate their newfound friendship.

To appease both sides, the two kings, Arthur and Francis, had agreed to meet at Balinghem in Calais, which, though it was geographically part of France, belonged to English territory since the Siege of Calais by King Edward III in 1346.

And it was there that the Field of Cloth of Gold would take place.

"Will I get to meet my betrothed, the Dauphin of France, Lady Mother?" the five-year-old Mary asked upon her arrival at court a month before the event.

They were walking together in the palace gardens, Katherine having always made sure to spend private time with each of her children, so that neither of them would ever feel less special than the other, for though England deemed princesses as less favourable than princes, Katherine did not. As the daughter to the former Queen Regnant of Castille, as well as the sister to the rightful current ruler Juana, Katherine knew of a girl's worth. And she believed them to be just as capable as their male counterparts.

But England was not yet ready to accept that truth.

"No, Mary," the queen replied, smiling down at her youngest child, "You and Artie are to stay here and look after England for us."

Mary did not return her mother's smile and instead she sighed and frowned, "But I would have liked to see France."

"Ah, but this summit is to be held in Balinghem, Mary," Katherine replied, smiling fondly at her daughter, "which belongs to England. So, you are not missing a visit to France, because we too will not be in France."

While Mary was only five, she was aware that her mother was jesting with her, but she knew that the decision had been made and that no amount of pleading would change her royal parents' minds.

March 1521

Artie, as the male heir and therefore next in line to the throne of England, was left in nominal charge of the kingdom upon his parents' departure to attend the Field of Cloth of Gold a month later. He and his sister Mary watched from the window as the royal procession of over five-thousand people departed through the palace gates.

"Now the fun begins," eleven-year-old Artie grinned at Mary as soon as the gates were safely closed behind the last rider, "Until father's return, *I* am your king."

The little princess frowned up at her older brother, trying to appear outraged at his silly remark, but Artie only laughed.

"Come on, Mary," he said, "Let's organize a dance!"

Mary picked up her skirts and side-stepped him, "You do as you please, Artie," she called as she walked away, displaying an aura of someone much older, "I shall be maintaining my studies as Mother has asked of me."

Artie *tutted* and hurried to catch up with her, "While Mother and Father are away, I am in charge. Why not have some fun? The palace is ours!"

Mary raised her chin and turned her face away, but Artie could tell that she was trying not to smile.

"Oh, my little Mary, my dearest, sweetest sister," Artie teased, "Do say you will attend my ball when it is organized?"
She did not reply right away, having arrived at her chambers, and waited a moment while the guards opened the doors for them. As she spotted the Lady Bryan and two ladies embroidering by the window, Mary felt a pinch of tedium at the image before her. She turned to Artie, who was leaning expectantly against the doorframe, his arms casually crossed.

"Fine," she said curtly, "I shall attend."
Artie grinned victoriously and turned to leave, but not before his little sister's voice called after him.

"But I will *not* be calling you 'king'!"

Two weeks later, three days after Artie's extravagant ball, Mary was summoned to the great hall where she found Artie sitting on their father's throne, his tutor the Lord Chancellor Thomas Wolsey, and Wolsey's page, standing beside him. Mary's auburn eyebrows twitched to see Artie upon the king's throne, the image never appearing quite right to the no-nonsense princess.

"Whatever happened to your smaller, makeshift throne made of wood?" Mary asked matter-of-factly as she approached.
Artie looked down at his father's gold throne, "This one is more comfortable."
Mary raised her eyebrows and nodded in feigned understanding, her expression making it quite clear she did not believe him.

"We have received word from your royal mother and father, Your Grace," Thomas Wolsey said as his young page, Sir Henry Percy, passed him a letter, "the queen writes that their arrival at Balinghem has been a success but that the French king and his queen were not best pleased that Your Grace was not with them," Mary shot Artie a worried look then, which her older brother replied to with a shrug of his shoulders.

The Lord Chancellor continued, "Your lady mother writes that France may send envoys to check on Your Grace's health. She urges Your Graces to maintain your composures and to entertain their concerns with the utmost care, for your betrothal may come in jeopardy if they fear Your Grace is feeble."

April 1521

As their mother had predicted, French ambassadors soon arrived at the English court without a word in advance.

At the French envoy's entrance, the few courtiers within the great hall stopped their conversations and games mid-way, and began to gather before the thrones, hoping to catch any gossip which might ensue from the impromptu meeting.

At their approach, the ambassadors were surprised to see that the young princess was not weak and sickly as they had been led to believe, but standing strong and majestic beside her brother as he greeted them from his father's throne.

"My lords!" Artie called in greeting with a wide grin, then waved for Mary to step forward.

When she did, her back was straight and her hands were clasped elegantly before her. She was the very image of her royal mother. With a pale complexion, rosy cheeks and a ready smile, the princess was quite clearly in such obvious good health that the French ambassadors were good enough to look uncomfortably at one another, displaying their shame at their unannounced intrusion by bowing apologetically and beginning to retreat from the hall.

But Mary would not let this moment to flaunt her skills pass her by.

"Please, *mon seigneurs*," Mary called after them in perfect French, "Do not trouble yourselves. You did your duty to your king and queen by paying us a visit. But as you can see, I am in perfect health, and I ask that we put this behind us."

She waved her little hand to one of the servants then and reverted to speaking in English, "To celebrate this special visit I request for strawberries to be served to our visitors," she said prettily, and the servant hurried away on their errand.

Artie was chuckling behind her, as were several of the observing courtiers, hugely entertained to see the French ambassadors squirming under Mary's adorable authority.

"Now, gentlemen, let us be merry while you are here!" Mary continued cheerfully as she walked down the three steps and around the bearded men, escorting them towards a virginal in the corner of the great hall, "This visit need not be in vain."

Then she took a seat at the great instrument and began to play a jolly tune as several servants entered carrying silver platters of strawberries.

The French delegation enjoyed them gratefully as they watched the princess' proficient musical performance, and when the time came for the French to return to their masters, they did so with nothing but cheerful news that the Princess of England was not only well and full of life, but also as pretty and graceful as any princess in Europe.

May 1521

Upon their return to England following a successful conference in Balinghem, Katherine felt only pride for her husband's clear-headedness throughout the hectic event, as well as for the exceptional manner in which her children received the French delegation while she and Arthur were away.

It gave Katherine great joy to know that Mary had inherited her self-assurance, and that she would one day prove to be an excellent Queen of France.

"I would like to expand Mary's education," Katherine informed her husband one morning as they made their way to the chapel for their morning prayer, "I have consulted with Juan-Luis Vives to draw up an excellent programme on the education of girls. He calls it *De Institutione feminae Christianae,* 'The Education of a Christian Woman', and it is a remarkable programme, Arthur, it includes all she may need to become a true model of feminine virtue."

Arthur nodded as he listened to Katherine's request, interested to know more, her passion for expanding the education of women in England having been a matter of great discussion between them of late. He admired her enthusiasm for women's equal rights, her own mother having reigned Castille in her own right had given Katherine a front row seat in observing a woman's ability as equal to that of a man, and Arthur was keen to listen to what she had to say.

"It will include not only learning the basics of language and oration," Katherine went on as they turned a corner down the palace hallways, "but also philosophy, history, as well as outdoor pursuits – hunting, falconry and archery."

At that, Arthur frowned, "Archery?" he repeated, "Whatever for? It is not suitable for a girl."

Katherine raised an eyebrow but did not argue, for they had reached the chapel entrance, "I ask only that you consider it, my lord," she said quietly, in respect for the house of God.

Arthur smiled down at her and quickly pecked her on the lips, "I will think on it," he promised.

June 1521

The following month, the matter of their daughter's higher education was broached again during a most unexpected visit.

"I wholeheartedly agree with it. If it was more widely agreed upon that a woman is as capable as a man, I might still be serving as Regent for my son."

Margaret Tudor, Arthur's eldest sister who neither he nor Katherine had seen in over ten years, had returned to England upon being run out of Scotland following her scandalous replacement as Regent by the Duke of Albany.

Katherine watched Margaret from across the table as she ripped meat from the bone and stuffed it angrily – and not to mention, most unladylike – into her mouth.

Katherine did not dare to point out that it had not been Margaret's lack of education or the Scots' doubt as to her ability to rule which had caused her shunning, but rather her rash decision to marry one of their clans' noblemen instead of maintaining her neutrality among the kinfolks. But her sister-in-law was speaking *for* Mary's higher education, and so Katherine would not think to correct her.

Arthur and Katherine watched as Margaret picked up her cup of wine with greasy fingers and swallowed its contents in one, and they shared a look of both shock and concern.

Her time in Scotland had changed Margaret. Before them sat a woman of thick-set build, with a downturned mouth and an angry glint in her eyes, and Katherine felt a pang of guilt as she realised it was likely after the Battle of Flodden that things had begun to go south for her sister-in-law – though, of course, there was no way of knowing for sure.

"Where is our sister, Mary?" Margaret asked then, her time in Scotland having given her a slight accent.

Arthur inhaled, "She and her husband remain in Flanders."

"In Flanders?" Margaret echoed, her eyebrows bunching together, and Katherine noticed her forehead was no longer smooth but etched with fine horizontal lines, "Whatever is she doing there?"

Katherine and Arthur shared a look but Katherine quickly looked away, saddened by her poor communication with her younger sister-in-law over the years, life having become too busy to remember to write each other frequently, or even at all.

"She was banished some years ago. Did you not receive our correspondence?" Arthur was saying.

Margaret waved her hand in the air, "Yes, yes," she said, "But I'd have thought they would have been allowed to return by now."

Katherine picked up her spoon, hoping that Margaret's remark would open a discussion as to the possibility of their banished sister's return, for Katherine had missed Mary dearly ever since her sudden removal from court, so much so she had named their daughter after her.

"I hadn't considered it," Arthur admitted dismissively, "It has been rather hectic around here of late."

"Ha!" Margaret exclaimed, wiping her hands on the silk napkin on her lap, "Ruling a kingdom has not been as easy as you had expected it to be, eh, brother?"

Arthur cocked his head to one side, "Whatever gave you the impression I had believed it to be easy?"

There was humour in his voice, but Katherine knew her husband well enough to have heard the twang of defensiveness, and she only hoped that he would not take too much offense to Margaret's disparagement, for she was clearly hurting to be away from her young son and the country she had called home for the past decade and a half.

"What of your new husband?" Arthur asked, returning Margaret's back-handed comment with one of his own, "The Earl of Angus, did he not wish to visit England?"

Margaret looked down at her plate and cleared her throat, "He returned to Scotland shortly after crossing the border into England," she said, her upper lip twitching with rage, "He has scurried back and made *peace* with Albany. He has betrayed me! After everything I have given up for him…"

Katherine pressed her knee against Arthur's under the table, silently beseeching him not to aggravate Margaret further, for she had clearly been played for a fool and lost everything for the love of a man who abandoned her at the first opportunity.

"Margaret –" Katherine began, but her sister-in-law cut her short with a hard look.

"Don't, Katherine," she whispered harshly, though Katherine detected a hint of sadness in her voice, "I do not need anyone's pity."

Katherine nodded and resumed eating, respecting Margaret's need to put on a hard front to protect herself from external reproach. For upon having lost her regency in Scotland as well as custody of her only surviving son, the young King James V, there was no doubt in Katherine's mind that Margaret was chastising herself enough already as it was. And despite Margaret's extremely altered persona to the happy-go-lucky young girl she had once known, Katherine was glad to have her sister-in-law back at court, and she only hoped that Margaret's presence would remind Arthur of the other sister he had once loved.

Chapter 19

January 1522

At the age of twelve, Prince Artie was officially betrothed to the eighteen-year-old Princess Isabella of Portugal – much to Katherine's disappointment, who had hoped to see him wed to her sister's daughter, Catalina de Castille.
But Spain had been too slow to respond to England's offer two years prior, and Arthur had been too anxious to obtain a bride for their son to wait around.
Though Artie had not once complained of even a stomach-ache since his near-fatal illness four years earlier – the king's physicians being quite amazed at the young boy's sturdiness – Arthur would not be completely at ease until Artie married and produced an heir of his own.
The young couple was betrothed by proxy – just as Arthur and Katherine had been nearly twenty-five years ago – due to Princess Isabella's distance in Portugal. It had been agreed that upon Artie's fifteenth year, Isabella would make the journey across the channel with her household to commence her life within England, and that she and Artie would be officially married shortly thereafter.
There was no more planning to be done. Only waiting.
And in the meantime, Arthur turned his mind to other matters, a king's list of duties never failing to grow if left unchecked.

"Martin Luther has been excommunicated, as threatened by Pope Leo X," Wolsey informed the king and his council as he sat down at his self-appointed seat to the king's right. He handed him a letter, "Luther has been condemned an outlaw by the new Holy Roman Emperor, your nephew King Carlos V, and is now in hiding."

"In hiding?!" Harry repeated indignantly from across the table, visibly flustered at the mere mention of the man, "Martin

Luther is the Devil himself, I have no doubt about it! Whyever he was not burned at the stake for his heresy, I do not know!"

"He escaped with aid," Wolsey explained, "He has been hidden away and until he is found and punished, there is nothing we can do."

"There *is* something we can do," Harry countered triumphantly, presenting Wolsey and Arthur with a pamphlet, "and I have already done it,"

"What is this?" Arthur asked, taking the document from his brother.

"This, brother, is my theological treatise, dedicated to Pope Leo X, where I condemn Luther's heretical teachings," Harry explained, "I call it the 'Defence of the Seven Sacraments', and I ask that you send a copy to the Pope and publish it as far and wide as possible."

Arthur scanned the document, "Harry, this is excellent work," he said after reading a paragraph where Harry defends the sacrament of marriage, further strengthening Arthur's belief that Harry's remark about casting Katherine aside for another some years ago had been no more than an attempt at deflection.

"Did you write this yourself?" Arthur asked as he leaned over to Wolsey and indicated a paragraph for him to read.

"Bishop Fisher aided me somewhat," Harry admitted, "And Thomas More."

Arthur raised his eyebrows in wonder at the mention of Harry's co-author, as the well-known lawyer turned literary intellectual of humanistic rights and strong Catholic beliefs was widely respected throughout London.

Wolsey nodded as he read the paragraph pointed out by the king, "Well done," he said to Harry, which, for the Lord Chancellor, was high praise.

Harry beamed with pride at Arthur and Wolsey's compliments, glad to have been able to do something to defend God and the true faith of Catholicism from the sacrilegious ramblings of a madman.

Following the publication of Harry's treatise, the Pope himself assigned Harry the title of Defender of the Faith, a title which had previously only ever been bestowed upon a king, the late King James IV of Scotland.

"It is a great honour, Harry," the Duke of Suffolk Griffith Rhys said as the two men stood outside the council chambers, following the great announcement.

Harry bowed his head in humble thanks, "I only did what I believed to have been right. No one should be able to attack the one true faith without receiving some retaliation. And perhaps this way, if Luther were to respond, we might flush out where he has been hidden."

Griffith raised his eyebrows, "Very tactical thinking," he said before clapping Harry on the shoulder, "You have grown up, Harry – finally. I no longer see any hint of that foolish young man you were not long ago. Time at the abbey has clearly been good for you."

Harry nodded up at the older man, taking no offense, "That immature young boy is gone, Rhys, and in his place is someone who wishes for nothing more than to serve his king and his God."

February 1522

Other than Princess Margaret's support of Katherine's wish of a higher education for Mary – which had swayed Arthur in agreeing to it – Margaret's return to England had brought nothing but trouble.

Since her replacement with the Duke of Albany as her ten-year old son's Regent, Margaret had spent many hours at her desk furiously writing letter after letter to her new husband the Earl of Angus, the Duke of Albany, and to her young son.

She never received a reply from any of them, and it led to a tense atmosphere within the English court.

"My reckless, useless, *swine* of a husband has abandoned me!" Margaret would call loudly during banquets, after one too many wines had been consumed.

"He's played me for a fool, wrote me some sappy poems and I fell for it," she'd say, chastising herself for believing his flattery to be true, "I was putty in his hairy hands."

Some courtiers would laugh uncertainly, some would excuse themselves from her presence.

"Men!" she'd shout, glaring angrily around the court at the male courtiers, the guards, and even the king, "They are all the same! Lying, cheating *scoundrels*!"

At first it had received a nervous chuckle from the crowd, but each night it grew less and less comedic, the atmosphere at court having been significantly soured with each drunken outburst from the Dowager Queen of Scotland. It seemed that if Margaret's time in Scotland had taught her anything, it was that, to be taken seriously by men, a woman had to be boisterous.

But in England, and as the sister of the king, Margaret need only to have asked.

"I have been in contact with Albany," Arthur told his sister one day after she had thundered into the great hall yet again upon receiving no word from her homeland, claiming loudly to anyone who'd listen that she had married a cheating crook and been separated from her son by a treacherous brute.

"You have?" Margaret replied in surprise, her Scottish accent still strong after almost a year away, "He won't reply to a single one of my letters!"

Arthur gave her a look that said Albany had likely replied to Arthur because he was both the King of England and a man.

Margaret clicked her tongue and shook her head, her point about being disrespected as a woman being made for her.

"We have been discussing a treaty of reconciliation between you and Albany, so that you may return and act as Regents together, amicably," Arthur said, "Wolsey has already drafted it up. Albany need only sign it."

Margaret could hardly believe her ears, and in a rare moment of speechlessness, she could do nothing other than embrace her older brother in thanks.

Lina de Cardonnes had met and fallen in love with a crossbow-maker just three months prior, a young man also of Moorish descent such as she, who had promised his queen, Lina's mistress, that he would take care of Lina until his dying breath if only Katherine were to grant them permission to marry.

Katherine and Arthur had, of course, approved of this union, the queen being overjoyed for Lina's happiness as well as equally saddened to know that, soon, Lina would likely leave her service, her lady having often hinted throughout the years that she would wish to raise a family back in Spain.

And that terribly sad day came much sooner than Katherine could ever have predicted, for Lina announced her swift conception of a child just six weeks after her simple wedding to her bowyer husband had taken place.

"Already?!" Katherine asked, unable to quash the unwelcome stab of jealousy at Lina's obvious fertility. But she shook her head free of such sinful thoughts and forced a smile, her happiness for her friend being just as real as all the other emotions she was being flooded with at the prospect of Lina's departure from her household.

"I am just as surprised as you are, my lady," Lina said, her dark eyes shining with excitement, but then their shine flickered, "I did not expect to leave you so quickly."

Katherine took her friend's hands and squeezed them, "Do not let our parting take away from this joyous gift. You have been lucky to find a good man such as yours, and I give you my blessing to pursue the life you wish for back in Spain."

Lina inhaled deeply and smiled, pressing a hand to her belly though it was still as flat as it had always been.

"I am thankful for all you have given me," she said, "And I shall never forget your generosity throughout the years, of both in opportunity and kindness."

Katherine waved her hand in the air, "There is no need for all that," she said, hoping to keep her tears from falling, "This is not the end for us. You shall write to me of your new life, and I shall write to you. This friendship does not end simply because your service to me has done."

The women embraced then, sealing the promise before returning to their day, the two of them heartbreakingly aware that when Lina embarked on the ship back to Spain in the weeks to come, they would likely never see each other again.

April 1522

Following Margaret's return to Scotland and Lina's return to Spain, Katherine found herself feeling lonelier than she had felt in years and she decided that instead of letting it engulf her, she would instead begin her search for a new lady-in-waiting to fill Lina's vacated role.

The announcement that the queen was in search of a new lady for her household led to a vast influx of new young ladies from all across the country, each of them hoping to be the lucky one to be chosen.

"What do you think, Agnes?" Katherine asked her other lady, who had, with Lina's departure, been appointed Katherine's Lady of the Bedchamber.

Agnes looked up and down the long line of young ladies before them, three of which stood out to Agnes, "Thomas Boleyn's daughters are both well educated, my queen," she informed Katherine quietly, "As is Lucy Talbot."

The queen looked over at the lady Agnes was pointing out at the end of the line.

"She is a little older than I would like my ladies to be," Katherine said, dismissing Lucy Talbot from the final selection, "Tell me more about the Boleyn sisters."

Agnes cleared her throat and looked towards the two young women as they stared dutifully ahead.

"They had been selected to accompany the king's sister Princess Mary to Spain had the betrothal to your nephew, King Carlos V, gone ahead," Agnes explained, "Their father Thomas Boleyn has been a loyal courtier, as you know, Your Grace, and he and his wife Elizabeth Boleyn – formerly Howard – have given their daughters an excellent education, one equally as good as their son George's. They claim to have done so due to Your Highness' influence in women's education over the years."

Katherine was nodding as she absentmindedly perused the other ladies before her, "I do appreciate a lady with wit and smarts. Makes for good conversation."

Agnes nodded in agreement.

"Do they sing? The Boleyn girls?" Katherine asked then.

Agnes nodded, "Mary is said to have a beautiful singing voice. Anne less so, but she is witty and said to be charming."

Katherine smiled, having moved closer to the two girls in question. She stood before the plainer looking one with the darker complexion.

"This is Anne," Agnes informed, "the other, Mary."

"Mistress Anne?" Katherine said, to which the young woman curtsied elegantly, "Why ought I select you for my new lady over your older sister Mary? I am told she has a much better singing voice."

To Katherine's surprise, Anne smiled at that, her features brightening as she did so, "Mary can sing a pretty tune, Your Grace, there is no doubt about it. And if you would be good enough to take us both on as your new ladies, my family and I would be extremely grateful to you. But if Your Highness must choose only one and it is a question between us both, I would have to say that if it is a pretty singing voice you seek then my sister would be the perfect choice. But if it is a faithful companion you wish for, with a wider range of abilities and an eagerness to serve, then I would be the better option."

Katherine sensed the older sister, Mary, stiffen slightly at the minor snub from Anne, but Katherine was intrigued.

"A wider range of abilities, you say?" the queen asked Anne, "What abilities might those be and why would I wish for them?"

Anne swallowed, aware that she had insulted her sister but eager to secure this prestigious position for herself.

"Mary is an exceptional lady, with many talents," Anne said, "But my interests go beyond that of most people, and I hope to not only serve, but to learn all that I can from you, our most gracious queen."

Katherine glanced briefly at Agnes beside her before thanking the Boleyn sisters and walking steadily away and along the line of other candidates.

"My queen?" Agnes asked, wondering if either of the two young women had made the final cut.

Katherine nodded pensively as she perused the other ladies, some too old, some young enough to be her daughter's playmate.

"I like her," Katherine said quietly.

Agnes looked over her shoulder at Mary and Anne, Mary blushing angrily beside her younger sister, "Which one?"

Katherine pursed her lips, "Anne, of course," she said, "She has caught my attention. But I do believe I shall take on both of the Boleyn sisters, just in case. I was hoping to find a lady who can sing, and as the Mistress Anne herself admitted, her sister has the better voice."

May 1522

In honour of Prince Artie's betrothal, King Arthur organized a lavish celebration to take place where the prince would be shown off to the court as a reminder to the nobles that the Tudor line was strong.

A grand tournament was arranged where many lords jousted against one another, Griffith Rhys taking part in Arthur's honour, the king never having had much interest in barrelling towards another armoured knight on horseback with a great wooden lance pointed directly at him.

But the sport was enjoyed by many, Harry himself having been partial to it in his youth before he had departed for Oxford. But now as a priest, Harry cared little for showing off his physical attributes, his dedication to God being a far greater triumph to him.

And yet, it was during festivities such as these that Harry was reminded of the adrenaline rush one would get just before the moment of impact, the surge of excitement mixed with fear that would engulf the body in that moment before victory or potential death. It was a thrill which he sometimes missed.

But it was nothing compared to the thrill of a woman's touch.

Upon being ordained a priest and having taken his vow of celibacy, Harry had had every intention of forever setting aside even the *idea* of women. He had dedicated his life and his soul to serving God, never once having believed that his body's physical needs would ever surpass the needs of his soul.

But most recently, Harry's blood had been pumping quicker in his veins, his palms had become sweaty, and his breathing more erratic, as though he were a young man once again.

He knew what had brought this on, of course; his physical reactions only ever occurring when that one person walked by him. Or, in this case, when she was standing right beside him.

As the king's brother, Harry had the privilege of standing beneath the royal canopy as the court observed the jousting tournament taking place in the tiltyard at the bottom of the field behind the palace. He and the king would often mumble quietly about the jouster's form or discuss the morning's council meeting while the crowd before them clapped at the riders. But on this occasion, Harry felt as though the air around him had gotten thick, one of Queen Katherine's new ladies causing him to be hyper-aware of himself ever since her sudden appearance at court.

No woman had ever made Harry feel so uneasy before, his previous encounters with the opposite sex before his vow of celibacy having been no more than experimental, a taste of something he had known he would soon no longer be allowed to enjoy but finding that it wasn't actually that delicious after all, his love for God having surpassed his desire for any woman. But suddenly, *this* woman was causing his mind to become clouded, and he caught himself thinking of the hypocritical Thomas Wolsey and his not-so-secret mistress he'd fathered two children with in a non-canonical marriage. Despite Harry's previous contempt for the man's actions, Harry recently found himself wondering if perhaps he, too, would be so inclined to do the same.

He stole a glance in the young woman's direction then as she leaned forward to listen to something Queen Katherine was telling her over her shoulder, and his heart pounded unevenly suddenly as she opened her mouth and trilled a harmonious laugh, her hand coming up to cover her face momentarily, then straightening up and resuming her previous stance behind her queen as she tried to compose herself.

Harry inhaled deeply to settle his nerves, reminding himself that it was ludicrous to feel this way over someone he did not even know, and he forced himself to watch the tournament before them, Griffith Rhys having just in that moment knocked his opponent clean off his horse with a perfect strike to the other knight's boss. Harry clapped along with the rest of the observing crowd, nodding his head in appreciation for the sport, forcing himself to no longer look in the woman's direction.

She was Temptation, Harry told himself. She was a test sent from God Himself to see how devoted he was to serving Him. Or perhaps it had been the Devil who had sent her, to steer him off course and to destroy all that he had worked hard to achieve? Harry would have to steer clear of this woman, lest he be led down on a path straight to Hell.

No woman was worth tainting his immortal soul for. None.

Not even this dark-eyed vixen with a laugh as delicious as apple pie; this woman he knew nothing about other than that she was called Anne Boleyn.

Part V

You cannot teach a man anything,
you can only help him to find it for himself.

Chapter 20

3 years later

January 1525
London

The twenty-one-year-old Princess Isabella of Portugal had arrived upon the English shores with the coming of the new year in preparation for her wedding to the fifteen-year-old Prince of Wales, Artie.
Arriving in the dead of winter had been a huge shock to the princess, who had grown up in a land with much warmer temperatures, where snow was a rarity found only on the highest mountain peaks. But she did not complain about the weather nor about the choppy waters upon which she had had to travel to get here, for a woman's struggles did not matter so long as her duty was fulfilled.
Isabella had officially met Prince Artie the following day, on the morning of their wedding, the young man having come to her temporary lodgings in the Tower of London to introduce himself, and to hopefully put her mind at ease before the ceremony.
They had communicated in Latin – the only language they had in common – and Isabella was glad to see that the portrait that had been sent to her the year before had been true to its sitter.

"It is a pleasure to make your acquaintance, my lady," Artie had said with a smile, "I trust your journey was not too strenuous?"
Isabella had shaken her head.

"Good," Artie said before looking around the room in hopes of finding something else to talk about, and Isabella took the opportunity to take a better look at her betrothed.
Artie, though younger than Isabella by six years, was a handsome young prince with a mop of curly, dark red hair and

a small straight nose with freckles splashed across it. As he looked up at the wood ceilings, Isabella noticed a small cluster of faint pits on his left cheek, the aftermath of a childhood illness no doubt. He was shorter than Isabella by quite a bit, but she was aware that he had yet to complete his growing.

He excused himself then with a peck of her hand and a friendly grin, and Isabella was pleased to note that, his satisfying looks aside, Artie appeared to be a well-educated, considerate young man; and following their meeting, she was much less anxious to walk down the aisle to wed him.

The wedding ceremony went by smoothly, Artie's mother, Queen Katherine of Aragon, smiling encouragingly at Isabella from among the crowd, another factor to have relaxed the foreign princess slightly.

The banquet to follow the union, too, had gone by without a hitch, her new husband introducing Isabella to his younger sister, the Princess Mary, who had taken her excitedly by the hand and led her to the dancefloor, where they discovered that Isabella knew not a single one of their English dances.

The bedding ceremony had been more awkward, however.

Due to Artie's age of just fifteen, the couple was not obligated to perform their marital duty on their wedding night, surrounded by the noble lords and ladies as witnesses; and Isabella had given thanks to God for her luck. However, once the Archbishop of Canterbury William Warham had blessed the bed and the many courtiers had left the prince's chambers, Artie had unexpectedly turned to her and laid a hand over her breast. Isabella had looked over at him, surprised that he wished to be physical on their first night when he was still so young; but as a woman, the princess knew not to question the young man who would henceforth be her lord husband, and she allowed his hand to linger.

"Is this alright?" Artie had asked in Latin without looking her in the eyes.

Isabella had nodded slightly, knowing that she could not have said 'no' if she'd wanted to. *This* was a woman's duty.

At her consent, her young husband awkwardly pulled down his hose before placing his hand upon her breast once again.

Isabella tried not to stiffen at his touch, but the idea of engaging in intimacy with this boy, whom she had only just met that morning, caused her to feel slightly sick.

She resolved to close her eyes as Artie inched towards her and positioned himself between her legs. She forced herself to breathe slowly and to think of home as she felt him lifting her nightgown and, without forewarning, entering her.

She winced slightly in pain, though Artie had been slow and gentle to begin with. But by the grace of God, once he had found his rhythm, it was over very quickly, Artie rolling off her with a big, dopey grin on his face.

Isabella lay on her back, looking up at the beautifully carved wood ceiling, compelling herself to examine the intricate Tudor Roses in each panel while she calmed her nerves, as Artie continued to breathe heavily beside her. Then he turned on his side and made himself comfortable, no doubt feeling suddenly as though he'd just become a man.

With the wedding and consummation behind her, Isabella thought, she was now part of the Tudor House. There was no going back. And perhaps – if she was lucky – this coupling would lead to the conception of child, so that she wouldn't have to lay with her boy-husband for another year.

February 1525
Greenwich Palace, London

Following Harry's rise in power in the last decade from a deacon to the King of England's Royal Almoner and advisor on the Privy Council, as well as being titled the Defender of the Faith by the Pope himself, Pope Leo X felt it befitting that Harry be appointed as his papal legate within England.

As papal legate, Harry would henceforth be a personal representative of the Pope himself within the English court and King Arthur's council, empowered on matters of Catholic faith and for the settlement of ecclesiastical matters.

It was a huge honour! One Thomas Wolsey had hoped to obtain for himself – and perhaps would have done, Harry thought, had it not been for his blasphemous relationship with Joan Larke.

Which was why Harry recognized that if his own secret were to come to light, he would likely lose much of his recently obtained respect among the clergy.

"Harry!"

Harry snapped out of his thoughts at the sound of his brother's voice calling his name, his mind having begun to drift to the night before where he and his secret had been alone in his chambers, her hair tumbling over her shoulders as she'd removed her hood –

"Harry, are you with us?" Arthur called again, and Harry nodded his head.

"Yes, my lord," he said, forcing the images of her bare shoulders from his mind.

"Wolsey has drafted the titles of the Lutheran books found within England," Arthur was telling Harry, passing him a document, "Do you have any more to add?"

Harry perused the list of titles, "I know of no others, Your Grace," he said, handing the parchment back to Wolsey, who took it without meeting Harry's eye and held it over his shoulder for his page Sir Henry Percy to take.

Ever since Harry's appointment as papal legate, Wolsey had given Harry the cold shoulder, his former pupil having surpassed him in this one way, giving the older man reason to dislike the younger priest.

But Harry shrugged off Wolsey's dismay, for he could hardly blame the man for his jealousy. And he silently thanked Thomas More for his help in writing the 'Defence of the Seven Sacraments' against Martin Luther's anti-Catholic ramblings, for without his insight, Harry might not have achieved the Pope's attention and high praise.

"See to it that they are all burned, Wolsey," Arthur ordered as he looked at the list in Henry Percy's hand as though it were a deadly vial of poison, "We will not allow for such heresy to be spread throughout England. I have also ordered for Bishop Fisher to preach a sermon against Martin Luther at St Paul's Cross. The message that England is against his heretical teachings must be made abundantly clear."

Wolsey and the rest of the council nodded their heads.

"Moving on," Arthur called, looking around to Sir Henry Wyatt and Griffith Rhys, "Have we received word from my son and his wife in Ludlow?"

Prince Artie and his new wife Isabella of Portugal had set off to preside over the Prince's Council in Ludlow Castle in Wales just as Arthur himself had done over twenty years ago when he and Katherine had been newly-weds. If court gossip was to be believed, however, it would appear that Artie and Isabella had not needed the orchestrated alone time in Ludlow Castle to consummate their marriage, the young couple having, apparently, managed to conclude their marital duty on the very night of their wedding. And though Arthur was a little surprised to hear the news, he was glad to know that his son did not seem to suffer with the same insecurities that he had struggled with at that age.

"The couple have settled in," Griffith informed Arthur as he ran a hand through his thinning hair. The Duke of Suffolk had chaperoned the royal couple to Ludlow, only returning to London when Artie himself had given him the order, which, to Griffith's amazement, had been just two days after their arrival. It appeared the young man had wanted to be alone with his princess as soon as possible.

"There should be news of an heir very soon, I would wager," Griffith added. A chuckle arose from among the Privy Council, and it made Arthur briefly wonder if Griffith would ever sire a legitimate heir of his own, having continued to remain unwed despite bedding many ladies of the court.

"It is g-good news," Wyatt said, snapping Arthur from his thoughts, "With the next T-Tudor generation in the making, England shall continue on a solid t-trajectory."

At that, Arthur nodded, "Hear, hear. Pray God the Princess Isabella is fruitful."

April 1525

Katherine and her ladies were enjoying a walk in the palace gardens, the weather finally proving dry after two weeks of constant rain, when a messenger came towards them.

Agnes spotted him first and held back from the group of women to receive the note and to read it to her queen, but the messenger shook his head.

"It is for the Mistress Anne," the young man said, "I was instructed to give it directly to her."

Agnes looked over her shoulder at Anne Boleyn, who appeared flushed to receive the note, then at her queen who mirrored Agnes' own deep frown of confusion.

"Is everything alright, Mistress Anne?" Katherine asked as Anne stuffed the unopened note into her sleeve, to be ripped open and read later.

Anne nodded and forced a smile, "I am sure all is well. It is likely news from my father about Mary's labour."

Mary Boleyn, the other Boleyn girl who Katherine had selected as a new lady-in-waiting, had found herself with child soon after entering into the queen's household, and had been sent back to her home in the country to give birth to her husband's baby.

Katherine nodded her head, though the frown between her brows remained, "Please do let me know if you wish to visit your sister during this time."

Anne smiled sweetly, "Thank you, Your Grace."

The ladies resumed their walk in silence, Katherine and Agnes walking ahead and briefly sharing a look which suggested neither of them had believed the young lady in regard to the contents of the letter, for Katherine had often found the Mistress Anne blushing at the proximity of a certain noble lord, and stealing coy glances across the dancefloor at him.

Katherine smiled at the thought of young love, her own love story flashing before her mind's eye then as she and her ladies wandered past the rose bushes beginning to bloom, and she wondered if perhaps in this very moment, her son was feeling his own heart soar at his pretty wife's proximity, just as Anne Boleyn's heart surely soared at the proximity of Sir Henry Percy.

Henry Percy was the eldest son of the Earl of Northumberland, and therefore the heir to the Earldom of Northumberland. He had been sent to serve as a page in Thomas Wolsey's household from a very young age to learn about the aristocratic society and to make connections within the court. He had been knighted for his services some six years earlier, King Arthur having recognised him as a loyal vassal not only to Wolsey but, by extension, to the crown.

The young Lord Percy, due to his high status as well as his good looks, received much attention from the young ladies at court, and it had not been uncommon for Wolsey to find numerous love letters sent to the young man over the years. But he had never engaged in sinful behaviour, much to Wolsey's admiration – for he himself had not been able to deny the lusts of the flesh.

But over the last year, Wolsey had noticed a change in his young attendant. A change which was most unwelcome, since it stemmed from the attentions of a certain lady, the Mistress Anne Boleyn.

The Lord Chancellor had found the two of them, on more than one occasion, walking together – *alone!* – through the palace gardens late at night, or abruptly breaking apart in dark corners when they heard Wolsey's approach. And Wolsey had not liked this development one little bit, for as a member of his household, Wolsey had been entrusted with keeping his page from making reckless decisions such as marrying a woman below his station.

"You will break off all interaction with that Boleyn girl," Wolsey had told his attendant some months prior, when word had begun circulating that the couple was planning to wed in secret, "As the heir to your father's Earldom you must marry a woman of higher standing. Not some nobody!"

Henry Percy had inhaled deeply and puffed out his chest, much to Wolsey's surprise.

"With all due respect, it *is* my intention to marry Anne. If I am to spend the rest of my life with a woman, I should be allowed to marry one of *my* choosing."

Wolsey had shaken his head at his page, a humourless laugh escaping him, "Your father has other ideas, my boy," he had said, "You would do well to cut all ties and break all promises to this woman, or forfeit your inheritance."

And that had been that. The following week court gossip had been thick with the young woman's heartbreak at the hands of Henry Percy, and Wolsey had been glad to not ever spot them together again.

But Anne Boleyn had not been fooled by her lover's meagre excuse as to his revoked betrothal, and she had known straight away that there had been more to it than he had let on.

"There is only one way to get a former lover to come back to you," Mary Boleyn had whispered to her younger sister one night, some weeks before her return to Hever Castle to have her baby.

When it came to matters of seduction, Anne would take any advice her sister had to offer, for she had been known in her youth to attract more attention from men than she could handle, causing their parents to have swiftly married her off to her now-husband William Carey.

Mary had giggled at Anne's wide eyes as she'd eagerly awaited her sister's suggestion.

"If you want this Henry Percy, then you must make him jealous."

Anne had frowned, her dark eyebrows bunching together, "Make him jealous?"

Mary had licked her lips and taken her sister's hand in hers, "Take another lover, Anne, and I swear to you, Henry Percy will come crawling back to you with his tail between his legs begging you to marry him."

And Anne had done just that, wasting no time at all in finding the perfect man for the job: a man who had been quite clearly besotted with her for years. A man of high status, with great looks, and a close relationship to the king. A man who she had noticed ogling her one too many times despite his respectable status – the priest Harry Duke of York himself.

As soon as Anne Boleyn was alone, she unfolded her letter with as much care as she'd given had it come from the King himself.

She knew what the contents would hold, and yet she wondered – as she did every time – if during *this* rendezvous, the Duke of York would want to sleep with her.

They had been meeting in secret in several different locations throughout London for the past two months now, and each time, the priest had asked her to undress slowly in candlelight as he'd watched with hungry eyes from across the room. Sometimes, Anne had even noticed his desire quite evident from underneath his robes; but he had never acted upon it, and Anne often thought how very unpleasant that must feel.

He had touched her once, just brushed her hair over her naked shoulder one time to allow for a better view of her bare breast before taking his usual seat on the other side of the room. That one touch had sent a shock wave of excitement to course through Anne, even though she had previously felt nothing for the king's brother but silent gratitude for not wanting to use her as another man would have done by now.

By taking the Duke of York as her lover, Anne was doing what her sister had suggested in making Henry Percy jealous, had acquired someone to make eyes at whenever Henry was nearby so that he would know that she had moved on. And in choosing the king's brother, she had been able to maintain her virginity so that *when* Henry could no longer deny his love for her, that she would continue intact for their wedding night.

But ever since that brush of the priest's fingertips on Anne's shoulder, Anne had been looking at him in a different light.

Previously, he had been no more than a means to an end, the perfect candidate to obtain what she truly wanted. And she *did* still truly want to marry Henry Percy.

But now, as she read the priest's carefully handwritten note, a thrill began to flow through her, and as she made her way to meet him, Anne wondered what it would feel like to have Harry's hands roam more firmly over her skin.

Chapter 21

May 1525
Ludlow Castle, Ludlow, Wales

Prince Artie and Princess Isabella were enjoying the break from the wet Spring weather by leisurely riding their horses up and down the field behind the castle grounds.
Isabella had yet to conceive – much to the princess' disappointment, who had been hoping to have a year to abandon her marriage bed and to give her young husband time to mature. But on the positive side, she was still free to partake in other activities that she would no longer be allowed to enjoy once she did conceive, horse riding being her favourite pastime.
"We should go back inside," Isabella said after an hour of trotting around the field, looking up at the grey clouds that had begun to gather.
The princess' grasp of the English language had improved immensely since their arrival at Ludlow, Isabella requesting twice daily lessons from her tutor as well as asking Artie to only converse with her in English from then on, so that she may learn as swiftly as possible.
Artie had admired that determination and commitment in his wife, and they had since her request nevermore spoken in their common language of Latin, even when the princess found herself not understanding a certain word or phrase.
It had led to many stunted conversations and frustrating interactions in the weeks that followed, but as time had gone on, the pair had learned to laugh at the princess' slight errors, and before long, there were less and less of them.
Artie followed her gaze to the darkening clouds, "It will not rain," he assured her.
Isabella lifted her hand to her cheek, "But it is…raining," she responded.
Artie laughed, "Hardly."

Isabella looked to her young husband with a frown, "Is it not 'rain' if it is water falling from the sky?"

The prince shrugged, "It's only drizzle," he said, releasing his horse's reins and holding a hand horizontally in the air, "I can hardly even feel it."

Isabella raised her chin, "Well, I can."

Artie turned to her, "Does my lady insist we make our return?" Despite Isabella's continued aversion to being intimate with her much younger husband, she had begun to enjoy his company. Yes, he was more immature than her in some ways – as would be expected for a young prince not yet in his sixteenth year.

Yes, he cared little for her comfort during their couplings.

But outside of the bedroom, Artie had proven himself a very sweet and funny young man, one who always made sure she was warm enough, or who cheered her up when she felt homesick. He was a good boy, and Isabella only hoped that as time went on, he would grow up to become an even better man.

"I would like to return, *sim*," she admitted, offering him a pretty smile.

Artie clicked his tongue in his cheek to spur on his horse, "Very well, then," he said, flashing his wife a playful grin, "But not before we have some fun."

And then he kicked the heels of his boots into his horse's sides and hurried ahead, Isabella realising a second too late that he wished to race. She breathed a surprised laugh at his dupe and whipped her reins against her own steed's neck, hoping to gain on him as he galloped ahead, laughing over his shoulder.

Greenwich Palace, London

It was a bright and sunny morning on the day that would change England forever.

Word had just come from Ludlow. A letter which would destroy Katherine's happiness. A letter which held within it the potential to bury the Tudor name forever.

"There must be a mistake," Katherine said with a quiver of disbelief, her eyes pleading with Arthur for him to be wrong.

But Arthur shook his head, his own eyes appearing dull and dark, as though the news had sucked the life right out of him.

"There is no mistake," he muttered before swallowing hard, "Artie…is dead."

At the confirmation, Katherine exhaled a shaky breath, her eyes wide and her mouth hanging open as she collapsed slowly to her knees, her hands coming up to cover her mouth. Arthur was by her side in an instant, though he too felt like breaking down. But, as the king, Arthur knew he could not show weakness. He would have to be the one to stay strong, to be the one to keep Katherine from falling into despair, and to keep the country from descending into civil unrest.

Katherine's shoulders shook as she cried without sound, her body unable to take in enough air to form even the smallest noise.

Arthur folded his long arms around her and awkwardly rocked her back and forth. He rubbed her hunched back and whispered into her ear for her to breathe, but all she could do was gasp for air.

He bent his head to look at her face then and was shocked to see her lips turning a pale shade of blue. He grabbed her by the shoulders then and squeezed them, hoping to snap her out of this shock.

"*Katherine*," he whispered harshly as the tears fell down her cheeks, but she continued to be unable to breathe, "Katherine!" then he shook her until her head lolled back and forth, her mouth opening and closing like a fish out of water as her neck muscles began to strain.

He pulled her roughly to her feet suddenly and took her face in his hands, "Katherine, breathe!" he pleaded as their eyes locked, and he saw the hopelessness in her stare.

"Please," Arthur begged, his mouth downturned as he tried not to weep, "Think of Mary. Think of us…"

At that, Katherine closed her eyes and tried to nod. She leaned her head against his chest and forced herself to calm down, however painful it was.

Finally, she felt her throat relax and she took in large gulps of air, to which Arthur responded by thanking God as he kissed her cheeks and forehead.

"Think of our daughter. Think of us."

Arthur continued to chant those seven words as he held her tightly to him, the pair glued together by their grief and their fear for the future, and all the while knowing that the pain of this loss would never, ever, leave them.

"How did it happen?"

Arthur was sitting stiffly upon his gold throne in the great hall, the smaller throne beside him vacant due to Katherine's breakdown at the news. She had been taken to her chambers and given a draught by Dr Butts to help her sleep.

The young messenger before Arthur was wringing his cap in his hands, quite clearly distressed to be the bearer of such terrible news.

"He – the prince fell from his horse, Your Grace," the boy said.

"Fell?" Arthur repeated, dumbfounded, "But he is an excellent rider! How could he have fallen?"

The messenger licked his lips, "Prince Artie and the Princess Isabella, they were racing," he said, "The princess saw it happen right before her eyes."

A gasp was heard from the small crowd that had gathered in the great hall, and Arthur reminded himself that he must remain composed, for as king, no personal tragedy was ever private.

He waved the messenger away then, unable to hear any more.

Wolsey and Griffith were by the king's side suddenly, mumbling words that Arthur could not make out, the blood rushing through his body causing them to sound as though he were underwater.

"Bring him home," Arthur mumbled as he stared blindly down at the floor. He closed his eyes and swallowed his tears, "Bring my son home."

The country was in mourning, but none more so than Katherine of Aragon herself.

As the city of London descended into a silent gloom, with no other sound than that of the constant tolling of the church bells that signified the death of a royal, Katherine of Aragon's chambers rang loud and desolate as the Queen of England sobbed and screamed uncontrollably.

It had been three days since the news of Artie's death had broken all over England, and as Arthur arranged their son's funeral with as much poise as he could muster, Katherine was yet to accept that their son's death had been an accident.

"Someone must have done this to him," the queen insisted when Arthur would visit her in her chambers each evening, "Perhaps he was pushed, or poisoned. Perhaps the horse wasn't shoed properly…"

She had yet to rise out of bed since the physicians had advised her to rest, and by the looks of things, she had failed to sleep much since that first day. Dark, sunken circles surrounded her bloodshot eyes. Her skin was blotchy and red from the constant crying. Her loose hair hung tangled and messy over her shoulders. Her lips were cracked and ashen from dehydration. She looked almost as dead as Artie himself.

"Someone must have hurt him," Katherine continued, "You must open an investigation. Send Griffith to Ludlow to enquire, please, Arthur, please, *please*. He cannot have fallen. He cannot. Artie was a good rider…"

And so it would go on until Arthur left, with his wife ranting and imploring him to find out *why* their son had been taken from them. Unable to accept the tragedy for what it was: a faultless accident.

He would leave Katherine's chambers feeling worse than when he had arrived, always having to be the one in control, to be the one who *didn't* show his emotions.

For what good would that do? What good would a desolate king do for his country?

A king was expected to be strong, to lead.

Arthur did not have the privilege to break down and cry and never get up again, as he so wished he could do in this very moment.

But sometimes, just before he entered Katherine's chambers, Arthur hoped he would find her sitting up and able to soothe *him* for a change. Because despite not showing it, despite being the man, the father, the king, Arthur was hurting just as much as Katherine was.

Prince Artie's funeral was held three weeks after his untimely death, having given the city just enough time to prepare for the grand, yet woeful, event.

Thousands of mourners lined the streets of London as the coffin covered with black velvet was carried through the city towards Westminster Abbey on a horse drawn hearse, with a canopy held over it by four Knights of the Garter. A procession of over two hundred people from the prince's and the king and queen's households walked behind the coffin, all of them clad in black robes of mourning.

As was tradition, the king and queen were not to attend their own son's funeral. It was believed that the king and queen's royal presence at such an event would bring into question their own mortality, and for the sake of the country's stability, the sovereign must never be associated with death. Especially not now that the king's only son and heir was being buried; the continuation of the Tudor dynasty having come to an abrupt and screeching halt.

But it was probably for the best that they could not attend, Harry thought as he watched the procession approach the church, given Queen Katherine's appearance of late, the people might begin to fear that a second funeral was yet to come.

In the royal parent's stead, Thomas Howard Duke of Norfolk was appointed as Chief Mourner to represent them, the position being both an honour and a misery; and it was he who led the procession into the abbey.

Upon entering the church, the coffin was laid in the quire as a funeral mass was led by the Duke of York, after which all mourners offered the mass penny.

The choir, comprising of fifty boys and twenty adult singers, began singing their gloomy anthem as the time approached to lay the body in the grave, an eruption of weeping having ensued from the congregation causing the choir to have to increase the intensity of their song. More anthems were sung then by the whole congregation as the bishops gathered to cense the coffin, and as it was laid in the ground, Harry started to say the final prayers. But he could barely speak the words for crying.

With great effort, Harry completed the prayer through blubbering sobs before placing a cross on the coffin in the grave.

He was weeping, of course, for the loss of his nephew and for his brother's and sister-in-law's heartbreak. But he was also crying for the uncertainty that now lay ahead, England's future being utterly altered in the blink of an eye.

Would Arthur once more expect Harry to give up his life and become his heir? Would Harry even be willing to do that, for the sake of the country?

Perhaps Arthur would look to others from their family tree to become his new heir? Or perhaps Arthur would think on what Harry had said to him all those years ago, about taking another wife and obtaining an heir through a new alliance?

Harry shook his head at the distant memory and hoped Arthur would not. Despite having been the one to suggest it, the thought of Arthur sending Katherine away to a nunnery – or, worse yet, divorcing her – caused acid to burn Harry's throat, and he reproached himself for ever having suggested such blasphemy against the sanctity of marriage.

Prince Artie was dead. The last thing the country needed now was more upheaval from within the monarchy. What England needed was stability. And if God saw fit to take away England's heir, then there must be some other path He wished for Arthur to take.

But due to the dark cloud of sorrow that had enveloped the Duke of York, he was struggling to see just *what* God's plan for the country's future might be.

June 1525

Queen Katherine was devastated.

If she wasn't crying, she was numb. If she wasn't numb, she was suffocating. If she wasn't suffocating, she was crying. And so the wretched cycle went on.

She thought she had known of grief. The stillbirth of her baby Elizabeth having felt both unbearably painful as well as agonizingly dulling, as though Katherine had fallen down a deep chasm of darkness, the impact of the fall breaking her heart and the darkness surrounding her numbing her senses.

Losing a child at birth, never getting to know them, or hear them laugh, or hold them, or console them. It was earthshattering.

But *this*…

Losing a child you *had* gotten to know, *had* held in your arms, *had* kissed away their tears, *had* fallen in love with…it was unlike anything Katherine had ever known.

Grief now had an entirely new degree of intensity, one where she felt completely alone despite those others who had loved him sharing the same pain.

But was it really their pain? No, it wasn't.

It was so much worse, surely, for a mother. The only person who had experienced his heart beating in sync with her own.

The only one to sense his little kicks inside the dome of her belly when music had played.

Sometimes, when Katherine lay awake at night, the grief felt so intense that she thought if she stretched out her arm, she could physically touch it. It made the air around her feel heavy, and with each inhale it suffocated her more and more.

There was a lesion inside her now. A lesion which was growing with each day that passed, slowly ripping and tearing her up inside. Nothing could stop it or slow it down. Not even Arthur's daily promises that they would overcome this grief together. *Nothing.*

Because Arthur could not understand her sorrow. Not really.

Nobody could. Katherine was alone with her pain. And no matter how often people repeated that great lie 'time could heal all wounds', no amount of time would heal this hurt inside her: a wound that was beginning to fester deep in her heart.

"What is to be done with the Princess Isabella?"

It was the question on everyone's minds following the young prince's death just five months after his marriage to the Portuguese *infanta*.

If the court gossip was to be believed, Artie and Isabella had consummated their marriage at least once, which meant that there was still a fine flake of hope for the Tudor dynasty's continuation.

"Princess Isabella has been questioned as to the nature of their marriage," the Lord Chancellor said as he looked around at the other advisors sitting around the table, "She has assured us that it was consummated and that there has been more than one occasion thereafter where the couple shared a bed. She may be carrying an heir as we speak."

Henry Wyatt and Griffith nodded sombrely; it was little consolation.

"And what if she is not?" King Arthur asked quietly then.

The council members all turned to look at their king.

He was sitting forward with his elbows resting on the table, his fingers intertwined together before him as his head drooped heavily between his shoulders, his hair hanging limply, his face in shadow. He made no attempt to meet his advisors' eyes, caring little for formalities, his sorrow weighing him down more and more each day.

"If the princess is not with child, who then should we look to?" Arthur asked.

Harry swallowed, his Adam's apple bobbing anxiously as he looked to Wolsey, then to Griffith.

"Our sister, Your Grace," Harry said carefully, as though he feared spooking the fragile king, "Send for Mary to return. She and Charles Brandon have been shunned long enough. They have paid their price for their betrayal. If you could forgive me, then you must forgive them."

Arthur raised his head ever so slightly.

"You say I must forgive them. And then what?"

"They have a son, Arthur," Harry informed his king, "You could name him your heir."

The room fell silent, nobody daring to add to the Duke of York's suggestion.

"A son?"

Harry nodded, "Two, in fact."

Arthur inhaled deeply then before expelling the breath sharply. Katherine had failed to mention that Mary and Charles Brandon had had sons, Arthur thought, remembering only that one letter Katherine had received informing them that Mary had given birth to their first child – a girl – some years earlier.

These boys must be no more than toddlers; hardly promising candidates to safely inherit the throne. For Arthur knew just how easily children could perish…

He rubbed his hands over his tired face, his stubble scratching at the palms of his hands.

"Very well," he said after a moment, "Send for Mary and her husband. If the Princess Isabella is not with child, I shall offer them my pardon in exchange for their eldest son."

Henry Wyatt looked, wide-eyed, from the king to the Duke of York, "Just like that?" he said, "You are to p-proclaim this boy your heir without meeting him? Without so much as a word to your queen?"

Arthur did not even flinch at the judgemental tone from the old man, his blue eyes moving lazily to meet Wyatt's.

"If you think Katherine will hear a word I or anyone else has to say, then please be my guest and inform her, Sir Wyatt. She has been unresponsive for the better part of a month now and I do not believe her to come out of her misery any time soon."

Wyatt huffed in disbelief.

"It is not set in stone, Wyatt," Griffith interjected in his king's defence, "Let Mary Brandon return and have the Tudor siblings reunited. When all are together once more the monarchy will be at their full strength to tackle the matter of a successor."

Lord Chancellor Thomas Wolsey nodded in agreement with Griffith, then turned to observe the king. But he had already returned to staring glassy eyed at the table, and for the first time since King Arthur's coronation, Wolsey suddenly felt apprehensive as to the survival of the Tudor House.

Chapter 22

July 1525

Since Artie's fatal fall two months prior, Princess Isabella had been kept under strict supervision for any sign of pregnancy. Though the young woman kept guaranteeing the physicians that she knew she was not with child, even the queen could not simply accept her word.

Every day, the Portuguese Princess' linens were checked for any sign of bleeding, the queen herself requesting to have them brought to her chambers for her own personal inspection when, a month after Artie's funeral, Isabella had not yet bled.

But still it had not been enough to rouse Katherine from her bed; and nothing would, not until she could be sure that Artie's wife was indeed carrying his child.

The physicians continued hopeful for a while that an heir may well be within the princess' womb, and when she one day fell ill with nausea, Katherine grew more and more anxious with each hour that passed.

But it had been no more than wishful thinking, for the following day, the princess had begun her monthly courses, and Katherine's final hope of retaining some small part of her beloved son had been lost forever.

Following the disappointing news, the Portuguese Princess and her household were allowed to return to their homeland, to complete the widowed princess' traditional year of mourning in her own country, and to no doubt be married off to another soon thereafter.

And with that final beacon of hope being snuffed out, the queen fell – if possible – into an even deeper depression.

August 1525

Having heard of Arthur's plan to allow his sister Mary to return to England after years of banishment had brought a brief glimmer of light back into Katherine's life, who had for so long hoped to be reunited with her dearest friend.

But that light had soon been extinguished upon learning the reason for Mary's return, and Arthur's distasteful idea to replace their perfect son with Mary's.

"Where is he?" Katherine called as she threw open the doors of her chambers, emerging from them for the first time in weeks.

"Where is the king?!"

Her ladies hurried after her, but it was the shocked courtiers that they passed along the way that pointed her towards the great hall.

"I won't allow it!" Katherine called angrily as she stormed her way towards Arthur, who sat upon his throne at the end of the vast chamber, Griffith Rhys standing before him in quiet discussion.

"Katherine," Arthur said in dumbfounded surprise, dismissing Griffith from before him, "What is the matter?" the king worried, rising from his throne.

"I have heard of your plan!" the queen replied, her eyes blazing, only just managing to control her tone, "I will not have our son replaced so easily!"

Arthur's eyebrows twitched, understanding the reason for Katherine's burst of life then.

"My plan?" he asked, trying to gain time to adjust his thoughts.

"To replace Artie with your nephew! I will not agree to it!" she fumed, standing before her lord husband as stiffly as a statue.

Arthur did not reply and instead took in the woman that stood before him.

Katherine was, despite her obvious wrath, graceful in her stance. She stood with her back straight and her hands clasped before her. Her gable hood encrusted with diamonds and rubies was placed neatly on her head, her gown matching the hood in colour and fabric. If he didn't know any better, she could have passed for any queen of Europe. But the sunken sockets of her eyes gave her away, the dark shadows beneath them a frightening contrast to the wan complexion of her skin.

If Arthur was being honest with himself, he hadn't liked the idea of his sister's son becoming his heir either. But what other alternative did he have? What else could he do?

Other than perhaps what Harry had suggested years ago...

But Arthur would not go down that route. Even to entertain the thought was insulting to everything he and Katherine had been through together. This *was* the cleanest course of action, no matter how they felt about it. But Arthur was suddenly aware that this could be the very thing to guide Katherine out of her gloom.

The king raised his chin and cast his eyes over the courtiers who had, upon Katherine's livid entrance, abandoned their games and conversations, and turned their heads to witness this public outburst.

Arthur's mouth twitched. It was not ideal to proceed with this delicate matter in public. But he could see that her anger had birthed a fire within her, had risen her from the sombre pit she had been wallowing in. And if it meant he would be saving Katherine from herself, Arthur would gladly stoke the fire inside her and see it burn her sorrow to ash. Even if it meant that he would bear the brunt of her umbrage.

"You *will* allow it," Arthur replied then, as firmly as he could, "This matter goes beyond pride, Katherine. Though I know your Spanish blood runs thick with it."

Katherine flinched at his words, her eyes narrowing at Arthur's out of character remark.

"How can you think to replace Artie like this?"

She had whispered the accusation, but the ire in her words had carried her voice.

"You know why, Katherine," Arthur replied, their lack of a spare male heir never having been quite so evident.

He hated himself for speaking the words but knew them to be necessary to fuel the flames.

It had the desired effect, Katherine's neck and cheeks blotching bright red with fury and shame.

"How dare you?" Katherine spat, no doubt feeling as hurt as Arthur had felt cruel to even broach the subject that had so long haunted the royal couple.

"I *dare* because you have failed me, Katherine!" Arthur called out then, forcing himself to sound cruel.

A gasp escaped his wife as well as several courtiers behind her, her lady-in-waiting Anne Boleyn even raising a hand to her mouth to hide her shock.

Noting his success, Arthur went on, "Without a spare male heir, England is now weak and in need to regroup. Had you done your duty by me and given me more sons, this day would never have come!"

The great hall had fallen silent as Katherine stared up at her husband, her mouth pinched so tightly it was all she could do not to look around herself in burning shame.

So, this was how he *truly* felt?

After years of reassuring her, telling her that he did not blame her for their losses, coaxing her out of her guilt.

Had it all been a lie?

"'Had I done my duty?'" Katherine repeated, stunned by his heartlessness.

Arthur raised his chin, trying hard not to break eye contact. He needed her to hold onto her anger, needed her to believe that she had something to fight for.

"Until you provide me with a male heir," Arthur declared as he stared her down, "I shall seek to find one elsewhere!"

September 1525

King Arthur's announcement that he would be seeking other means to obtain a male heir had led to an influx of new ladies at the English court.

Many nobles and high-born families from within London and the surrounding areas who had heard of the king's newfound distaste towards his wife had gathered up their daughters, married or unmarried, and promptly brought them to court to flaunt them before the king.

And Arthur had never been so disappointed in his countrymen.

"What do they hope for?" Arthur asked as he closed the door to his chambers behind him, Harry and Griffith having slipped in just in time before being clipped by the door as it swung on its hinges.

"Never in my twenty-four-year marriage have I so much as looked at another woman," Arthur said frustratedly, "And, what? Now that my son is dead the nobles think it's the perfect time to offer up their daughters to me?"

Harry walked over to the table at the centre of the room and picked up the silver jug of wine, "The nobles hope to alleviate some of your stress," he said as he filled three cups with the dark red liquid.

Griffith claimed one cup and took a seat at the table, Harry holding another up to his brother, "A little fun to distract you from your woes."

"What do you know of that kind of fun, or of my woes?" Arthur asked rhetorically as he grabbed the cup from Harry and took a sip.

Griffith chuckled into his cup. Harry did not reply, though a memory of the Mistress Anne laying naked on his bed flashed before his mind's eye.

Arthur was right, of course. What *did* Harry know of Arthur's stresses and what might alleviate them? As an unmarried, childless man who had had the opportunity to follow his life's calling and had his brother as the most powerful man in the country to help him achieve greatness that much quicker; what could Harry even say that would suggest he understood?

He *didn't* understand. And he likely never would, since he was yet unwilling to give up this life to reclaim his position as Arthur's heir.

Arthur hadn't asked Harry to consider it again, hadn't threatened to defrock him as he had done the last time his succession was in question. Perhaps he had accepted that Harry would not be a suitable heir due to his unwillingness for it. Perhaps he feared Harry would suggest, yet again, that to divorce Katherine would be a better alternative.

Regardless as to why, Harry was grateful to his brother for not laying that pressure upon his shoulders. For, in truth, Harry was not as strong as Arthur, and given just a little too much strain, Harry wasn't sure he could handle even half of what Arthur had endured.

"Despite my lack of personal experiences, I am aware that distraction, in whatever form, can soothe the mind," Harry replied after a moment as he sipped his wine and took a seat before the roaring fire.

"I don't wish for distraction," Arthur said as he knocked back the contents of his cup and reached for the jug of wine.

Harry nodded as though he understood, watching as Arthur filled his cup to the brim and took another large gulp.

"So, you still hope for a son by Katherine?" Griffith asked from his seat at the table.

Arthur sighed through his nose and looked down at the burgundy liquid swirling around in his cup, the memory of their most recent coupling flashing through his mind.

Arthur had called Katherine to his chamber the previous evening to discuss the development of their daughter's continued education. Katherine's anger had allowed for very little discourse, her answers to his questions having been short and dripping with indifference. But her resentment had wavered as Arthur had edged closer with each rebuffed question, his proximity and her passion having suddenly sparked an urgent need for each other – the thin line between love and hate becoming blurred. An intense night of lovemaking had followed, Katherine leaving quickly thereafter without so much as a word to her husband.

"Even if I did take a mistress," Arthur said then, leaving Griffith's question unanswered, "Any child born from the relationship would not do for an heir. As an illegitimate, the child would not be accepted."

Harry stared into the flames in the fireplace, "You could always have a boy child legitimised," he said pensively.

"The people would not stand for it," the king replied immediately, raising his wine to his lips.

Harry and Griffith nodded. Arthur was right of course.

"Not to mention that it would not be something I would wish to pursue. I could never do that to Katherine," Arthur said as he took a seat on the lounger beside Harry, "and no other woman has ever interested me."

The two brothers sat in silence for a moment, the younger looking up to the elder though they sat at equal eye level.

Arthur's revelation had made Harry think of his own love life – or rather, lust life – and how not even Anne Boleyn had appealed to him enough to break his vow of celibacy, though she had been the only woman he'd ever known to stir that *want* to. Even after months of secret meetings and dozens of opportunities to have her, Harry had never so much as kissed her. Sure, he had come close to once, had had sinful thoughts and dreams about her. But never once had he *actually* lain with her. And what went on in his mind was not against the rules of his vows.

Nevertheless, despite Harry's desperate attraction to Anne, not even she had managed to make him betray God, and he suddenly thought that, in some strange way, perhaps God was to Harry as Katherine was to Arthur.

The Tudor brothers both possessed a love for another being so great that none other would ever measure up, even if – in Arthur's case – they could give him the one thing that he needed most in that moment.

"This displeasure you have developed for Katherine," Harry said before pausing, choosing his words carefully, "It has not been enough to drive you into the arms of another."

Arthur frowned, "There is no displeasure," he admitted quietly before taking another long swallow of his wine, "There never has been."

It was Harry's turn to frown, and he looked over at Griffith who too looked at Arthur in confusion.

"So, the court gossip is not true?" Griffith asked, "I was there, Arthur. You were most displeased."

"What I have chosen to share with the world is that I am displeased with my wife," Arthur explained, "It is precisely what I wish for her to believe. But it is not what is true in my heart."

The wine had already gone to Arthur's head, Harry noticed, for his words, though clear, had a slightly emotional undertone. One which Harry knew Arthur would not be showing were he in complete control of his emotions.

"Why then – ?"

"Because she needs me to," Arthur admitted with a heavy sigh, standing up to refill his cup yet again before sitting back down, "Our love, our daughter, time…none of it worked in shaking her from this loss. But the idea that our sister's son might take Artie's place…"

"It has fired her up," Harry concluded.

Arthur raised his cup and tapped it to Harry's before taking a sip, "Precisely."

Harry nodded, understanding that Katherine really was everything to his brother. So much so that he would risk pushing her away only to see her through her melancholy.

Arthur sat back heavily in his seat, breathing deeply all of a sudden. Harry looked over to his king. His eyes were closed. He had fallen asleep.

Harry noticed as he looked upon him then, that Arthur looked older than his thirty-nine years, his auburn hair sporting more greys than reds. But it was the sallow hanging of the sides of his mouth that added ten years to his age, his sorrow quite literally pulling his older brother down in appearance as well as in mood.

The Duke of York looked to Griffith and jerked his chin towards the door, wordlessly suggesting they depart. Griffith swallowed the last of his wine and headed for the door, holding it open as he waited for the Duke of York to follow.

"Rest now, my king," Harry whispered as he stood up and squeezed Arthur's shoulder, "By the grace of God, soon everything will fall into place."

And they made their way out of the king's chambers, leaving him to sleep off the wine and the strain.

October 1525

Mary and Charles Brandon's return to England was not a happy one, as Katherine had always imagined it would be.

Ever since Arthur's proclamation that he would look to others to provide him with an heir to the throne, Katherine had been dreading her sister-in-law's return, despite so often having longed for it over the years.

It came as no relief then when, upon their entry into London, Katherine and Arthur were presented with not one but *two* legitimate male children of the Tudor line by Mary Brandon.

And to merely look upon them felt like a punch to Katherine's gut. Mary had lied to her.

Of course, they were both in good health and of a strong build like their father, the eldest of the two standing almost to his mother's shoulders though he was but six years old.

"Sister!" Arthur called in merry greeting as they approached, as though their banishment had never happened.

Mary curtsied and Charles Brandon bowed at the waist before their king and queen.

"Your Highnesses," Mary said as she rose, "We thank you for your invitation to court."

Arthur nodded, then turned to allow them entrance into the castle.

In the days that followed, preparations were made to inaugurate the eldest of the two boys to become Arthur's successor and to establish whether he would be accepted not only by the people but also by Arthur himself, who had yet to make a final decision on the matter.

The boy – named Henry, after the late King Henry VII, Mary's father – would be sent away to begin his higher education and to learn how to – perhaps – one day become the next King of England, King Henry VIII.

Despite never before even having set foot within England in his lifetime. Despite being utterly unprepared for the role. Despite being not half as smart or regal or charismatic as Artie had been. And Katherine could feel hatred beginning to brew inside her.

"It will take years before he is ready," Wolsey was telling his king during one of their council meetings following Mary Brandon's return to the English court, "His earlier education was good, but it is hugely lacking for that of a future king."

Arthur waved his hand, "Of course it is!" he said, "What else did you expect from a boy brought up in exile. Son of a princess or not, I am just glad the boy can read."

"He will need to do m-more than read to run the country, my lord," Henry Wyatt said with an air of disgruntled superiority, "I do not think this to b-be the right path to take."

"What other path is open to me, Sir Wyatt?" Arthur asked, trying to keep the frustration from his voice.

Wyatt turned towards Harry, his stare alone speaking volumes.

Arthur followed Wyatt's gaze, then exhaled sharply before reaching over to brush invisible crumbs from the table.

"The Duke of York is too important in the position he is in for me to have him defrocked," Arthur admitted, "With any luck, Harry will be the next Archbishop of Canterbury."

All heads snapped up from their documents. This was news to all of them, and many wide eyes turned to gawk at the king, Harry's in elated surprise while Wolsey's in disgusted horror.

"Archbishop?" Wolsey spluttered as he looked from his king to his former apprentice, "Your Grace, surely someone more experienced –"

Arthur cut him off with a flick of his hand, "This is not the time for that discussion. I only broached it to explain to you, my council, why my brother is no longer an option as my heir. There is only my sister's lineage who possesses that. With her sons, I gain *two* would-be successors."

Wolsey clenched his jaw shut to keep from expressing how offended he was at the king's blasé announcement. Wolsey's wisdom and experience superseded that of Harry's in leaps and bounds – after all, Harry had learned much of what he knew from Wolsey himself! – and to be so easily overlooked for the respectable title of Archbishop of Canterbury...he could not allow it to happen.

"The queen continues troubled by your sister's return," Griffith added, casting a knowing look to his lifelong friend and king.

Arthur nodded his head sombrely, saddened by the gulf he had had to form between himself and his wife for the sake of fuelling her anger.

"Yes," he agreed, "So, she does."

Anne Boleyn averted her gaze just before Henry Percy turned to look her way, and the two former lovers crossed paths without so much as a nod of acknowledgement. But Anne had felt his eyes on her as she walked away, as she did every time their paths crossed, and she smiled to think that her plan was working. He clearly still felt something for her.

"A letter, my lady," a messenger said as he handed Anne a note before hurrying away. She did not need to open it to know who it was from, so she tucked it safely into her sleeve, to be read later. And as she continued ahead, Anne risked one quick glance over her shoulder in the direction of Henry Percy, who had returned his attention to the group of men around him, wishing – not for the first time – that these forbidden letters were coming from him.

Later, once Anne Boleyn had been dismissed by her queen, she found herself alone for the first time since receiving the Duke of York's note.

Looking around herself to make sure no other lady had entered the queen's chambers, and that Queen Katherine was not stirring in her bed in the other room, Anne pulled the letter from her sleeve and peeled it open to discover Harry's chosen place of rendezvous. And she was surprised to see it was not a secret location away from prying eyes as it normally was, but merely in the courtyard. She frowned to think he would select such a place where, though they would meet at night, would not be secluded enough to fulfil their usual ritual.

Their meetings had continued as strange as ever, Anne thought, the handsome priest wishing only ever to look upon her as she stood naked before him. He had progressed, however, to occasionally brushing the tips of his fingers slowly over her breast, never *quite* touching the skin. Or leaning in – closely enough that she could smell the incense clinging to his robes – and grazing his lips so lightly along her neck and jawline that she thought he might lean in and kiss her. But he never did, dismissing her an hour later, more often than not without having uttered a single word.

And it would seem that tonight he wished to do even less still, given his choice of location.

Feeling satisfied that the queen was deep enough asleep to slip out and meet her lover, Anne tiptoed towards the door and flashed the guard standing sentry outside a smile, the queen's guards no longer surprised to see ladies sneaking out past nightfall.

Anne hurried through the candle-lit hallways and down the staircase, quickly emerging outside and into the courtyard, spotting the Duke of York immediately.

"My lord," Anne mumbled in greeting as she approached.

Harry turned around to face her and smiled, to which Anne could feel herself blushing, and she was glad they had met in the shadows.

"Mistress Boleyn," Harry said, his voice deep but quiet.

Anne looked about herself subconsciously then, ashamed to be feeling elated at their continued meetings. It had not been part of the plan to develop feelings for the king's brother.

On her pursuit to make Henry Percy jealous, Anne had chosen the Duke of York as her lover for the simple fact that he had shown an obvious interest in her. His higher status to that of Henry Percy's had been a fortunate addition, as Anne knew it would serve to bruise Henry's ego that much more to hopefully want her back.

But after six months of sneaking around with Harry, using him to obtain what she *truly* wanted, Anne was ashamed to admit that not only had Henry yet failed to fight to get her back, but Anne had also begun to have feelings for the redheaded Duke of York.

"You asked to see me?" Anne reminded him then, forcing herself to meet his gaze.

Harry was still smiling down at her, and in the moonlight, Anne could not help but wonder if perhaps she should just forget about Henry Percy.

Harry nodded, "I did," he said, before turning in a way which said she should follow. Anne hopped into step beside him.

"I asked you here to…to talk," the Duke of York said.

Anne blinked, "To talk?"

"Yes," Harry replied, his hands clasped behind his back as they walked slowly through the courtyard. They passed a couple of guards and a servant girl carrying linens. But otherwise, they were completely alone.

Anne could feel her heart hammering in her chest. Perhaps this was the moment in which he would confess that he wished for more than their secret meetings. Perhaps he wished to take her as his would-be wife as Thomas Wolsey had done with his woman, Joan Larke.

She found herself breathing unevenly and forced herself to calm down. She licked her lips.

"Talk about what, my lord?" she asked.

Harry inhaled deeply and briefly looked up at the dark sky, his lips pursed as he tried to arrange his thoughts.

King Arthur's recent announcement that Harry was on a path towards becoming the next Archbishop had both excited and surprised Harry. The current Archbishop William Warham was old and likely in need to be replaced soon, yes, but Harry had never thought himself to be up for the job. Not yet, at least. And certainly not when others had served the crown for so much longer than he.

If looks could kill, Harry had no doubt that Wolsey would have blown him into a puff of ash with the look he had given him from across the table at the king's proclamation. It made Harry chuckle to think of it now, despite having been just as shocked as everyone else.

But it had made Harry wonder as to *why* Arthur would think to appoint him to such an enormous task when Wolsey was a more experienced candidate? Of course, being the king's brother came with advantages – advantages which he knew he had been privy to for most of his career – but *archbishop*?! Before the age of forty?

It begged the question as to what failures Wolsey had made for him to be overlooked.

Harry, as a man of the cloth himself, knew that many saw Wolsey as an embodiment of clerical sin. He was an absentee priest, who appeared to care more for riches than God, his open disregard to his vow of celibacy irking many of his peers.
And Harry could not be painted with the same brush.

"I believe our...association...has run its course," Harry said quietly then, looking over his shoulder briefly to make sure they continued out of earshot of the guards.
He glanced down at Anne, a friendly smile on his lips, "I free you of whatever obligation you thought you had to me. You may henceforth wish to pursue a more suitable suitor."
This was not what she had thought to hear, and Anne was not sure how to respond. She stayed silent for a moment in which her eyes blinked furiously.

"You 'free' me?" she said, repeating the odd choice of word he had used, as though she had played no part in choosing him at all.

"Yes," Harry replied with a small shrug, "I believe you and Sir Henry Percy have eyes for one another?"
At that, Anne stopped in her tracks, worried suddenly that he had played *her* all along. Had Wolsey set him up to keep her away from Henry?
Harry, sensing her having trailed behind, stopped and turned to find Anne ashen faced, and Harry was surprised to feel a little aroused by her worry. He let out an amused scoff.

"Do not fret," he said, taking a step closer, "It is not the reason why I wish to go our separate ways."

"Then why bring him into it?" Anne asked accusingly, her eyes flashing briefly with anger.
Harry scoffed again, "Because I believe you need me if you wish to be considered worthy of the heir to an Earldom."
Anne recoiled at his words. Had he always considered her as 'unworthy'?

She raised her chin, angry at herself for having read more into their relationship and forbidden meetings than what they had always been: a means to an end.

"Why would you help me?" she asked, "What would you get in return if not my body."

"Ah!" Harry said, raising his eyebrows and taking another step closer. Anne looked about herself swiftly, sensing that he did not wish to be overheard, but she saw only one guard in the distance by the archway.

"What I wish from you in return," Harry said, his voice no more than a whisper as his gaze dropped to her slightly parted lips, "Is for your silence."

November 1525

Just six months after Artie's fatal fall from his horse, England received news that his widow, Princess Isabella, was to be betrothed to Katherine's own nephew, Carlos V of Castille.
And Katherine was outraged.

"King Carlos has asked the Pope for a dispensation, he and Isabella being cousins," Griffith informed his king and queen as they received the news in the great hall, "And they plan to wed as soon as her year of mourning is complete."

Everyone was moving on, Katherine thought. It was as if Artie had never even existed. It was just six months later, and the world was already forgetting him.

Her nephew's disrespect did not go unnoticed either, Carlos' swift claiming of Artie's widow just months after his demise feeling like a slap to the face from her home country. And she felt betrayed both in-house as well as out; no one seeming to realise that the wound of her loss was still as fresh as the day it had been inflicted. Or perhaps it was simply that no one cared.

Katherine refused to see her once dear sister-in-law.

If they were to cross paths in the mornings on her way to chapel, Katherine would make a point of staring straight ahead, as though no one were there at all, her face turned slightly away to emphasise her snub.

At banquets when Mary was seated beside her, Katherine would utterly ignore Mary's attempts to make conversation, and it had not gone unnoticed by Arthur or the courtiers. But Arthur was simply glad that Katherine hadn't made a scene about the entire situation, as he knew would have been her right to do.

But, despite Katherine's inability to mask her newfound disdain for Mary and her family, was nothing if not loyal, and though she had confronted her king in the great hall some weeks prior, Katherine had never again allowed her anger towards him to show, letting it continue to bubble inside her instead.

Her resentment and disappointment in both Arthur and Mary had had the desired effect at least, for she was no longer wallowing miserably in bed; and Arthur only hoped that now that she had accepted Artie's loss, she would slowly be able to move on.

But days had turned into weeks, and still Katherine was openly hostile to the sister of the king, so much so that the court had begun to gossip about the fragile stability of the royal family.

Until one day, the king had had enough of his wife's enmity.

"You will make amends with my sister, Katherine," he told her one evening, having found her quietly reading the Bible in her chambers, "Enough of these mind games! By now all of England knows of your aversion to Mary's son becoming my successor, but it won't change the fact that it is our only remaining option."

Katherine glared up at him, then closed the Bible with a loud *thud*.

"Of course, Your Highness," she said icily before rising from her seat and curtsying exaggeratedly.

The next morning, Katherine had invited Mary to breakfast with her in the queen's chambers after their morning prayers,

Katherine being slightly irritated by the princess' immediate reply accepting the invitation. She had hoped Mary would not be so utterly desperate to settle their differences, for once this matter was put to bed, what would Katherine have left to hold onto if not her hatred?

Conversation was sparce once they had taken their seats and servants had placed silver trays of freshly baked bread and cheese in front of them, Mary receiving more warmth from Katherine's new ladies Anne and Mary Boleyn than from the sister-in-law she had been so looking forward to reuniting with. During her time in Flanders Mary had, of course, heard the tragic news of her nephew's untimely death, information about the royal family having always travelled fast throughout the country and beyond. She had cried many tears over his loss, had prayed for Artie's soul on the day of his funeral, and even written Katherine a long letter detailing her sympathies.

But like so many others over the years, the letter had never been sent, Mary being too aware that their lives had gone their separate directions, and to receive a letter in this most painful of times after years of silence would only have led to resentment.

But it appeared resentment had formed nonetheless, and in truth, Mary could not even blame Katherine.

"The weather has been glorious," Mary Brandon was saying, continuing to attempt to mend the broken bridge between them, "I expected storms by now. But our journey across the waters was very pleasant."

Katherine nodded slowly, as though she couldn't care less about her sister-in-law's safe travels.

It made Mary sigh in frustration, and after three weeks of the same painfully bland exchanges, Mary had had enough.

"I'm really trying, Katherine," the princess said, pushing her half-eaten breakfast aside, "Please, speak with me plainly."

Katherine turned a pleasant face to Mary, "Whatever do you mean, sister?"

"Enough of the feigning pleasantries," Mary said as forcefully as she dared, for she was still, after all, speaking to the Queen of England, "I know you do not care for my family's return. Under these circumstances it is understandable. But this is not my doing, Katherine. I never wished for this."
Katherine had dropped her half-smile and now stared wide-eyed and red-cheeked at the younger woman.

"You lied to me, Mary," Katherine said, meeting her glare, "You wrote to me following Henry's birth. You told me you'd had a daughter!"
Mary flinched, she had not been prepared for *that* accusation. She licked her lips and looked away, "That is true, I did lie to you."

"So you see there is more to my disdain," Katherine said, reaching over to pick up her cup of small ale.
Mary looked over at Katherine, her eyebrows bunched together in saddened frustration, "I never wished to offend you. I never thought you would find out – I hoped you never would! We were shunned, ordered never to return under pain of death!"

"Then why?"
Mary shook her head, "To protect my boy!" she exclaimed in exasperation, opening the floodgate of emotions she had been holding in since their return.
Katherine narrowed her eyes at her, "Protect him?"
Mary breathed a humourless laugh, "You think I wanted to return to a land where I have been labelled a reckless, disloyal fool?" Mary continued, evading Katherine's questioning look and moving past her previous remark, "My own brother banished me for following my heart. And now I must return and give up my son for the sake of the crown I had previously disrespected. How could I deny my king that? What more would be done to us if we had not accepted his offer?"

"Nothing more would have been done to you," Katherine replied monotonously, as though it were obvious.

"How can you know that?"

Katherine shot Mary an insulted look, "Do you really think so little of your brother? Of your king? Arthur would have likely accepted your decision not to return. As he accepted Harry's decision to remain within the church."

Mary shook her head and dabbed at the corners of her eyes with her handkerchief, exhausted from her short burst of emotion.

"It no longer matters," she said, defeated, "My Henry will be sent away to Ludlow to further learn how to become the next king. And I won't see him for months."

Katherine flinched, "Be glad you'll get to see your son again at all."

Mary met her old friend's glowering gaze, an apology in Mary's eyes, "Forgive me. I know my sorrows are nothing compared to yours."

They fell silent, the tension between them having risen and then ebbed upon finally speaking their thoughts.

"It is a strange world we live in," Mary said absentmindedly then as she stared down at the wooden table, "Boy children are preferable in a world of men, but I prayed for girls every time I was with child. I did not want this life for my children."

The queen did not respond, did not acknowledge that Mary had even spoken, for suddenly the thought of her other sister-in-law Margaret and her own struggles in Scotland came to mind.

If it was more widely agreed that a woman was as capable as a man, I might still be serving as Regent for my son.

Katherine blinked, unsure why the memory had suddenly dawned upon her. Then she heard it again, except this time it wasn't Margaret's voice, but a deeper, calmer voice.

If it was more widely agreed that a woman was as capable as a man.

With a gasp, Katherine froze with her hand halfway up to her mouth.

"I have to go," the queen suddenly said as she stood up abruptly, her chair clattering behind her.

"Your Grace?" her lady-in-waiting Mary Boleyn asked as she bent over to pick up the chair, her light eyebrows bunched together as Agnes and Anne appeared from the other room, curious to what had caused the commotion.
Katherine turned this way and that, desperate to leave, "I have to go," she repeated, "I have to speak to Arthur."

Katherine burst through the doors to the king's chambers to find her husband and the Duke of York sitting hunched over a chess table, and by the looks on their faces it appeared Harry was – as ever – on the losing side.
"Arthur!" Katherine called ecstatically, forgetting her discontent with him, for now that God had spoken to her it no longer mattered, "Arthur, I must speak with you."
The two men looked up from their game and Harry rose to his feet before bowing his head at his queen and looking to Arthur to be dismissed.
Arthur nodded and Harry quit the room, closing the heavy doors behind him.
Katherine sank to her knees before her husband, her great gown of red and gold velvet ballooning around her. She took his hand in hers.
"I have a matter of great urgency to discuss with you."
Arthur looked down at his wife, his eyebrows raised in question. He wondered if perhaps she was about to tell him that she was with child, but thought it better not to ask, lest risk sullying her joyful mood.
"I have had the most wonderful realization," Katherine said, "The answer to all our questions and the very reason as to why we were joined together by God. It has been before our very eyes all along. Right under our noses the entire time. It's the only thing that makes sense!"
She was rambling, Arthur thought. Perhaps her grief had progressed into madness.

Katherine closed her eyes and shook her head in disbelief, breathing a laugh, "I cannot believe I did not see it sooner. God has had to test me again and again. He has had to push me to the very brink of despair for me to see it. But I have seen it now. I see it as clearly as I see you before me, my love."

"Katherine, please," Arthur said, removing his hand from hers and standing. She followed suit.

"What is this about? What has happened?" Arthur asked.

"Where I come from, a woman is worthy of the throne just as much as a man is. Princesses are not only brood mares to be married off to create alliances. They have the ability to reign in their own right! My mother, the great Isabella de Castille, ruled over Castille as Queen Regnant. My sister Juana was her successor. Where I come from girls *can* inherit their father's thrones!"

"What is your point, Katherine?" the king asked, raising a hand and pressing it to her forehead and cheek, "Are you unwell?"

Katherine shook her head and pulled away from him, grinning widely throughout, "No, Arthur. I am better than I have ever been. For I have finally received God's message!"

"*What* message?" Arthur asked, his blue eyes searching his wife's face.

Katherine sighed, "Don't you see? It is Mary," she said, "It has always been Mary. Our daughter. *She* will be your successor. It is why God led me to be your wife: to guide England into the future. Mary will be your heir, and England will finally see a woman upon the throne!"

Chapter 23

January 1526
Greenwich Palace, London

By now, all of England had heard of the king's plan to name his Flanders-born nephew, the son of a traitor, as his successor; and the people were not best pleased.

"There is public outcry in the northwest, Your Grace," Griffith informed his king gravely, his forehead creased with many additional lines to that of the constant one between his brows, "The people are petitioning against Henry Brandon *or* his brother to become your heir, and in Wales the crowds have gathered in Ludlow to protest against his arrival."

Arthur shook his head and exhaled, "I am thirty-nine and without a male heir. If England does not accept my nephew –"

"There will be c-civil unrest," Wyatt interrupted, "Your father's marriage to your mother ended the th-thirty-year War of the Roses within the country. They put an end to the c-conflict between cousins. If you do not leave the country to a successor that the p-people will accept, you face leaving the country in ruin. To return to war, cousin against cousin!"

"Surely, given enough time, the people will grow to accept the boy?" Harry Duke of York countered, leaning forward and resting his elbows on the council table.

The fire in the hearth behind them cracked loudly then, as though God Himself were present in the conversation, protesting to Harry's remark.

Arthur shook his head, "Wyatt is right," he said, more to himself that anyone else, "He has lived through the unrest of the Cousin's War, has more insight into the people's minds at the time than any of us do."

The king looked to Wyatt as if for confirmation, and the old man nodded his bald head once, his slack cheeks hanging as though the memory of such times was wearing him down even today.

Arthur inhaled deeply then and nodded his head. He had made his decision.

"Recall the boy from his kingly education," he said, addressing the Lord Chancellor Wolsey, who began furiously scribbling in his notes, "Reunite him with my sister and renege his title of Heir Apparent. He has no use for it anymore."

"And the family, my lord?" Wolsey asked, "Are they to return to Flanders?"

Arthur sighed deeply, as though to repress his nerves, "Send word to my sister that I wish to speak to her. I expect a private audience with her this evening."

"Your Grace," Mary Brandon said as she curtsied before Arthur later that day.

Her brother smiled and waved his hand, "Stop it, sister," he said before embracing her, and they both realised as they broke apart that they had never before held each other as adults.

Mary smiled tightly, "You wished to see me?"

"Sit," Arthur offered, turning to the loungers by the fire.

Mary did as she was asked, running her hands over the soft maroon seats.

"My husband and I are grateful to you, Arthur," she said, addressing the day's developments, "We are looking forward to having Henry back with us."

Arthur nodded, "Don't mention it," he said.

"No, truthfully, brother," Mary replied, "We did not wish for that life for our sons. It was not why Charles married me, to have a claim to the throne. He never wished for any of it."

"I understand."

"Do you?" Mary asked, searching her brother's face, "For so long we feared you questioned Charles' intentions by marrying me in secret. When our children were born, we wondered briefly if you would send spies to keep an eye on us. We purposefully didn't seek to educate them beyond the basic skills so that you would know we weren't pushing them towards anything –"

Arthur held up a hand, his eyebrows furrowed at her confession, "You thought all this? For so many years?"

Mary nodded, looking down at her hands resting on her lap.

"When we were banished, it was the happiest time of our lives," Mary recalled joyfully, "We had nothing but each other, but we were happy. But when we conceived...we prayed it would be a girl so that you would not think of him as a threat to Artie's throne, the way father had looked to his relatives."

Arthur thought back on their childhood, and the many people of the Plantagenet bloodline Henry VII had married off or sent to the block for being a potential threat to his throne, his wife's own cousin Teddy Plantagenet being one of them.

"I would never have done that," Arthur whispered, his eyes fixed on Mary's, "I am not like our father."

Mary hung her head once more, "I know that now," she said, "But at the time, we only wished to protect our children."

Arthur understood his sister's woes of course, the Tudor siblings having been brought up on tales of spilled blood in the name of the crown.

But Arthur had never felt the sting of paranoia quite as fiercely as their father had done, a man who had feared usurpers around every corner – no doubt because he himself had been one.

"This was why you wrote to Katherine that you'd had a girl," Arthur realised then, remembering the last letter exchanged between his wife and sister, many years ago.

Mary nodded, "A girl would have been safer. Girls do not inherit the throne."

Arthur nodded pensively, Katherine's epiphany contradicting that very tradition echoing within his mind as it had done every day since she had uttered it.

It had been two months since Katherine had shared her belief that it was God's will that their daughter Mary sit upon the throne as England's first Queen Regnant. Two months since she had animatedly explained that all her losses finally made sense. That Artie's death made sense...

It still did not make sense to Arthur, who – though he put on a brave face for the sake of his kingdom – was still grieving the tragic loss of his son, and likely always would.

And yet, the more time Arthur thought about it, the more he began to wonder if perhaps Katherine was right...

He had been shocked into silence at her suggestion at the time, had had to stop himself from laughing aloud at the idea. Never before had a *girl* successfully ruled over England. And the last time it had been suggested four centuries earlier when Henry I had named his only surviving child, his daughter Matilda, as his heir, the country had fallen into civil unrest for nineteen years due to the nobles' inability to accept a female as their ruler. But Katherine's reminder that her own mother *and* sister had ruled over Castille in their own right had struck a chord within Arthur, who had always looked to Spain for a more modern perspective on things.

England *was* behind in so many aspects. Arthur himself had dedicated his reign to furthering England's better understanding of medicine, arts and culture, to leading England towards the future, attempting to get on track with Europe's Renaissance.

But was England ready for *this*? Arthur was not sure.

"What do you think..." Arthur said then, choosing his words carefully and breaking the comfortable silence that had ensued, "...of the idea – and this is just hypothetical. But what would you say to the idea of a...female ruler?"

Mary raised her eyebrows, blinked, "A female ruler?"

"Yes, a Queen. A Queen...Regnant. Of England."

His sister only stared at him, her small mouth set tightly as she thought.

"You mean, for your heir? Instead of...my Henry," Mary asked.

Arthur nodded once, keeping his eyes fixed upon his youngest sibling so as not to miss a single fleeting reaction on her face.

Mary inhaled deeply as she thought, crossed and uncrossed her ankles as she fought to keep herself from smiling.

She could sense Arthur was holding his breath as he awaited her answer. But surely, he must already know what she would say.

Finally, after what felt like an age, Mary rose to her feet and crossed the space between them, the fire now behind her hiding her face slightly in shadow. She leaned down and pecked her older brother on the cheek, her eyes shining with pride and wonder at having been part to such a pivotal moment in England's history: the moment in which a King of England realised his daughter's worth.

"I think England is ready."

February 1526

Mary Brandon and her family had been reunited and granted a royal pardon despite Arthur's decision not to proclaim Henry Brandon his heir.

"You may remain in England if that is your wish," Arthur told the family upon their son's return, his sister smothering her eldest boy with kisses until he squirmed, embarrassed to be fawned over in public.

"As my sister I would grant you lands of your choosing and an annual allowance," the king proclaimed from his throne in the great hall, the courtiers mumbling approvingly at their monarch's generosity, glad to bear witness to the return of Good King Arthur.

"Alternatively, you may go back to your former life with the knowledge that you and yours are always welcome within my court."

Mary thanked her brother with a sincere smile, "Thank you, Your Grace," she said as she held little Henry before her in a loose embrace, "We will think on your generous offer."

The Brandons chose their former life outside of the public eye, their short stint at the centre of England's politics having cemented their wish to live a simple life. They did, however, accept Arthur's offer of an annual income as well as a small manor in the countryside just outside London, a residence to call their own if ever they were invited to visit England or attend an important event.

And thus, Katherine and Arthur bid farewell to Mary Brandon once more, this time with much less shedding of tears but a lot more love between them, the air having been cleared in a most unexpected way.

"A *girl*?!"

"The people won't –"

"Surely not!"

"Gentlemen!"

The king's Privy Council was up in arms, Arthur having that morning announced his decision to proclaim his daughter as his heir.

"You cannot expect England to agree to this, my lord," Wolsey was saying as he shook his head at his king, flabbergasted, "It has never happened before!"

Arthur turned to Wyatt, who was equally as flustered, "Wolsey is r-right, Your Grace! Women are not f-fit to rule!"

They continued to squabble as Griffith and Harry interjected on Arthur's behalf to try to quieten the older men, hands waving and spittle flying as they disagreed.

But in the end, it was Arthur's voice of authority that would ensure their silence, his firm tone notifying them all that his decision had been made. And there would be no changing it.

"My lords!" he called, allowing for a moment's pause until all eyes were on him, "I have reflected upon this day and night since it was brought to my attention. Trust me when I tell you that no amount of bickering and outdated doubt as to the people's acceptance of the Princess Mary will alter my fervent belief that England is ready for a Queen."

"But, my king –"

Arthur held up a hand to silence Wolsey, Harry smiling to himself to see the king and Wolsey in disagreement. Their growing discord would work in Harry's favour, given that he had just last night, during a private meeting with Arthur, broached the subject of the marriage between Henry Percy and Anne Boleyn. Such a union would normally need the king's consent due to Percy's highborn status – and had previously been denied by Wolsey – but if the king himself were to go over Wolsey's head and grant them permission to wed, Harry would rid himself of Anne Boleyn as well as bury any connection to her; therefore securing his promised position as the next Archbishop of Canterbury.

Harry was getting stirred up just thinking about it. More so than he had ever been during his private meetings with Anne.

"My daughter shall officially be declared my heir," Arthur was saying in response to Wolsey's interruption, "and Parliament will insert her as first in line of succession. Female or not. If, in the meantime, Queen Katherine bears me another son, he would automatically be placed ahead of Mary. But if that day should never come, my daughter shall be crowned upon my death, and as such, she should be taught to rule as any heir ought to."

Arthur looked around at his most trusted men, Wyatt continuing to shake his bald head, yet unconvinced that this path was the right one to take.

But Arthur had made his choice, and he was proud of his wife and sister for having shown him the light.

"Make arrangements for the Princess Mary to be sent to Ludlow to preside over the Prince's Council," Arthur ordered, to which Griffith began scribbling in his notes and Harry smirked to see the colour drain from Wolsey's face.

"No girl has ever been entrusted with this honour," Wolsey muttered, shooting a swift glance over at Wyatt who nodded his head at him in silent agreement.

Arthur noted the exchange but did not let it fluster him. Instead, he simply smiled.

"Then it's about time we make history, gentlemen."

May 1526

As part of her elevation to Heir Apparent to the King of England, ten-year-old Mary was called to return to London from her residence at Hunsdon House, to be officially titled as Princess of Wales – a title which had never before been granted to a female in her own right.

Mary had stood tall and elegant during the grand ceremony at Westminster, a cheerful yet modest smile playing on her lips throughout. The ceremony was one equivalent in splendour to that of Artie's own, showing the country that though Mary was a girl, she would be granted the same honours as her male counterparts.

The city of London celebrated widely, many gathering inside and around Westminster to bear witness to the young girl's investiture as Princess of Wales – an entirely unique moment in English history. And the people's acceptance of the princess came as a great surprise to Sir Henry Wyatt and Thomas Wolsey, the older men not having expected such eagerness from the public to one day be ruled by a woman.

"The p-people accept her," Wyatt stuttered dumbfounded as he, Wolsey, and Wolsey's new secretary, Thomas Cromwell, walked through the castle grounds the following day on their way to the great hall, "How can th-this be?"

Wolsey shrugged and shook his head, "All I care about now is returning to the king's good graces," he admitted, glancing over at Cromwell as though embarrassed to admit to such a thing in front of him.

"Let the girl be named heir," Wolsey hissed, "no doubt she will run the country into the ground when she is queen. But before that time comes, I wish only to improve my own circumstances. There's plenty of life left yet in our king, and I for one have bigger fish to fry at this present moment."

Wolsey's lip curled up in distaste as he thought of the Duke of York, who's mere existence confined Wolsey to mediocrity.

"So, you will support this?" Wyatt asked, his watery eyes wide.

They turned a corner and paused, not wanting to be overheard as two ladies walked past them.

Wolsey leaned closer to his colleague, so close Wyatt could smell his stale breath, "As I said, if it benefits me at present to appear in agreement, then that is what I'll do."

Wyatt stopped in his tracks and watched as Wolsey and Cromwell continued ahead and through the huge archway to the great hall, Wolsey plastering on a forced smile as he made his way inside. Wyatt shook his bald head and followed, disturbed by the lengths some people would go to, to attain the king's favour. Some of them going so far as to go against their own conscience and risk sullying their soul in exchange for earthly luxuries.

With Mary's new status, many changes would be made to the young girl's household and education to befit that of a would-be Prince.

Her governess, the Lady Bryan, was henceforth replaced with the princess' own godmother, the Countess of Salisbury Margaret Pole.

Margaret Pole was the only surviving daughter of George Plantagenet, who had been the brother of Arthur's grandfather, King Edward IV. She was the last of the pure Plantagenet bloodline and therefore of noble Yorkist blood but had been a loyal supporter of the Tudors for decades. She had been named Princess Mary's godmother upon her birth and had held her during her swift christening ten years prior. And she was honoured to be appointed as head of the princess' new household.

As well as a new governess, Mary was assigned many more tutors to accompany her to Ludlow to ensure she received an education befitting the king's heir – and though she had been given a much broader education as previous princesses already due to Katherine's introduction of Juan Luis Vives' influence in her teachings, Mary was now to be taught a wider curriculum which would include a deeper understanding of history, logic, oration and grammar, as well as Greek and Latin.

But there would be no more outdoor activities.

"No archery, no hawking and absolutely *no horse riding*!" Katherine of Aragon said as the princess' new household stood before their monarchs in the great hall.

Arthur nodded his head to emphasise this order from the queen.

"The Princess is never to go even *near* the stables, is that clear?" the queen asked as she eyed the servants, tutors and new ladies-in-waiting.

They all nodded or curtsied to show their understanding, the Lady Margaret Pole smiling up at her queen in the hope of reassuring her that her daughter would be in good hands.

June 1526
Ludlow, Wales

As the royal party made its slow ascent through the town of Ludlow and its bustling marketplace, curious onlookers began to gather, eager to sneak a peek at England's very first Princess of Wales in her own right.

The Princess Mary, equally as curious of her new surroundings as the people of Ludlow were of her arrival, looked out of the window of her carriage as dozens of enquiring faces searched the convoy for a sign of their beloved princess. As people caught sight of her and word spread through the crowd, many cheered and waved with delight.

Mary smiled and guardedly waved back at the crowd that had gathered, before becoming overwhelmed by their proximity and shrinking away from the open window, resuming her seat between her new ladies-in-waiting Cecily and Frances.

Margaret Pole, who sat on the opposite side of the carriage, smiled at her young ward.

"Never fear, princess," she said, Mary sensing a soothing tone in her voice, "The people are happy to see you."

Mary took another peek out the window and, noting the people's gentle smiles and joyful mumblings, she allowed herself to relax a little, wondering if her brother Artie had felt similarly as anxious when he had been sent to preside over the Prince's Council.

The memory of her beloved brother's loss stung in her chest then, the little princess not yet fully believing that this entire turn of events was not some elaborate and terrible nightmare. A guard rode up beside them then and announced that they would be approaching Ludlow Castle soon, and sure enough, within mere moments, they were approaching the magnificent palace. Mary stuck her head out the window and looked up at the tall, grey walls as they made their way through the gatehouse and to the vast outer bailey. The surroundings were considerable, containing stables, storehouses, and workshops, and Mary looked about herself in awe, her mouth hanging slightly open.

The princess' carriage came to a halt and as her ladies and her governess gathered up their fur blankets, they could hear commotion all around them as orders were being barked at servants and the guards dismounted their horses, their heavy boots thumping loudly upon the ground.

When Mary emerged from her wagon, she breathed in deeply and smiled; the air smelled cleaner here somehow.

"Come now, Mary," said her governess as the servants began heaving their trunks off the carriages, "Plenty of time to look around. Let me show you to your royal apartments."

They walked through a beautiful, arched entrance and made their way through the great hall and up a spiral staircase to the uppermost storey where the royal apartments were.

"These are your chambers, princess," Margaret Pole said as the guard standing sentry threw open the heavy wooden doors to a warmly decorated and open room.

They entered and Mary nodded approvingly as she took in the high ceilings and exquisite tapestries that hung on the walls. On the far wall was a great, four-poster bed with an upholstered seat at the foot of it. On the other side of the room was a magnificent stone carved fireplace, and Mary was relieved to see a roaring fire blazing within it.

As Mary soaked in her beautiful surroundings, she wondered briefly if her brother Artie had resided in these very rooms, which had now been assigned to her, and whether she should thank God for this incredible honour that had been bestowed onto her, or if she should resent Him for having taken her brother away.

Part VI

Trickery and treachery are the practices of fools
that have not wits enough to be honest

Chapter 24

2 years later

September 1528
Richmond Palace, Surrey

A lot had happened in the two years that followed. But not all of it had been good.

"The spread of the sickness continues, Your Grace," Harry informed his king, standing tall in his new robes befitting his latest advancement to Archbishop of York.

Arthur had granted his brother the prestigious title the previous year, Harry having continued to prove himself a most loyal servant of God and king.

It was not the coveted title of Archbishop of Canterbury – the most powerful station to hold within England, lesser only to the King and Queen themselves – for at seventy-two, William Warham was still very much the proud holder of that title.

But as Archbishop of York, Harry answered *only* to William Warham, giving Harry authority over other bishops – including Harry's former mentor Thomas Wolsey the Bishop of Lincoln.

And if Arthur were to stay true to his word – as Good King Arthur was known to do – Harry would undoubtedly be granted the position of Archbishop of Canterbury when the old man popped his clogs.

In private, Thomas Wolsey had not taken being overlooked yet again very well, and though he too continued on the rise within Arthur's court, it was at a much slower pace than the king's own brother. And Wolsey had just about had enough of that young man's smugness.

"How far?" Arthur asked now as Harry handed him a document.

He scanned the names on the page as he had done every day since the outbreak, a list containing hundreds of names. Hundreds of deaths.

"There are reports of fatalities all the way up to the north," Harry replied, "Though Scotland sends no reports of infected yet."

Arthur dropped the document into his lap and rubbed a hand over his tired face.

"If the spread continues for much longer, we will face a harsh winter," the Archbishop of York continued, "Farmers are dying. And their crops are left to perish."

Arthur nodded sombrely. There was nothing he or anyone could do.

He and Harry stood alone within the great hall of Richmond Palace, the only hope of avoiding infection being to remain as secluded as possible, for there had even been reports of infected within the king's own court, Queen Katherine's own lady, Anne Boleyn, being one of them. Luckily, or perhaps due to her new husband's title of Earl of Northumberland – Henry Percy having inherited the title from his late father the year before – she was able to procure a decent physician, aiding her to survive it.

"Any news on my heir?" the king asked then, looking up at the sound of the door opening in the distance.

Harry followed Arthur's gaze to find Griffith Rhys entering the hall, his footsteps echoing loudly in the empty rooms. He bowed his head in greeting and stopped a few feet at a distance from the Archbishop of York.

Harry nodded at Griffith in greeting, the two of them having developed a mutual respect for each other over the years, and turned back to the king.

"We have received word just this morning that the Princess Mary is well and showing no symptoms," Harry reassured his brother, "Her household has been greatly diminished since one of her servants succumbed to the illness last week, but the princess is continuing her studies secluded in her chambers."

Arthur nodded, "Good," he mumbled, "And what of the Princess Alice?"

Harry smiled, the birth of the new royal baby just three months earlier had been a blessed surprise to the whole country, it having been widely believed that at the age of forty-three Queen Katherine had been past her childbearing years long ago. But as it was, she had borne her lord husband one more healthy child, and she had brought light back into the king and queen's eyes following Artie's death, the two of them having managed to find their way back to each other.

"The princess is safe in Hatfield, brother," Harry reassured him, "There have been no reports of infection within her household. And your orders to maintain a rigorous routine of cleanliness are being followed, the servants scrubbing the walls and floors twice daily as you requested."

Arthur swallowed his anxiety and inhaled deeply before waving a hand to dismiss his brother.

Harry bowed at the waist and turned to leave, allowing Griffith a private audience with the king.

"What is it?" Arthur asked as soon as Harry had quit the room, his voice echoing slightly.

Griffith Rhys stood before his king, the permanent frown between his brows deeper than ever before, "I bring news of Wolsey in the west wing," he said, "He has been taken ill. Fevers, chills."

"He is infected."

Griffith nodded once, "We must make haste and move."

Arthur was up from his throne in a flash, "Send word to Katherine to pack. I wish to be gone within the hour."

"Where shall we go to this time, Your Highness?"

"Hampton Court Palace," Arthur replied, "The renovations will have to wait. It is the only area as yet to have no reports of the sweat. With any luck it shall be our last stop this summer."

October 1528
Greenwich Palace, London

But luck had not been on England's side, and the sweating sickness continued to take thousands more lives until the end of October, when it suddenly vanished just as quickly as it had appeared.

Much to Harry's quiet disappointment, Wolsey had survived, but a devastating total of fifteen thousand lives were lost in London alone, almost a third of the city's population, and several more hundreds of thousands throughout the rest of the country.

England would take years to recover, and Arthur made a mental note to increase the crown's charitable giving in the following months to come.

But by the grace of God, the royal family had come out unscathed, the king, queen, and both their daughters having survived the terrifying epidemic. Perhaps He had decided that they had already suffered enough.

With the sickness finally having ebbed, the royal court was able to return to Greenwich Palace in London, and Arthur was more eager than ever to return to normality.

Though he and Katherine had resided under the same roof as each move throughout the summer, they had isolated from one another in separate wings to ensure each other's safety. It had reminded him of the first few months of their marriage in Ludlow.

He smiled to recall those days, back when their whole lives had been ahead of them, before they had ever known real problems and real heartache.

But they were both in their early forties now, seasoned warriors to troubles and grief, the fine lines and wrinkles on their faces like a map of their arduous journey together. And he could hardly wait to be alone with her again and to trace those lines with his fingers, after many weeks apart.

But first, other matters needed attending. Matters which had needed the king's urgent attention for months, which had been left unresolved while England had faced the fiercest wave of the sweating sickness it had ever known.

Namely, the preparations for Princess Mary's wedding.

"Due to their young ages, a marriage by proxy shall take place to ensure the finalisation of the peace treaty with France," Arthur was saying, his council nodding along as he spoke, "Mary being my heir means some changes must be made to the contract, however. She can no longer be shipped off to France to take up her role as Queen Consort of France. Her primary place is here, in England, so that she may become Queen Regnant when the time comes."

He did not need to utter the words, for those closest to him knew of Arthur's mistrust of certain members of his council to stay true to their sworn oaths of fealty to his female heir. Wolsey and Wyatt had continued to show a dislike to Arthur's choice of successor, the two older men never going so far as to actually speak up on their distaste to be ruled by a woman, but making it very clear nonetheless, Arthur being able to pick up their subtle changes in attitude whenever the topic was broached. And he did not trust them to abstain from usurping Mary if she were to be out of sight in France with some distant male of royal blood when Arthur's time came. Not that he believed his time to be coming to an end any time soon, but he need only look back to the only other female to be named heir in English history – Henry I's daughter Empress Matilda – to know that men in power did not always stay true to their vows of fealty.

"King Francis won't like it," Griffith Rhys was saying with a heavy sigh, running a hand through his once-thick blond hair which now hung limply to one side in an attempt to mask his hair loss.

"He won't want to send *his* heir here to reside away from his country either," Rhys continued, "A wedding by proxy is fine but a marriage by proxy? A royal couple cannot be separated by land and sea if they wish to obtain heirs for their countries."

A chuckle escaped the new Archbishop of York, Harry swiftly shaking his head in apology.

"Griffith is right, brother," Harry said with only a trace of a smile remaining, "Our treaty with France may need to have some adjustments made to it."

"Such as?" the king asked, leaning back in his throne at the head of the table and stretching his long legs out before him, his knee having begun to ache of late if he sat down for too long. Growing older really was irksome.

Harry shrugged, "He has another son."

Arthur narrowed his eyes at his brother, "And what good is a second son to me?"

"Well, Your Grace, what good is Francis' first son to you?" Harry asked rhetorically, "An alliance with France will go ahead through marriage. Whether it be with the king's heir or his spare, you do not need to marry Mary off to a future king if she herself is to be the queen of her own country. All we need is a noble born Prince of France to sire heirs for England. And Francis would be a lot more willing to give up his spare to move to England permanently to conclude the marriage, rather than send the heir to *his* throne and have the important young man travelling the dangerous seas every month to copulate with our princess."

Only a brother to the king could have delivered the point in such a manner, Wolsey, Wyatt and Griffith looking away or raising an eyebrow at Harry's brashness.

Arthur stared Harry down for a moment with heavy eyelids, for though he did not like to hear Harry speaking so casually of Princess Mary's virtue, he knew him to be right in the grander scheme of things.

Francis, like Arthur, would not want to send his heir to England and away from *his* country, and an alternative option would have to be discussed without risking the alliance.

Arthur nodded to Harry, "Send word to Francis that we wish to discuss new terms," he said, "Do not mention your suggestion just yet. Let's see what Francis himself comes up with. But make it clear that Mary is not to venture to France. My heir is to remain in England. There will be no argument about it. Either his heir comes to us, or we consider another for Princess Mary." And Arthur's stomach lurched to see Wolsey and Wyatt exchanging a sly glance.

November 1528

"I feel a shift within the Privy Council which I no longer wish to entertain," Arthur was telling his two most trusted councillors, Griffith and Harry, one evening.
The three of them were sitting by the fire in the king's chambers, all three leaning forward with their forearms resting on their knees as they drank wine from silver cups, their faces illuminated by the crimson flames.

"Do you have anyone in mind who might replace them?" Griffith said, already knowing of what Arthur spoke, for his king's doubt as to Wolsey and Wyatt's loyalty had been a topic of private discussion for quite some time.

"What about Thomas More?" Harry said then before Arthur could speak, the thought suddenly springing to mind, "Forgive my interruption, brother, but More is a man of brilliant intellect, a lawyer by education but a humanist at heart. He has steadily been gaining respect among the nobles throughout the years for his speeches and humanistic writings. He has shown his loyalty to the crown and the true faith, giving up a career in law to pursue the life of a simple man of the church, at the risk of losing his father's inheritance I believe."

"More," Arthur replied, "Thomas More."
It wasn't a question, but Harry nodded.

"He aided you in your writing of the 'Defence of the Seven Sacraments', did he not?" Arthur asked, scratching pensively at his chin, his red stubble now sporting patches of white.

"He did," Harry replied, "And he is a competent spokesman and general patron of the poor."

Arthur was nodding along, having heard nothing but good things about the man in recent years, his known literary works befitting that of an intellectual who fraternised with leading European Renaissance humanists. And Harry's enthusiasm at the mention of him did not go unnoticed.

He was precisely the kind of man Arthur wished to have within his council.

"Send word that I wish to have a private audience with him," the king said, "With such high praise from you I can only imagine he is a man worth meeting with, at least."

Harry grinned then, scooting forward in his seat and licking his lips excitedly at the prospect of booting Wolsey out of office, "Which one will he replace?"

Thomas More was not a man who chased fame and glory, but when he was approached by the new Archbishop of York with a proposition to replace a bad apple within the Privy Council, More saw this as the perfect opportunity to do good on a grander scale. Advising the King of England himself was a most noble and sought-after opportunity, especially when he and the king appeared to agree on so much.

"I was most pleased with your decision to name your daughter as your heir, Your Grace," Thomas More said during a private meeting with the king, "England is following in the footsteps of the great countries of Europe, not only in open-mindedness as to the equality in gender but also in medicine, arts and economy. I am glad to be alive during a time such as this, to bear witness to such a great king."

Arthur was not keen on the flattery, never having been comfortable with it, and he let it slide over him like water off a duck's back for now, choosing only to focus on More's mention of his daughter.

"You do believe then, that a woman may rule a country as well as a man?" Arthur asked, glad to have found what appeared to be a perfect replacement for the old Henry Wyatt and his archaic views.

More nodded as he stood before the king in his simple brown robes, such a great contrast to Harry's own expensive red mantles.

"With the right guidance, a woman is just as capable as a man," More said enthusiastically, "Just as yourself, my king, the princess will have a carefully selected council to guide her. It is no different to your own reign or that of your father's and any other king that came before. She is the daughter of Good King Arthur! I have no doubt Princess Mary shall one day be an excellent queen."

It was what the king had wanted to hear, but Arthur had sensed a genuineness in the man's words. He had not simply said what he had thought the king had wanted to hear, as Wyatt and Wolsey so often did of late. *Their* growing dislike of a girl as the king's heir was so strong it was almost a palpable thing during council meetings, and it was not the atmosphere Arthur wished for from his advisors.

And this Thomas More. Well, he was like a breath of fresh air.

December 1528

By the Christmastide, Arthur had requested that the old Sir Henry Wyatt retire from his position. No reason was given, only a heartfelt thanks for his long service to the crown, and compensation of an annual pay to see him through until the end of his life – which, judging by the man's old age of sixty-eight, would likely not be too long.

Wyatt took the decision as well as would be expected, grumbling as he exited the king's chambers that England would likely face ruin under the rule of a woman. And it was exactly what Arthur had needed to hear, being more certain than ever that he had done the right thing in replacing him.

Wolsey had watched Wyatt's exit with a wide-eyed disbelief, turning slowly back to face his king when the door had closed behind the old man, and offering Arthur an unsure smile.

Arthur hoped this act would be enough to remind Wolsey who was in charge, for – despite his and Harry's unspoken tête-à-tête – Arthur sincerely hoped to keep his Lord Chancellor, Wolsey's advice and connections being of great value to the crown.

But when Arthur spotted Wolsey looking about himself sheepishly, he only hoped that he was not making a grave mistake in allowing Wolsey to keep his position of power within his council.

February 1529

"Now, promise me you will listen to all I have to say before you respond."

It was early afternoon and Arthur and Katherine were walking leisurely through the palace gardens while there was a break in the weather. The thick grey clouds had parted earlier in the day, allowing for a ray of sunshine to peek through after the rain had been a constant and depressing downpour since the Christmas festivities two months prior.

Katherine looked up at her husband and clenched her jaw, already knowing that she would not like whatever news he brought, the topic of Mary's betrothal to a Prince of France having been one she had disliked from the first moment it had been uttered. She would have much preferred for Mary to marry into her Spanish family.

"Following our announcement that we would not send Mary overseas, Francis I has since also refused to send the Dauphin to England to conclude our treaty," Arthur said carefully as he continued to walk slowly beside Katherine.

Katherine nodded and tightened the furs around her shoulders, perhaps there was hope for an alliance with her country of birth after all.

"The possibility of Mary therefore becoming engaged to his second son, Henri D' Orleans, was suggested by Harry."

Perhaps not. Katherine continued only to listen.

"But Francis I has replied with his own suggestion," Arthur said, his eyebrows bunching together slightly, "His suggestion being that *he* take Mary as his bride instead."

Katherine stopped walking. She cocked her head to one side and narrowed her eyes as she watched Arthur. When he did not speak further, Katherine clenched her teeth once again. France…

"May I speak?" she asked.

"I already know what you will say," Arthur said, raising his eyebrows.

"Then why am I even here?" she asked, before turning around and heading back towards the castle.

"Katherine," Arthur called after her with a chuckle.

She stopped and half turned.

"I wished only to inform you of all the developments," the king said, taking her hand in his and pulling her gently back onto the gravelled path in the gardens.

"Though, it is not unheard of," Arthur was saying, "Francis I is but thirty-five, not much older than James IV of Scotland was when he and my sister Margaret wed."

Katherine *tutted*, "But we do not wish uncertainty for Mary."

"No," Arthur agreed before raising his gaze to the darkening sky.

"And Francis is not the only option."

"Which is why an answer has already been dispatched," Arthur said, smiling down at his wife, "If not the Dauphin, then Henri D' Orleans, or no one."

Katherine tugged lightly on Arthur's hand and reached up to peck him on the cheek.

"You're a good father, Arthur," she told him, grateful to have him by her side.

March 1529

"France is threatening to break off the alliance altogether." It was the last thing Arthur had wanted to hear.

"Break it off?" he asked, rising from his throne, dumbfounded, "What has brought this on?"

"Francis I is unwilling to put forth his second son for the union between England and France. Henri D' Orleans is to be betrothed to Catherine de Medici, arranged by her own uncle, Pope Clement VII, and Francis would not wish to insult the Pope in such a manner."

Arthur sat back down slowly, "No, of course not," he agreed as he thought, "Has he come back with a counteroffer?"

"Francis I reiterates that the options remain himself or his eldest son, the Dauphin," Wolsey continued, "He urges you to consider his terms carefully before responding, as he does not wish to continue this back and forth any longer."

Arthur nodded for Wolsey to continue.

"He proposes that if you choose to maintain the original plan of a marriage between our princess and the Dauphin, that Francis I would allow the Dauphin to make the relocation to England in three years' time when he has reached his fourteenth year."

"He has agreed to send the Dauphin?"

Wolsey raised his eyebrows and continued reading the letter from the French ambassador, "Only under the condition that the Dauphin then return to France by his eighteenth year, whether their union has produced an heir or not. What should follow is to be reassessed when the time comes," he folded the letter in half and passed it to the king.

Arthur reached over to take the letter. He inhaled deeply as he stared at the document, then let his breath out slowly before replying.

"Send word that England agrees to France's terms," he said, "As long as our peace with France is maintained and my successor remains in England for the time being, I am happy to oblige to this proposition. Time is of the essence, and the sooner England is on its path toward the future generation, the better."

May 1529

"There is talk that the Pope is to make the Duke of York a Cardinal."

At first, the news stunned Wolsey. His expression froze entirely, then his ears began to ring eerily. A high pitched crescendo, as though a mosquito was hovering closer and closer before embedding itself inside his brain. And then, as his mind digested the information, it felt like a cold slap to the face.

"Cardinal," Wolsey echoed to make sure he hadn't misheard.

His informant nodded before bowing once, twice, three times in quick succession as he quit the room backwards.

Wolsey stared straight ahead, the cup of wine in his hand beginning to shake as the anger boiled inside him.

This simply would not do!

Chapter 25

June 1529

Princess Mary was to return to London after having spent the last three years presiding over the Prince's Council in Ludlow – which, in Mary's opinion, really ought to be renamed the Heir's Council.

During that time, the princess had learned a thing or two about what it meant to rule, her father having made sure to give her the best tutors in the country, many of which had previously taught her late brother. She did, however, miss the more entertaining side of her royal education, horse riding, hunting and hawking having been deemed too dangerous for the king's heir after what had happened to Artie.

She understood her parents' decision, of course. They could not risk losing another child to a reckless accident.

But now that she was to return to London to be married by proxy, Mary was hopeful that fun may yet return to her daily life, court always being that much more entertaining, with many festivities, events, and banquets being organised for most evenings.

She may not be allowed to partake in any activities herself, but to simply be back within the court atmosphere was enough for the young princess, and she could hardly wait to sit underneath the canopy with her royal mother and father, watching a joust or a play together.

It was these events that Mary was choosing to focus on during her journey back to London. Anything to keep from thinking of her proxy wedding.

At the age of thirteen, she and her betrothed the Dauphin of France – who was just eleven – were not old enough to be officially married to one another. But like many noble marriages where the two individuals are in separate countries, a proxy wedding – where a gentleman of noble birth would stand-in for the young Prince of France during a wedding ceremony to Mary – was essential to secure the alliance made between two nations. It was completely natural. A totally standard procedure for royal children of the period. And yet, Mary couldn't help but feel anxious about it.

"You won't even need to touch the man," her governess the Countess of Salisbury Margaret Pole had said when the invitation to court for the event had come some days earlier.

"It is no more than a legally binding ceremony, a promise to France that the Princess of England shall wed no other in the years before the official marriage," she explained, though Mary already knew, "You will not need to kiss or dance or consummate with this proxy. He is no more than a puppet, a symbol, to represent the Dauphin in his stead. Much like at your betrothal where the Lord Admiral of France presented you with a ring. Do not fret."

But it did little to settle Mary's nerves, it being a grand event where all eyes would be on the young princess for the first time since her move to Ludlow, where she would be judged for her elegance, grace and beauty.

And though Mary had no doubt she had perfected her stance and demeanour, she was not too arrogant to know that beauty was not one of her attributes.

She had inherited her mother's pale skin and her father's auburn hair. Her mother's pale blue eyes and her father's straight nose and thin lips. Nothing about her looks necessarily screamed ugliness. But her features were bland and expressionless at the best of times, having completely failed to inherit her mother's warmth or her father's quiet charm. And she often wondered what her betrothed would think of her upon their meeting in the not too distant future.

Upon her arrival at Greenwich Palace, Mary was met with a cheerful fanfare, dozens of courtiers having gathered to welcome their princess home, some clapping, some merely grinning and craning their necks to catch a glimpse of her.

But Mary had made an immediate beeline towards her mother and father, who had stood at the entrance of the courtyard, ready to welcome their daughter home after three years apart. She was met with such a warm welcome – a long embrace from her mother and a proud nod of his head and squeeze of her hand from her father – that Mary almost forgot about her insecurities, feeling merely overjoyed to be home.

Later that night, after the first of many banquets organized for the coming week was cleared and the court had retreated to their quarters, Mary and her parents were enjoying a moment alone in the queen's chambers playing cards.

"How go your studies?" her mother asked Mary in Spanish, catching her off guard, a playful smile tugging on her lips.

"*Muy bien, mamá*," Mary replied with a smug smirk, having perfected her Spanish many years ago, "And you will be pleased to know that my Latin and French are of equal ability."

Katherine nodded her head in approval, before laying down a card and picking another from the deck.

They played on in silence for a while, Mary losing a round and frustratedly shuffling the deck for a rematch.

She had just dealt out the cards and fanned hers out in her hand when she looked across the table at her mother.

"What if the Dauphin finds me dull?" Mary asked her mother suddenly, unable to contain her worries any longer.

Katherine looked up from her cards, furrowing her brows, "Finds you dull?" she repeated, unsure she had heard right.

Mary pressed her thin lips together as Katherine looked over to her husband, who had been sitting on the lounger by the fire reading the Bible.

Arthur looked up from the book in his hands and raised his eyebrows to his wife.

"Why would he find you dull?" Katherine asked, turning back to Mary.

Mary only shrugged, did not meet her mother's gaze.

Katherine put down her cards and *tutted*, "You are not to meet the Dauphin yet," Katherine reassured.

"But when I do," Mary replied, "I am not…" she left the revelation unspoken.

Katherine looked back at Arthur, who's expression was one of saddened empathy. He knew this unspoken feeling all too well. Well enough to notice it in his own child when he had battled with the same question of self-worth for most of his childhood and adolescence. Katherine confirmed his realisation with a tight-lipped smile, the look in her eyes a mixture of nostalgia and sympathy.

"You are a young girl in the process of blossoming, Mary," Katherine assured their daughter from across the small games table, "A budding rose only just beginning to bloom. You are a terrible card player," Katherine jested, "but you are not dull."

Mary smiled at that, and her mother reached over and squeezed her hand.

"Give yourself time to flourish, my princess," Katherine added, before looking over at Arthur, who was observing the touching moment, "We were all unsure of ourselves at your age. Trust me."

Mary followed her mother's gaze and frowned, "You, Father?" she asked in surprise.

Arthur closed the bible and sat up, "Growing up is no easy task," he said, trying to sound as though he could hardly remember, though his teenage awkwardness still haunted him from time to time.

He stood up and walked towards them, "But believe me when I tell you, Mary," he said before taking her chin in his hand and looking into her pale blue eyes, "When the time comes for you to meet your betrothed, in no time at all, he will learn just how wonderful you are."

September 1529

Katherine's lady-in-waiting Anne Boleyn was rather useless of late, her belly great with child impeding her from doing the most basic of tasks.

Following Anne and Henry Percy's simple wedding – approved by the king himself, much to Wolsey's chagrin – they had wasted no time in conceiving child after child, the young woman proving to be just as fertile as her sister Mary Boleyn, who had retired to the country to care for her many children following the death of her husband William Carey during the outbreak of the sweating sickness the year before. But Anne did not wish to retire to the country, for not only was she the queen's favourite, but court life was far too entertaining to give up; especially now that she was the wife of the Earl of Northumberland, Henry Percy inheriting his father's title upon his death in 1527.

The Boleyn family was on the rise within the English court, and though her sister Mary preferred the quieter life, Anne was more than happy to continue serving her king and queen. But this pregnancy was proving to be more difficult than the previous two, and though Anne was but six months along, she could hardly lace up the queen's corset without getting out of breath.

"Sit down, Lady Anne," Queen Katherine said over her shoulder.

Even after two years, Anne still felt a thrill every time she was styled as 'Lady', having earned the title through her prestigious marriage to an Earl.

"You are no good to me if you work yourself too hard," Katherine said, swatting Anne away gently and turning to Agnes to continue dressing her.

Anne smiled in thanks and took a seat on the lounger, "Thank you, Your Grace," she said, "This child is carrying much heavier than I am used to."

Katherine observed the younger lady with a careful gaze, "Do you feel him moving each day?" she asked, her own experiences of loss having made her more aware than others of the warning signs.

But Anne nodded, rubbing a hand over her bump, "Oh yes, he kicks each night when I am ready to fall asleep."

Katherine breathed a knowing laugh, then gasped as Agnes pulled the corset tightly.

"Not too tight, Agnes!" Katherine scolded the older lady, frowning at her over her shoulder, "I plan to breathe today."

Anne and Katherine shared a smile, Katherine shaking her head lightly in mock disbelief.

"I'd wager this is one thing you do not miss," Katherine admitted light-heartedly to the Lady Anne, hoping to make her feel better about her strained pregnancy.

Later, as Katherine and her ladies were headed towards the great hall, which had been lavishly decorated in preparation for Princess Mary's proxy wedding, Anne suddenly felt a pang of nervousness, much as she often did at the prospect of being confined to the same space as Harry. Though Anne was happily married to the man she loved more than any other, she sometimes caught herself thinking of those forbidden meetings she and Harry had shared. He had awakened something inside her which she had yet to experience with her beloved husband, a sense of carnal danger that caused the heart to beat out of sync.

She smiled to herself just thinking about it. And though the path that included Harry was now firmly closed to her, she could not help but sometimes wonder what might have been. But she pushed the thoughts out of her mind. Lust did not trump love, and Anne had achieved what she had hoped to with their strange affair; as well as maintained her virtue for her wedding night to Henry Percy due to her carefully chosen celibate lover.

In hindsight, she could not have planned it any better.

*

Princess Mary stood beside her proxy betrothed, the French Ambassador Antoine de Castlenau, as Bishop Fisher performed the ceremony. Ambassador Castlenau was older than she had imagined, his great, grey beard concealing the entire bottom half of his face as well as his neck and part of his chest.

It made her think of other, less fortunate princesses, who were so often married off to men much older than them, when they themselves were young enough to be their new husband's daughter or granddaughter.

She shuddered to think of it and said a silent thank you to her parents for having arranged for her to marry a boy almost the same age as she.

Her royal mother and father sat proudly upon their thrones throughout the short ceremony, Fisher the Bishop of Rochester mumbling the Latin words of ritual as she and the many courtiers in attendance listened in silence.

As she stood perfectly still beside the proxy, Mary felt suddenly silly to have voiced her worries about being found too dull by her future husband. As her mother had reminded her, not only would they not meet for another two years, but – as this ceremony reminded her – their union was not one of love or intrigue into one another's soul, but of political means; and one which she would not allow herself to romanticise.

She snuck a peek at her mother, who caught her eye and smiled before raising her eyebrows, wordlessly urging her to pay attention. While it was true that her parents had found love in each other despite their marriage, too, having been one of political unity, Mary was no fool. She understood the rarity of their fortunate situation.

They were two kindred souls, no doubt destined to have found one another.

But she felt no such fantasy about her own marriage. After all, how likely would it be that she, too, would find such complete marital bliss. This proxy wedding was the first step in unifying England and France, and when the time came for her to marry her betrothed for real, Mary would not dare to utter even a single word of doubt about it. She would do her duty, as was instilled in her from an early age, and provide England with the next Tudor generation.

That was all her union to the Dauphin of France would be. A diplomatic merger of two strangers for the greater outcome of their countries. And if God was good, Mary would soon be the proud mother of the next King – or Queen – of England and France.

October 1529

Thomas Wolsey had been gracious for far too long.

Word had now spread throughout the court that the king's brother – the very man the king had once banished from court for his disloyalty and abuse of power – was to be made a Cardinal. Archbishop of Canterbury be damned! *Cardinal* was an even higher position! Granted by the Pope himself!

Wolsey shook his head in frustration to think how far he might have climbed were it not for the Duke of York's spoiled self existing.

For too long had Wolsey stood by and watched as the entitled and smug brother to the king got handed every title that should have been *his,* on a silver platter.

Wolsey had worked hard to get to where he was, had clawed his way up from *nothing*! A butcher's boy! He had the smarts and the drive to achieve greatness – and would have done, too, if the Duke of York – his own former *apprentice* – hadn't come along.

But who was he kidding? No one could compete with one of such tight royal connections. No matter *what* Wolsey were to do, say, or achieve, Harry would always come out on top.
But no more.

"The Archbishop of York," Wolsey's servant announced before moving aside to allow Harry to enter.

Wolsey rose from his seat by the fire and plastered on a smile.

"Ah, Harry!" Wolsey called in feigned delight, "I am honoured you found the time to join me this evening."

"Your invitation intrigued me," Harry admitted, choosing to maintain at a distance for now, not yet fully convinced that he would remain for supper as Wolsey had requested in his invitation.

"Was there a particular reason you wished to see me?" the younger of the two men of the church asked.

Wolsey dropped his gaze as he nodded, hoping Harry could not sense the seething hatred that emanated from him.

"I believe congratulations are in order," he said, "No doubt the Pope will make his official announcement soon?"

Harry couldn't help but smirk. He disguised it quickly by clearing his throat, but not quickly enough.

Wolsey's chest tightened with loathing, and he wanted for nothing more than to rip the heavy gold cross from around Harry's neck, preferably drawing blood.

"Please," he said instead, gesturing to the table beside him. Harry eyed the empty silver plates and cups suspiciously when the door behind him opened and a handful of servants entered carrying many fine dishes.

"Won't you join me?" Wolsey asked, taking a seat at the head of the small rectangular table.

The servants placed the trays of food down, bowed their heads and left, closing the door behind them.

"You serve yourself?" Harry asked as he watched Wolsey spooning food onto his plate. He approached the table and pulled out the seat opposite Wolsey.

Wolsey shrugged, "What's a little humility?"

Harry did not reply, opting instead to take heed of which dishes the older man chose and making sure to select only from those same trays.

"Wine, Cardinal?" Wolsey offered, holding up a silver jug.

Harry breathed a laugh, "That is a little premature, is it not?"

"What?" Wolsey replied naively, setting down the jug of wine at Harry's lack of an answer, "I would have thought you would appreciate my admitted defeat."

Harry's eyebrows twitched as he took a careful bite of his food.

"You and I have long seen the other as healthy rivals," Wolsey admitted before taking a long reassuring sip of his wine, "This is but my humble way of declaring to you that you have come out the victor."

Harry noted Wolsey's long pull of his wine and nodded toward the silver jug. Wolsey passed him it with a friendly smile.

Harry watched his host carefully as he poured himself a cup, allowing Wolsey's confession to hang between them.

Wolsey only kept on eating in the silence, not once lifting his gaze to watch Harry pour his drink. And Harry allowed himself to relax.

"I appreciate the gesture," Harry admitted finally, placing the near-empty jug of wine down between them, "And I wish to extend my own."

"Oh?" Wolsey said, looking up as Harry lifted his cup.

Harry took a small sip, then smacked his lips and raised his eyebrows in appreciation of the fine wine. Wolsey nodded his head once in simple thanks.

"Yes, well," Harry said, picking at the sweetmeats on his plate, "I would be lying if I did not enjoy surpassing you."

Wolsey did not respond and instead focused on chewing the food in his mouth slowly.

"And I am not too proud to admit that I know my connections have led me this far," Harry said, unable to meet the older man's eyes as he spoke.

Wolsey allowed the revelation to linger in the air, glad to have heard it come directly from his opponent's mouth. The validation of his anger felt good. But it did nothing to quash the hatred he felt towards the man.

Wolsey raised his cup, "To confessions," he said, meeting Harry's gaze from across the table.

The younger man lifted his own cup and smiled before the two of them brought the cups to their lips. Wolsey finished his in one gulp and immediately refilled it.

"Reginald!" Wolsey called then, to which the doors to his chamber opened and his servant entered carrying another silver jug of wine.

The young boy locked eyes with Wolsey for no more than a second before nodding ever so slightly and placing the full jug of wine beside the empty one and taking it away.

"So, Harry," Wolsey said as he popped a lump of cheese in his mouth, "With your future title of Cardinal looming, how do you feel about the king's offer to make you the future Archbishop of Canterbury? With a step above that title as Cardinal, I should say Archbishop of Canterbury ought to fall to another?"

"You, you mean," Harry replied, wiping his mouth with the back of his hand.

Wolsey spread his hands and shrugged as if to say *of course*.

Harry sighed and took another swig of wine, raising the cup to empty it completely, then reached for the new jug to refill it.

"Why would I simply hand you the honour?" he asked.

Wolsey couldn't help but smile, "You wouldn't," he said, not at all surprised at the greedy man's answer.

"Would you? If you were in my position?" Harry countered before placing the jug of wine down with a low thump.

Wolsey's heart was beating wildly in his chest, and he breathed in deeply to try to disguise his agitation.

He pretended to consider the question for a moment, hoping to gain time as well as to allow Harry to finish what would be his final meal.

After all, it was the least he could do.

"I would like to think that I would," Wolsey said eventually, not even he believing his own words.

Harry scoffed as he picked a piece of meat from between his teeth with his fingernail.

"Well, you and I are different creatures it seems. I am sorry," Harry said.

Wolsey digested the apology and found it tasted insincere.

He shrugged his shoulders and, having finished his plate, leaned back against his chair and folded his hands over his belly as he observed the younger man.

Harry took one last mouthful and chewed in silence, then picked up his cup of the excellent wine and washed the meal down with one long pull.

And Wolsey could not help but stare wide-eyed as he did so, his body coming forward slightly as Harry lifted the cup and emptied it in one.

"A splendid feast, Wolsey," Harry said then before slamming his hands down in appreciation and rising from his seat, "What a shame it has taken us this long to show one another our true colours. But the game has been an entertaining one."

Wolsey pressed his lips together to keep from laughing, the poor fool had no idea just how dark Wolsey's colours ran.

"Yes," he agreed half-heartedly, knowing that it was now only a matter of hours before all his troubles were behind him, "You have been an excellent opponent."

Harry flashed Wolsey a grin as he turned to leave, one which assured Wolsey that the younger man had absolutely no idea that he had just lost.

Chapter 26

The following day, a Sunday, the king and queen were attending mass when suddenly quick and heavy footsteps disturbed their calm, and a dishevelled servant came running through the open doors of the chapel.

Such a blasphemous interruption could only mean terrible news, and Arthur was on his feet in one fluid motion despite his bad knee screaming in protest at the quick movement.

"My king!" the servant called, collapsing to his knees before Arthur, his hands clasped together as if in prayer, "Forgive me, sire!" he sobbed, "I found him that way. I found him – I had nothing to do with it!"

"Nothing to do with what?" Katherine called from behind them, having risen from the altar a moment after Arthur, her brows frowned in alert confusion.

"Found who?" Arthur urged the man.

"The Archbishop of York," the servant sobbed, his head hanging and his clasped hands shaking over his head, "Your brother, Your Grace. He is dead."

In his haste, Arthur's shoulder crashed into the open doorframe to Harry's bedchambers, the crowd that had gathered having parted at their king's hurried arrival down the long corridor.

"Harry—" he had begun to call, but the name died on his lips at the sight of his brother's body on the bed.

Lying on his back still in his robes, Harry stared up at the ceiling glassy-eyed, a white foamy substance dribbling from his slightly open mouth.

"No, no, no," Arthur mumbled desperately, reaching for his brother and holding his upper body in his arms.

A sharp gasp sounded behind him then which Arthur knew, even without looking, to have come from Katherine.

At the gruesome sight, the Queen covered her mouth with her hand, unable to tear her eyes away from the terrible scene before her. One of Harry's arms hung limply as Arthur shook him in vain, the other by his neck as though he had been clawing at it in his last moment before death.

There was foul play at hand here.

"Guards! Clear the area!" Katherine called then, to which the soldiers keeping the crowd at bay began to push them further back.

"You two, secure the door," Katherine commanded two guards, "Do not let anyone inside. *No one*, do you understand?"

The men nodded their helmeted heads.

"Come, Arthur," she coaxed her husband, taking hold of his arm. Arthur swallowed his horror and lay Harry back down where he'd found him.

With one last look at his brother, Arthur and Katherine exited his chambers, the guard shutting the door behind them and blocking it as their queen had ordered.

Katherine flashed Arthur a loaded look as they accelerated away and towards the great hall, both of them disturbingly aware that a murder had taken place within the safety of their castle.

"Everyone out!" Arthur ordered as he and his queen entered the great hall.

Dozens of surprised courtiers, who had not yet heard of the latest gossip, rose from their seats at games tables or by the windows and hurried out the main doorways, their king and queen rushing against the crowd as they headed towards their thrones.

"We must send riders to the princesses' residences," Katherine mumbled as they watched the last of the courtiers exiting the hall, "Until we know if this was a singular attack, none of us are safe."

Arthur only nodded, his jaw clenched as he worked to control his anger, shock, and pain.

Katherine tore her gaze away from her husband as the Privy Council members rushed into the room, followed by two guards who stood before the closed wooden doors, their halberds crossed before it.

The castle was on high alert.

"Gentlemen," Arthur called, "There has been an attack on the royal family," he said, his voice cracking ever so slightly to think of his younger brother lying dead in his bed. He cleared his throat as he looked down at Wolsey, Griffith and Thomas More.

"My brother, the Archbishop of York, has been slain."

"Slain?" Wolsey spluttered.

Arthur cast his eyes over his advisors, could he trust them?

"Until the culprit is found, the queen and I shall remain here," Arthur declared as he looked to Katherine, who nodded her agreement, "More, send guards to check on the princesses' well-being at their residences. We must know if –"

"Leave it with me, Your Grace," Thomas More interrupted, though Arthur was glad not to have to finish the sentence.

"Griffith, double security around the castle," the king continued, "Whoever did this might still be within its confines."

Griffith bowed and turned to leave.

"Inform Dr Butts that he is needed in the Archbishop of York's chambers, Wolsey," Katherine added, "If someone did this to the king's brother, he will be found."

Wolsey bowed deeply at the waist before retreating from the great hall, cursing Harry for being able to cause him problems even in death.

Monkshood was a beautiful yet highly poisonous flower found in most gardens in the southern parts of England.

The royal gardens were of course cleared of any trace of the deadly plant, but it didn't take travelling far to find the purple flower growing in the wild.

Wolsey had chosen it purely for its befitting name, Monkshood being named as such due to its resemblance to a hood worn by monks. The irony that this plant would be his greatest clerical enemy's downfall had not escaped him, and at the time that he was hatching his plan Wolsey had chuckled to himself for his wit.

According to the esteemed father of botany William Turner, Monkshood served, in small doses, as medicine against gout. But in doses even slightly too high, it was recorded to have caused diarrhoea, vomiting, and for patients' hearts to beat out of rhythm before collapsing to their deaths.

The latter side effect had been Wolsey's desired outcome for his nemesis. A death which, following their lavish feast and Harry's taste of that second, tainted jug of wine, would have occurred in the late hours of the night, preferably in his sleep, so that when he was found there would have been shock and sadness at his untimely demise.

But Harry – continuing to be a thorn in Wolsey's side even in death – just *had* to go and choke on his own vomit instead.

And now the castle was on lockdown and the king and queen on the lookout for a murderer.

Him.

Wolsey knew that it would not take the king long to learn who Harry had spent his final evening with – the same man who would be the only one to benefit from Harry's demise.

Thomas Wolsey breathed a shaky sigh, had he just signed his own death warrant?

"Poisoned?" Arthur whispered sharply back at Dr Butts following the old man's examination of the body.

The body.

Harry, son of a king, brother to a king, respected member of the clergy and future Cardinal and Archbishop of Canterbury, had not been dead half a day and already he was reduced to no more than his fleshy form.

Dr Butts nodded, "The body had tried to eject the offending toxin and would likely have succeeded if the Archbishop of York had not been lying on his back. Alas he choked on his own vomit."

"But it was murder?" Katherine pressed, craning her neck over the physician's head at the sound of the heavy doors to the great hall opening and Thomas More returning with news about Mary and Alice.

Dr Butts nodded again, "The yellowing of the fingernails would suggest as much."

Arthur and Katherine shared a look, then the king dismissed the physician as More bowed his head in a quick greeting.

"The princesses are both well and in good spirits," he announced, and relief washed over the royal parents, "The Princess Mary sends her warmest regards and sympathies."

"So Harry was targeted," Arthur mumbled under his breath, running a hand over his stubbly chin.

Katherine, having been near enough to hear him, reached over and rested her hand on his forearm, "We will find the one responsible, my king," she promised passionately, her eyes blazing with tormented determination, "They will be punished."

Arthur stole a glance at Thomas More before them and then back to his wife, unsure if to speak his mind would be the best course of action.

"More," Arthur called instead, "What are your thoughts? You have known Harry a long time."

"I have," the humble advisor admitted.

"And so? Did my brother offend within the clergy? Did he have enemies?"

More licked his lips, wrung his hands together, "My Lord, I do believe you know –"

"Your Grace!" a guard called then as he burst through the doors, "Your Highnesses! We could not stop him. He has fled the castle on horseback."

"Who?!" Katherine asked, rising from her throne, her anger at this attack on the monarchy overriding even Arthur's.

The king and Thomas More shared a knowing look, "Wolsey," they said, Arthur's more in question, still partly unable to believe what was right in front of him.

But then the guard nodded his head in confirmation.

Thomas Wolsey, Lord Chancellor to the King of England, had not gotten far from London before being caught and arrested by the King's Guard, a blubbering confession falling from his lips like blood gushing from an artery.

"What is to be done with him?" Griffith asked the following day, "This is the most despicable of treasons. To outrightly target the royal family!"

Arthur inhaled deeply to calm his temper.

He had lost many throughout the years: a father, a mother, a grandmother, siblings in infancy, a son, a daughter and countless unborn children.

But this loss was different. This had been malicious. A violent act against his family for the sole purpose of – what? Wolsey's own advancements? Jealousy? Both?

Had Arthur not bestowed enough recognition upon him? He had made him Lord Chancellor, the highest political position available within England! And he who had come from nothing – a mere son of a butcher! He should have been glad Arthur hadn't let him go years ago.

Perhaps he should have done; kept Wyatt instead of him…perhaps then, Harry would still be alive.

Arthur cleared his throat as he felt his anger dwindling into regret and lament. He sat up straight, looked his diminished council in the eyes. He could not afford to allow misery to take over yet. Now was time for justice. Now, it was time for revenge.

As punishment for his terrible crime, the king ordered to let Wolsey rot in the worst cell in the Tower of London while Arthur proposed a new Act to Parliament where death by poisoning, or even attempted poisoning, would henceforth be deemed as a capital offence, and to be punisheable in the most agonising means of being boiled alive.

"Boiled alive?" Katherine said, her mouth downturned at the gruesome imagery.

"Yes," Arthur replied, his tone clipped as he shuffled papers around on his desk in his chambers, his back turned to her.

"It could take weeks for Parliament to pass the Act," Katherine pointed out, "Don't you wish for swifter justice?"

Arthur did not reply nor turn to look at her when she spoke.

"Arthur?" she called.

He ignored her.

Katherine furrowed her brows and took a step closer, sighing as she looked about the room.

"Perhaps not a quick beheading, but hung drawn and quartered would be punishment enough –"

"No, Katherine!" Arthur exclaimed then, turning round sharply, his blue eyes flashing with fresh fury.

"No," he repeated, "It will not do! My brother was murdered! My *brother*! This is not some simple crime, but a direct attack on the Tudor House and *under my roof*!"

There it was. The guilt.

"Wolsey will suffer for what he did. For what he has taken not only from us but also from England! Harry was on a path to greatness! A Cardinal!" he fell silent for a brief moment, "Wolsey, too. Both were destined to achieve great things, I have no doubt about it. And now England shall be deprived of them both. Because Wolsey allowed the Devil to get to him and to commit a mortal sin. His soul is sullied for all eternity. And still it is not enough to quell my torment."

Katherine crossed the room then and put her arms around him, but his back was stiff against her palms and his body remained tense.

He moved away from her after a moment, and Katherine noticed not a hint of sadness lingering in his eyes. Only wrath. This was a side to her husband she did not recognise.

"Leave me, please, Katherine," he mumbled as he stood before the fire and stared into it, "I wish to be alone."

After decades of marriage and a myriad of shared grief, Katherine was all of a sudden out of her depth. Arthur had shut her out, a glimpse of his younger self flashing before Katherine's eyes, when he had been guarded and sombre.

She did not know what to do, other than as he asked.

She curtsied to her king and left the room, "My lord," she mumbled, hoping to catch his eye before she left.

But Arthur did not even hear her, too absorbed was he in watching the flames licking at the logs in the hearth, and no doubt imagining how Wolsey's pleading cries would sound as he was slowly lowered into a vat of boiling oil.

November 1529

It did not take Parliament long to pass the king's new Act to allow for poisoners to be boiled alive, and shortly thereafter, the date for Thomas Wolsey's execution was set.

At the king's request, it would be held on the same day as Harry's funeral, which the king and queen could traditionally not attend.

But executions...those *anyone* could attend.

"It will not look good for the king to watch his former Lord Chancellor be boiled alive!" Katherine insisted when Arthur told her of his plan to look Wolsey in the eyes while he met his maker.

Arthur shrugged his broad shoulders, indifferent to how it would look, indifferent to his queen's logic.

"He will plead forgiveness," Katherine continued, "you will appear unforgiving."

"I am unforgiving," Arthur replied monotonously before a flash of anger flickered in his eyes, "Don't you understand? When it comes to the safety of my family, I shall be relentless as to the pain and suffering I would inflict upon *whoever* might put us in danger."

He reached up and framed his hands, cold and trembling, on both sides of her face, and Katherine whimpered in fright at his sudden motion. But he did not let go.

"Don't you wish for people to know the Tudors will not stand for this?!" he said, "No one must ever feel so comfortable within my court that assassination is even *considered*! Perhaps if I'd been more ruthless to begin with, Harry might still be alive!"

He let go of her and ran a hand through his hair as he exhaled and shook his head.

"I am sorry Katherine," he mumbled.

The queen breathed a shaky breath, "It's alright," she reassured, the first lie uttered between them.

She allowed for a beat of silence before trying for one last time to remind him that there was still good in the world, for once being the one to talk *him* off the ledge.

"Never forget who you are, my king," she said softly, testing the waters, "One man's sins must not affect the realm. Punish him. Punish him severely. But once Harry is put to rest and his assassin is dealt with, England will need to feel safe. They will look to Good King Arthur to assure them they are safe. Don't let Wolsey's actions change who you are."

Arthur had stared at her as she had spoken, his jaw clenched and his brows knitted together, his body so tense in anger that she hardly recognised the man she had spent her life with.

"Good King Arthur is dead, Katherine," he countered coldly, "And he is not coming back."

Katherine did not reply, and instead watched wide-eyed as her once gentle husband straightened his blue velvet jacket and headed out the door to witness the horrific death of one of his former favourites.

Chapter 27

January 1531

Despite the court's heavy blow just over a year ago, England was continuing to thrive, much to Arthur's delight.
Thanks to his level-headedness and lack of interest in territorial expansion, Arthur's twenty-one-year reign had, so far, proven to be a fruitful one in terms of peace, and economic and military growth despite the recent epidemic. Women's literacy had increased three-fold in the past decade, women no longer being limited to mere signatures upon documents but writing entire letters in their own hand due to Katherine's influence and patronage of Juan Luis Vives, who believed that women were of an intellectual equal, if not superior, to men.
This, as well as their strong alliances with both Spain and France, meant that England was beginning to be recognised as a country to be reckoned with, one with a forward thinking and resilient ruler. England was on the brink of rejuvenation, and many European countries now wished to unite with them.
"We have marriage proposals for the Princess Alice from Portugal, the Netherlands, and Florence," Griffith Rhys informed the king, handing him several letters, then covering his mouth with a fist to clear his throat. A phlegmy rattle sounded from the man's chest.
Arthur narrowed his eyes at his friend, "Go see Dr Butts when we are done here, Rhys," he ordered as he perused the marriage proposals in his hands.
Griffith bowed and took his seat, wiping a sheen of sweat from his thick brow with a handkerchief.
"Florence," Arthur said, plucking their letter from among the others and scanning it, "The Medicis are an old and powerful family," he said, before laying the letter face down

upon the table, "But they are in a heated dispute with Carlos V of Castille which I would rather stay out of."

Thomas More and Thomas Cromwell nodded their heads in approval.

The vacuum left by Harry and Wolsey had been filled very soon after Wolsey's infamous execution with his very own former secretary, Thomas Cromwell, King Arthur's Privy Council having been in desperate need of new advisors. But Wolsey's position as Lord Chancellor had been filled by More, his wisdom and competence granting him that title above any others.

"Portugal offers their son Manuel," Griffith stated as Arthur singled out Portugal's letter, "He is but two months old, but we have reports that he was born very robust, with a head of thick, black hair."

Arthur nodded slowly, remembering the alliance with Portugal they had lost following Artie's death.

"Portugal intrigues me still," Arthur admitted, "Their naval capacity is exceptional."

"And their expansion across the ocean is promising," Thomas More added, "Already they have colonized many territories, most recently Goa in the west coast of India."

"Goa," Arthur repeated, mesmerized by the sound of it, "I like it."

"Should we send responses to any of these offers, Your Highness?" Cromwell asked, dipping his head into a respectful nod as he addressed his king.

"Yes," Arthur concluded, "Portugal must be eager to unite with us if they offer us a second marriage contract in recent years. Send word to King João III that England is happy to discuss terms."

September 1531
Ludlow Castle, Wales

Fifteen-year-old Princess Mary was more aware than ever of her changing body, and the inevitable path she was on to becoming a woman.

Ever since she had reached her twelfth year, the young princess would suffer terribly from intense stomach pains, chills, and dizziness every few months. Her belly would bloat, and her head would ache, so much so that she would sometimes need to lay abed with the windows covered and the fires burning low, the light hurting her eyes and head unbearably. The episodes would last anywhere between mere moments to entire days, and often subsiding with the arrival of the princess' monthly courses.

It is 'strangulation of the womb', the king's physician had informed the princess' parents following her second bout of illness in just two months, *There is no cure, but it is not fatal.* Katherine's shoulders had visibly relaxed at the wise man's words, Arthur taking her hand in his.

Is there a remedy or something we can do to alleviate the symptoms? Arthur had asked, his grip tightening on Katherine's hand.

Dr Butts nodded.

I can fix a tonic. But the best treatment to prevent it from occurring so often is exercise. Horse riding in particular.

Beside Arthur, Katherine tensed once again.

He'd looked to his wife, who had paled at the physician's recommendation, and they shared their fear with a brief look between them, Katherine shaking her head ever so slightly, making Arthur's decision for him.

Thank you, the king had said, dismissing the hunchbacked old man.

They had chosen to keep the physician's advice to themselves, neither of them brave enough to allow their daughter upon a horse, nevermind order her to ride it regularly as treatment for an illness that was not fatal.

Mary would have to suffer in order to stay alive.

But over the years, Mary had learned to live with it, the incidents becoming less frequent as each year had passed, the Princess being able to recognise when the episode was creeping in before it completely took over and quashing it with a cold cloth to her forehead and a nap before it developed into a full-scale attack of her senses.

But more often than not, no nap nor cloth nor Dr Butt's remedy could stop it, and Mary had begun to wonder if perhaps this rotten illness would hinder her from one day bearing children.

"It is *strangulation of the womb*!" Mary told her lady-in-waiting Frances harshly as they walked through the castle gardens one day, her two ladies at either side of her, "I can only imagine it means my womb is being strangled by my own body!"

Frances Aylmer was the daughter of Sir John Aylmer, a loyal courtier. She, as well as the princess' other lady Cecily Arundell, had been granted a place in the princess' household following her elevation to Heir Apparent, and the three young women had bonded greatly in those few years. Frances and Cecily were just one year older than their mistress, Arthur and Katherine having wanted their daughter to have company of similar age as she to hopefully form lifelong friendships.

And in this they had succeeded.

"Forgive me, Your Grace," Frances said then, glancing over at Cecily, for though Frances was the prettier of the two, with big hazel eyes and luscious lips, Cecily had always been more astute, "I did not mean to offend. I should have known."

"I would not fret, Princess," Cecily chimed in then, hoping to deflect from Frances, "You are young, and you will soon be married to a noble Prince. I have no doubt children will soon follow."

Mary sighed heavily, "I can only pray that you are right," she said, looking up as a skein of geese flew overhead, honking hoarsely at each other.

"Your wedding is but nine months away, Mary," Frances added then, hoping to regain favour with the anxious princess, "You may be with child by this time next year."

Cecily dropped her gaze and shook her head, stunned by Frances' continued lack of understanding.

"The Dauphin will be but fourteen when we marry!" Mary reminded her, "We won't be expected to consummate until he is fifteen or older still."

Frances blinked and stared back at Mary, her big doe eyes suddenly frustrating the princess.

Cecily pressed her lips together to keep from laughing, then watched as Frances opened her mouth to speak, and to Cecily's great surprise, her friend made a good point.

"But, Mary," she said, her light eyebrows twitching together, uncertain even in reason, "He is French."

October 1531
Greenwich Palace, London

The Duke of Suffolk Griffith Rhys woke up at the same time as he did each morning, his servant having been tasked to rouse him from his sleep promptly before dawn each day.

Griffith enjoyed that time of day the most, before anyone else was awake, the castle beginning to stir around him with the quiet movement of servants creeping about lighting fires and emptying chamber pots.

He enjoyed these moments of solitude, moving about his rooms in the dim light of pre-dawn, washing his face in the freshly filled basin and taking a seat before the open window to breathe in the fresh morning air and watch the first ray of sunlight peak over the horizon. And it was what he had done every morning for all of his adult life, nearly three decades having gone by without a single failed rising of the sun.

It was these moments of cherished silence that had kept him from marrying, no woman he had ever known having ever come close to that first ray of sunshine. No other than perhaps the queen herself – although she was, of course, out of his reach; taken by someone much more worthy than he.

But when Griffith awoke on this day, he did not feel so eager to meet the dawn, his chest having felt tight and heavy throughout the night, and for the past several days.

Dr Butts had warned him this day would come. That there was nothing to be done but to accept it.

And Griffith had accepted it, so much so that he heaved himself upright despite his painful back muscles from a night of fitful coughing. He dared not even look at his pillow for fear he would see more blood splatters as he had done the previous morning and the morning before that.

He glanced out the window. Already he was behind schedule, and he'd be damned if he missed what could be his last sunrise.

Griffith pushed himself out of bed and padded over to the metal basin by the fireplace, cupped his hands inside and lifted the shimmering water up to his face when a wet cough suddenly escaped him, and he spewed bright red blood into his cupped hands. Before he could even react, another uncontrollable cough rattled through him, and he grabbed the sides of the basin to gain some balance.

His body shuddered as cough after cough expelled more bright blood, and as Griffith Rhys fought to stop himself from choking on his own blood, behind him, the sun peaked over the horizon, his final chance to watch it rise in the distance having completely passed him by.

Arthur's face drained of colour at the news of Griffith's sudden death that same morning.

"By God! Must everybody die?!" the king exclaimed, not yet having recovered from Harry's murder.

The courtiers standing before him glanced left to right awkwardly, unsure how to answer such a question.

Sensing the wound of his sorrow reopening, Arthur worked to obstruct it with a bandage of frustration instead, for sorrow had aided him naught throughout the years.

"Help me to understand. He had but a cough…" Arthur said, looking to his physician in the crowd and his words trailing off at the old man's expression, "Dr Butts?"

"There was nothing I or anyone could have done," he confessed, "The Duke's symptoms progressed quickly."

Arthur's eyebrows twitched. He did not like to think of Griffith keeping this big of a secret from him. If only he had told him. He was the *king*! Surely he could have done something to save him!

Like you saved Artie? Or Harry?

Arthur shook his head at the intrusive thought, Artie's innocent, grinning face staring at him in his mind's eye, haunting him still.

Death, it seemed, was suddenly everywhere.

"We shall hold a grand ceremony for him," the king announced quietly, his council having to lean forward to hear him.

Lord Chancellor Thomas More nodded sombrely, "He was a great friend to the crown."

Arthur met More's eyes, "He was like a brother to me."

The funeral took place at St George's Chapel in Windsor Castle, paid for and organized by Arthur himself. Unable to attend, however, he watched the procession from the heights of his balcony.

"Another funeral," Arthur mumbled as he heard Katherine's footsteps stop short behind him.

She did not respond, merely offering comfort in her presence. Arthur stood on the balcony of his chambers, his hands planted firmly on the parapet and his head hanging low between his shoulder blades. In the distance, bells began to toll as though a royal was being buried – just as Arthur had requested – and he raised his head at the sound.

"I have buried too many of whom I love," he said quietly then as Katherine moved to stand beside him, looking down at the mourners gathered around the chapel.

She did not speak, for no words would soothe his soul.

She looked up at her husband. Through every tragedy they had faced over the years, he had always been the one to remain strong, a lifeline to hold onto.

Now that she thought of it, she could not even remember him mourning Artie's death – so poised had he remained, while she had been allowed to crumble in defeat.

And Harry's...well, Arthur had locked that particular pain away to fester, and it had taken shape as something ugly inside him: an anger that did not become him, and one he seemed unable to shake.

Katherine realised then that it was her turn to be the strong one, to be a lifeline for *him,* and perhaps in mourning his greatest friend, Arthur would be able to let out some of the grief he had been holding inside for far too long.

She reached over and touched her husband's shoulder, which, after many years of marriage, passed as an embrace. Then she took a step closer and tentatively rested her cheek on his upper arm, half expecting him to shrug her off and regain his usual composure.

But to her great surprise, his shoulders began to shake, and Katherine looked up to find her poised husband covering his crumpled face with his hand, his mouth downturned as he cried silently.

She reached a hand up to touch his cheek, "I'm here," she whispered tenderly, and it was then that he turned into her, his arms hanging limply at his sides like a child as Katherine enclosed his tall stature against her and held him while he wept.

And there they stood in sorrow, bells tolling in the distance, as the queen protected her king.

Chapter 28

January 1532

Finally, after years of much scandal and death, there was once again a happy occasion to be celebrated.

"I am being summoned to return to London," Mary said after reading the letter from her father, "The Dauphin is on his way."

Her ladies-in-waiting Frances and Cecily squealed with delight for their mistress, who they knew had been patiently awaiting this day for many moons.

"I am so ready for marriage," she had said on more than one occasion over the past few months, "I shall be glad if it is even half as happy as my mother and father's."

And she had grinned with excitement, her girlish giddiness over the new chapter in her life briefly overriding her more pragmatic belief that her marriage was no more than a political merger.

After all, a girl could only dream.

On her way from Ludlow to London, Mary's excitement for what was to come did not waver, and not even the downpour that met them but an hour into their two-day journey could dampen her spirits.

It had been two years since she had laid eyes upon her mother and father, the king having ordered for her, as well as her little sister Princess Alice, to stay away from court as much as possible following their uncle Harry's assassination.

The horrific incident had shaken her father, her mother had informed her in several letters over the years; but Mary had never truly taken her words to heart, unable to visualize her beloved father in any other way than completely in control.

As her party entered the castle gates, her agitation bloomed in her chest to see that the whole court had gathered to welcome her home, and that despite the persistent rain, banners had been raised and a fanfare sounded from inside the castle.

But that flame of excitement wavered within her at the sight of her father who, as her mother had cautioned, looked indeed much changed from the man Mary remembered.

As she stepped out of the carriage and hurried out of the rain and towards her parents underneath the canopy, she tried desperately to pinpoint what it was that made him appear so different.

It wasn't his growing age that had stood out to Mary, for his hair, though speckled with greys, continued a dark auburn in colour and shoulder-length. The lines on his forehead were no deeper nor more prominent than before.

"Welcome, daughter," he mumbled with a doting smile as she bobbed a quick curtsy and their eyes locked.

It hit her then, the change within him. The light in his eyes that had always been so warm and welcoming had dulled, and there was a slight but distinct stoop in his usually stark stance.

"Lord Father," Mary greeted him, before turning to Katherine, "Lady Mother. I am pleased to be back."

Arthur inhaled deeply then before reaching for his daughter and pulling her to him, holding her close, and Mary could sense the relief washing over him.

Mary looked over at her mother as her father continued to embrace her tightly, Katherine watching them with a troubled smile that said, *See?*

And she did. For it was suddenly so clear.

Mary's father was exhausted.

February 1532

Sixteen-year-old Mary Tudor was getting married.
According to the contract arranged over a decade ago, she was to marry the Dauphin, Prince Francis, to finalize the alliance between their two countries of France and England.

The Dauphin had arrived in the wet and grey country just two days earlier and had had very little time to adjust to the new weather, language, and customs before being prepared for the wedding ceremony.

As the son and heir to the great Francis I of France, the Dauphin had always known that his life was sacred and in need of safeguarding – which was why the fourteen-year-old continued utterly unconvinced that it had been right for *him* to have made the journey to another country, when it was widely agreed upon that a woman's life was of much less value.

His father must *really* want this alliance if he was ready to risk the life of his first-born son…

But the Princess Mary, whom he had only officially met upon his arrival, appeared less than worth the travels, the portrait England had sent as a gift for their betrothal three years prior having quite clearly been kind to its sitter.

And now, just two days after his arrival, Francis was already counting the minutes before he would be allowed to return home.

On the morning of her wedding, nervousness had taken over and erased any trace of giddiness Mary had been feeling over the past few weeks.

On the day of the Dauphin's arrival within London, he and Mary had made polite conversation following their official introduction, Mary even opting to speak with him in French to make him feel more at ease. They had arranged for the young couple to take a chaperoned walk in the gardens if the weather permitted it, and to play cards or chess by the roaring fires if it did not. And England being dependably wet in February did not ease up its light drizzle, leading the young couple to retire to the great hall and the games tables.

Mary had been kind, courteous and considerate of her future-husband, her mother having given her some insight as to how overwhelming it had felt following her arrival in England long

ago. Mary had taken her mother's experience to heart, allowing Francis to win at cards and making conversation about his country, hoping to ease his trepidation. But after a while it had become increasingly obvious that the Dauphin did not care for polite conversation – or indeed for his bride's company – when after most anything Mary had said, the young boy had sighed as though it were strenuous simply to be around her.
And Mary had not taken being snubbed very well.

"He did not ask one single question, and hardly answered any of mine!" the princess had fumed later that day as the servants had brought in tray after tray of wonderful food for the banquet. Her lady Cecily had leaned in closer, "Give the prince time," she'd advised, "He is surely nervous and perhaps a little frightened."
Mary had scoffed, "Frightened," she'd mumbled, glancing down the length of the high table to sneak a peek at her groom, who had in that very moment laughed loudly at the court Fool's performance before them.

"He does not appear to be frightened," Mary had muttered in judgement.
And now, as her ladies prepared her for one of the grandest days of her life, fluttering about her like bees on a flower, Mary could not bring herself to even smile at her own reflection.

"Now, now, princess," her governess Margaret Pole *tutted* from behind her as she spotted her glum expression, "It is a wonderful day to be wed!"
At the remark, Margaret Pole nodded at the sun shining through the window.

"If you speak of the weather then you are most certainly right," Mary replied, wincing as Frances tightened her corset.

"It is your wedding day!" the Lady Pole said, lifting her ward's chin with her finger, "Surely you can muster up a smile."
Mary did as she was told with as much sincerity as she could gather, choosing to focus less on the boy she would be marrying

and more on what their union would hopefully bring in the years to come.

Princess Mary travelled from Greenwich Palace to St Paul's Cathedral in a horse-drawn litter, wearing an embroidered white dress. Her long auburn hair hung loose and wavy down her back to symbolise her virginity, a gold-stitched white veil hanging delicately over her face and hair.
Thousands of people had gathered from all over London and its surrounding areas to witness the wedding ceremony of their very first future Queen Regnant of England, and the chants and cheers that reverberated throughout the city were intoxicating.
At least her people appreciated her, Mary thought as she made her way slowly through the crowds. That was all that she would need.
At the entrance to the cathedral, Mary was met by her father, who offered her a proud smile and the assurance of his sturdy arm.

"You look just like your mother," he told her, the adoration in his voice causing Mary's eyes to sting with tears.

"Thank you, Father," Mary whispered back as the doors to the cathedral were flung open from the inside.
Trumpets sounded as they took their first step down the walkway which was covered with a bright red carpet that had been tacked down for this special occasion.
Mary could feel the approving murmurs of the English and French nobility as her father escorted her towards the altar, and she silently thanked her ladies-in-waiting for helping her to look her best on this day; Mary feeling pretty for the first time in her young life.
At the high altar where the ceremony was to take place, King Arthur unlocked their arms and pressed a kiss to the crown of his daughter's veiled head before offering her hand to her groom. The Dauphin took it with little enthusiasm, his skin

feeling icy to the touch, and did not even meet his bride's eye. Mary's stomach dropped.

She quickly looked over her shoulder to her father as she climbed the steps to the altar, hoping to regain some of her previous serenity through his kind smile or a reassuring nod, but the king had already turned to join her mother in the crowd. Mary faced straight head, swallowed her resentment for her ignorant groom and knelt before Archbishop Warham to begin the long ceremony, praying that perhaps in time, the young man may yet grow to surprise her.

The nuptial mass lasted for three hours, the Archbishop of Canterbury uniting England and France with much ceremony and tradition, and to Mary's wonder, she had noticed Francis stealing glances in her direction from the corner of her eye. To begin with, the princess had purposefully forced herself to continue staring straight ahead and not to catch his eye, for she would not be played for a fool again. But after a while, his glances persisted, and she resorted to putting her stubbornness aside for the sake of their marriage.

Slowly, Mary turned her attention towards Francis as the Archbishop continued his long ritual, the old man's voice echoing throughout the cathedral.

She met the prince's gaze and offered a friendly smile, an olive branch to hopefully put aside the strange start to their relationship. Except, not only did her groom not return her smile, but Mary quickly realised that he was not looking at *her* at all, but past her entirely.

The princess turned her head, following his gaze to find the object of his attention to be her own lady Frances beside her, and Mary's heart sank. Her cheeks burning with humiliation, Mary snapped her head round to face forward once again, the ceremony progressing as though nothing at all had just happened.

But something had happened. For Mary had just caught a true glimpse of the young man she was pledging her life to before

God, the young man she had been so eager to finally meet and so keen to impress.
And she found that she did not like what she saw, not one little bit.

Due to Prince Francis' young age, he and Mary were not expected to consummate their marriage during the bedding ceremony, and the young couple was left to sleep off the excitement of the day following the traditional blessing of the bed.
Mary had pleaded her mother with her eyes not to be left alone with him, but Katherine had merely shot her daughter a sympathetic smile before closing the door behind her and the rest of the court as they hooted and cheered down the corridors on their way to their own chambers to continue the celebrations.
Mary had lain as stiffly as a board under the blankets, silently praying that her young husband would not wish to fulfil their physical obligation now that they were alone.
He is French.
Mary heard Frances' voice in her head, and she squeezed her eyes shut to block it out.
But to her great surprise, Francis did not turn to even look at her after the courtiers had left, and before long she could hear him breathing deeply. He had fallen asleep.
The princess lifted the blanket off of herself carefully and swung her legs over the edge of the mattress, her feet hovering just above the wooden floor as she listened for a change in the boy's breathing. When she was satisfied that she had not woken him with her stirring, Mary pressed the pads of her feet to the floor and arose.
She wrapped her slim arms around herself as a shiver ran through her, and made her way towards the low burning fire in the hearth. Kneeling by the fireplace she held her palms up to it, hoping to warm her soul and to burn away the misery of the day.

Francis snorted in his sleep behind her, and Mary looked over her shoulder to glare at him. They had not even been married one day and already he was infuriating her beyond belief. She turned back to watch the flames.

Mary had never been a hopeless romantic. She had always known, since before she could remember, that her marriage to the Dauphin would be a political merger. One that would obtain England's safety in more ways than one.

But lately she had allowed her girlish thoughts to cloud her judgement, her excitement over the potential of a happily ever after like that of her parents' loving marriage having blinded her to the reality of her situation. She and Francis were nothing more than two forced-together strangers with a slim chance of liking one another. Both of them were simply doing their duty. And Francis being male meant that he no doubt felt cheated out of his basic rights as the husband to not have to be the one to leave his home country.

But Mary's father and his had discussed the arrangement at length, and King Francis I had agreed to send his heir to England to conclude the marriage, as long as he were to return to France in four years' time. Whether Mary would join him in France had not yet been decided, and by the way she felt about her husband right now Mary could say with complete certainty that she would much rather live with a large body of water between them. She smiled at the thought of Francis being shipped back to France, Mary waving him off enthusiastically from the docks.

The fire cracked before her then, interrupting her thoughts, and Mary rose to take a seat on the lounger by the fireplace. She would sleep here tonight, she thought, the idea of laying next to Francis causing her lip to curl up in disgust.

Despite his disagreeable personality, the boy was not *entirely* unpleasant to look at. His hair was dark blond with a hint of redness to it, cropped short. He had a button nose, heavy eyelids, and a constantly bored expression on his face. Mary had also noticed during their vows that he had pale green eyes speckled with hints of gold, and Mary had found herself hoping then that their children would inherit that pretty feature from him. *As long as they did not inherit his arrogance!*

She shuddered suddenly to think of herself producing children with the conceited oaf, and she crossed herself to ask God to give her strength.

Despite who she was now married to, Mary not only wanted, but also *needed*, to bear children. For Mary, motherhood was something she had always longed for, to know a love deeper than any other on this earth. As a woman of noble blood, she knew it was also her basic duty. But as a future monarch in her own right, having an heir was essential for the continuation of the Tudor line. And realistically, she and Francis would need to produce at least one child if Mary wished to remain in England when the time came for him to depart back to France.

Mary craned her neck to look at her young husband then as he slept splayed out in the big bed. She wrinkled her nose at the sight of him, unaware and no doubt completely uncaring that she was not beside him.

With a deep sigh, Mary made herself comfortable on the lounger, warmed by her internal disdain as well as the fire beside her.

He is French.

She would not pressure him to do something that clearly neither of them wanted to do. But as Mary's eyes drifted shut, she found herself whispering her lady's words to herself as she fell asleep, suddenly hoping, for the sake of her future in England, that her lady would be right.

Chapter 29

September 1532
Greenwich Palace, London

"Archbishop William Warham has died, Your Grace," Lord Chancellor Thomas More informed his king with a heavy heart, not only for the respected man's death but also for the reminder of who was supposed to succeed him.

They had only just returned from their summer progress to Bristol and York, and already Arthur was being bombarded with problem after problem. This business of running the country was beginning to take its toll on the king.

Arthur nodded his head sombrely, "No need to look so dismayed," he said, noticing More's worried expression, "I have suppressed my anger at Harry's assassination when I boiled his murderer alive."

More swallowed, his Adam's apple bobbing uneasily.

"Have you considered who then might replace Warham?" More asked, hoping to move on from the sore subject as quickly as possible, his quill at the ready to make note of his king's ruling.

Arthur nodded, "There is no other I would trust with this honour than the very man who inspired a young Harry to follow his chosen path. He has been a constant source of loyalty and quiet dedication throughout my reign as well as my father's, and in truth, it causes me great shame that I did not consider him sooner."

"Who, Your Highness," Cromwell asked, his black eyebrows twitching.

"The Bishop of Rochester, John Fisher," Arthur declared, to which More nodded approvingly and began to scribble in his notes.

"Send a message to the Pope at once to propose Fisher as Warham's successor," Arthur ordered, "I have no doubt the

Pope will agree that, in Harry's regrettable absence, Fisher is the right man for the job."

"Moreover," Cromwell added as he handed Arthur a document, "We have received word from the Scottish borders which troubles me."

Arthur perused the document before him without taking it in, Cromwell knowing to enlighten the king himself.

"There have been increased raids, Your Grace. More than we have faced since the Battle of Flodden in 1515. It could cause a similar outcome if left unchecked."

Arthur handed the document back to Cromwell, "Scotland knows to stay in its lane," he said, "Queen Katherine defeated them herself while with child. If that alone is not reason enough to prove England will not be defeated by them then our Peace Treaty signed following the battle will. King James V is still being advised by my sister Margaret. I do not believe a war will come from this."

Cromwell bowed his head and dropped the matter, quietly scolding himself for having failed to pique the king's unease on the subject and to cause strife between the two Catholic countries.

At heart, Cromwell was secretly in favour of what Martin Luther had begun to preach in the late 1510s, and which had consequently led to the birth of the Protestant Reformation that was slowly but surely spreading throughout Europe. Cromwell believed that Catholicism was the religion of the past and that England would do well in accepting the new and improved religion.

But he should have known that King Arthur would not be swayed to become suspicious of his neighbouring Catholic country so easily; border raids having been an Anglo-Scottish problem for decades.

But to sow the seed of doubt was all that he could achieve for now, for to openly show his Catholic king his true colours would only lead to burning at the stake for heresy. And

Cromwell was far more interested in living a long life of luxury than to be remembered as the former advisor who died for his egotistical beliefs.

That he would gladly leave to be Thomas Wolsey's legacy.

October 1532

"If rumours are to be believed," Katherine's new lady-in-waiting Jane Seymour informed her, "The Dauphin and the Princess Mary are yet to consummate their marriage."

Katherine dismissed the news and took a sip of her warm ale.

"I should hope so!" she replied, "The boy is too young."

"But the princess is eager for children," Anne Boleyn replied casually from behind her queen as she folded linens into neat squares.

Katherine turned to her, "What makes you say so?" she asked, stunned to learn such important information about her own daughter from a third party.

Anne looked to Jane Seymour and then back at the queen, "It is the talk among her ladies," Anne admitted, "The silly one, Frances, she likes to gossip a little too much in my opinion."

"Yes, clearly," Katherine replied as she turned back around, "And you trust the lady Frances' gossip to be true?"

Anne put down the sheet she had been folding and approached Katherine, "I believe it would not be out of the realm of possibility. Princess Mary has always enquired as to the health of my three children, more so than even yourself, Your Grace. She has a keen interest in motherhood, of that I have no doubt."

Katherine smiled, remembering her eldest daughter's delight at the news of Katherine's final pregnancy when she had – by some miracle at the age of forty-three – conceived Princess Alice.

"Yes," the queen now said in thought, looking back over the years, "Mary always did love spending time at Alice's nursery."

"Does Your Grace remember when the princess went missing one night?" Agnes Tilney now chirped in, chuckling at the memory, "the Lady Pole was beside herself with worry to find the princess' bed empty one morning, only to find her curled up in baby Alice's crib with her. Very sweet."

Katherine nodded, her eyes shining with adoration for her only surviving children, "I suppose Mary would be looking forward to this next stage of her life," she said, lifting her small ale to her lips, "Such a shame her fourteen-year-old husband is likely not yet confident enough to take that step."

Ludlow Castle, Wales

The Prince of France rolled off of her with a satisfied exhale, each time they copulated feeling better than the last.

The pair lay side by side on the bed, breathing heavily as they stared up at the ceiling, her arm resting exhaustedly against his hairless chest.

The Dauphin turned his head to look at her, beads of sweat glistening on his forehead.

"*Et? Mieux qu'un Anglais?*" the prince asked mischievously, *And? Better than an Englishman?*

The girl looked over to him, her laboured breathing rendering her unable to voice a reply, but she nodded her head earnestly.

"*Bien*," he said, rising up on his elbow and running his index finger over her luscious lips, "It's about time England learn of France's superiority."

May 1533
Greenwich Palace, London

Queen Katherine of Aragon had not been feeling herself for quite some time.

It had begun with a feeling of anxiety weighing heavily on her chest every now and then, a feeling the queen had put down to nervousness about her daughter's wedding and her transition into womanhood.

But even weeks later, Katherine would suddenly feel tired throughout the day, the weight in her chest growing more and more bothersome as time went on.

"I'll send Dr Butts to you," Arthur reassured her when she had finally resolved to share her woes.

He pushed the hair from her forehead and kissed it, her skin still damp from their lovemaking.

"I feel fine today," she replied with a playful smile, "You have seen to that."

Arthur chuckled and pulled her closer, "Nevertheless," he argued, "Best to catch whatever ailment irks you before it develops. I cannot risk losing you."

At that, Katherine's heart sank at the prospect of being the first of them to die, for the thought of carrying on with life without Arthur was too much to bear, and she would hate to inflict such suffering upon him with her demise.

"With any luck we shall both die on the very same day," Katherine whispered half in jest, half in hope, "so that neither of us should ever feel the pain of the other's absence."

"You think God would be so good?" Arthur asked as he ran his fingers up and down her bare arm, the two of them staring off into the distance as they lay in each other's arms.

But before Katherine could reply, Arthur had untangled himself from her embrace and sat up, the sheet falling from his chest, his once effortlessly firm physique having become slightly laxer in his older age, both of them now having reached their forty-seventh year.

"Because I would not like to go on if you are not by my side," he admitted to her, his voice low and heavy with emotion.

He and Katherine locked eyes, the morbidly romantic statement hanging between them like a dark cloud.

Katherine sat up, grabbing a fistful of the bedsheet to cover herself, "Arthur," she said poignantly as she reached her free hand up to his cheek, "If I die…"

Arthur's mouth twitched and he started to turn away from her, but Katherine pulled him back.

"*If* I die before you," she said forcefully, her voice cracking slightly, "Then I would wish for you to take another wife."

Arthur shook his head and Katherine nodded hers in counter argument.

"Yes," she pushed, "Alice is too young to be left without a mother figure. And with any luck, you might yet sire another son."

Arthur looked down at the crumpled sheets between them, wrinkled and creased, as though time took its toll on a marriage bed as surely as it would a face.

"You still don't understand," he said after a moment, "after all these years. I have never wished for another son, nor have I ever wished for a male child over a female one. Our path has led us to this, with Mary as my heir: the Rose and the Pomegranate embodied. You, Mary and Alice are all that I will ever need."

"Yes, but –"

"Don't, Katherine," he interrupted, "all will be well. Whatever ails you, it will be naught we cannot defeat."

He leaned in to kiss her, a quick peck to conclude the matter. But Katherine was not satisfied, for whether it be this year, the next, or in ten years, as a mother she had to make sure Arthur would not let her passing affect him the way Harry's had.

"Promise me," she urged as he lay back down to go to sleep, "Promise me that you will go on."

Arthur looked up at her, her long hair framing her face much like on the day they got married.

"How can I promise such a thing," he asked, "When you will be taking my heart with you wherever you go?"

Following Dr Butts' assessment of the queen, Katherine was cleared to be in perfect health and advised merely to rest more and fast less.

"Fast less?" the pious queen had replied.

Dr Butts had nodded his old head, his white beard waving to-and-fro, "You are experiencing bouts of fatigue, Your Grace," he'd said, "To deny your body sustenance at a time like this will only increase your symptoms."

Katherine had nodded, quietly dismissing the man's advice, for surely all she needed to nourish herself was God.

"Thank you, doctor," she'd said before turning to leave.

That night, Katherine had decided not to attend the banquet in the great hall, choosing to listen to one of the doctor's words of wisdom and opting for an early night before court was to go on progress the following day.

She ordered her ladies Agnes, Anne, and her latest addition to her household Jane Seymour to attend the festivities without her, and to reassure the king that she was in good spirits.

For she hoped that when she awoke, the dizziness that had been troubling her of late would cease to be.

June 1533

"Dead?"

The question burst out of Arthur's mouth as though the news had winded him as the messenger boy before him nodded his head.

"Just yesterday, Your Highness," the boy said, "her husband writes that she never fully recovered from having caught the sweating sickness in 1528."

"My sister had the sweat?" Arthur whispered, his face one of misery and disbelief for not even having known that his sister Mary had caught the sweat and survived five years earlier.

The messenger nodded, "Charles Brandon asks that she be buried in England with all the honours of a princess despite their banishment –"

"Yes, yes, of course," Arthur interrupted, "That goes without saying."

Arthur held his head in his hands then as the great hall grew silent, the weight of the news making his head feel heavy.

He sniffed then as he raised his head, "What of Brandon? And the children?"

The messenger cleared his throat, wringing his cap in his hands, "Only one son survives his mother, their firstborn, Henry, died just this past winter. It is only Charles Brandon and their youngest, William."

Arthur nodded, stunned to learn of his sister's family's misfortune and feeling a stab of guilt at having sent them away all those years ago.

But in Mary's own words, they had been happy, and Arthur drew comfort from that at least.

"Send word that Brandon's wish is to be granted," the king said, "My sister shall receive all the honours worthy of a Princess of England. For that is what she has always been."

21st July 1533

Arthur laid his sister to rest at the Abbey of St Edmund.
It was a grand funeral, her body laying in state with candles burning all day and night.
King Arthur ordered for a Requiem Mass to be held at Westminster Abbey, and after her funeral, alms of meat, wine and money was given to the poor.
But, as was custom, neither the king and queen nor Mary's beloved husband could attend. And Charles Brandon was left to wander the Earth alone, feeling lost without his soulmate.

Chapter 30

February 1534
Ludlow Castle, Wales

Princess Mary and her husband the Dauphin of France had spent the first two years of their marriage completely ignoring the other's existence.
Francis had made it perfectly clear from their very first meeting – and every encounter they had had since, whether at a public event or bumping into one another in the hallways – that he cared nothing for his wife. And due to his vile behaviour towards her, now neither did she for him.
But an agreement had been made between the two just a few months into their marriage: that as soon as Francis was to reach his sixteenth year, that they would consummate their marriage. If not for their own pleasures, then for the sake of the alliance.
And that day had finally come.
"*Enlève ta robe,*" Francis ordered the moment he entered Mary's candlelit bedchambers.
She raised her chin defiantly, "You are in my land now," she replied, "It is about time you converse with me in my own tongue."
Francis stared at her with heavy eyelids, already bored. He sighed deeply and took a step closer to her, tugging his shirt over his head.
"Remove your nightgown," he repeated in English, his French accent strong.
Mary swallowed, suddenly nervous at the sight on his naked chest. He had filled out nicely in the past two years, the boy she had married making way for a young man.
Though she was the older one by two years, she felt suddenly as though she was a little girl under the scrutinous eye of a more experienced lover.

But of course that was absurd, Mary told herself as she pulled the cotton nightgown down over her shoulders and let it fall in a puddle around her feet. The whole reason behind their yet unconsummated marriage was because Francis had been too young to complete the physical side of their union. He was as much a virgin as she was. And tonight, they would see to it that they would both no longer be.

His green eyes roamed over her naked body like a slow caress, making Mary feel even more vulnerable than she already was, and she brought her long hair over her shoulder to cover her small breasts.

Francis sighed again as though he would prefer to be anywhere else, but then he jerked his chin towards the bed and pulled his hose down, kicking it off from around his ankles.

Mary lay down in the centre of the bed, pulled the thin sheet over her lower half and willed herself to ignore the fact that Francis had quite clearly not liked what he saw.

He crawled up the bed then and positioned himself over her.

"Look at me," he ordered, and Mary forced herself to meet his emotionless gaze.

He lifted a hand and ran his thumb over her thin lips, his mouth twitching slightly with obvious disappointment.

"Open," he said, and though his thumb was pressed over her closed mouth, Mary knew him to have meant her legs.

It was Mary's turn to sigh, though her need for it was more to do with calming her nerves than frustration. Though she felt plenty of that about her husband.

Slowly, she parted her legs as Francis pulled the sheet away from between them, then placed himself snuggly against her thighs.

Mary did not dare look when her husband reached down between them and began to work on himself, nor did she dare to even breathe when he cupped one of her small breasts in his hand and caused her nipples to harden. She turned her head to the side, but she was surprised to find that his hand on her did not feel entirely unpleasant.

She sensed him hard against her thigh then and she steeled herself for what she knew was to come when suddenly his fingers began to caress her instead.

She turned back to look at him then, her mouth opened in an involuntary gasp, and a smug smile pulled at Francis' lips.

Mary closed her eyes as Francis continued to stroke her, her hands having reached up to cling onto his forearm and shoulder, and just as she arched her back in pleasure, he pushed himself into her and – though Mary flinched slightly in pain – the pair erupted into spasm of ecstasy together.

As they regained their breaths, Mary thought that it had not been as awful as she had predicted it to be. In fact, she could get used to this side of her marital duty.

But as Francis rolled off of her, panting quietly as he lay naked on his back, Mary's unfamiliar satisfaction was clouded by the loud voice of reason in her head that screamed with certainty that Francis *had* done this before.

"What am I to do?!"

Cecily patted her friend on the back as she sobbed uncontrollably, so much so that snot was running down her upper lip and her eyes were scrunched shut.

"Is it the prince's?" Cecily asked.

The lady nodded and wiped her nose with a handkerchief, "Of course it is the prince's. I have been with no other."

Cecily raised her eyebrows, clearly unimpressed by her friend's situation.

"There is a tonic you can take –"

"No," she said, "I am too far gone, I have felt it quicken for over a week. There's nothing I can do."

Cecily shook her head, "Why did you not say anything sooner?"

"I hoped it would go away!"

By now, Frances had been blubbering in the servant's quarters for over an hour and Cecily had to get back to their mistress if they wished to avoid reprimanding. But Frances was in no condition to face the princess, whose husband's child she was carrying.

"Stay here and try to compose yourself," Cecily ordered, handing Frances a mug of small ale.

"With any luck, now that Mary and the Dauphin have begun being intimate, she will be with child soon and you may be sent off to the country to have your babe."

Frances shook her head, "Mary will never allow it, I have betrayed her for years with him. If the truth were to come out –"

"Then don't let it come out," Cecily interrupted, taking Frances' hand in hers, "What she doesn't know won't hurt her. This baby could be anyone's, and unless you tell her, she may never find out of your continued indiscretion. The best you can hope for now is to be sent away to have it."

"With child?!" Princess Mary exclaimed, turning round sharply to face her lady, "But, Frances, you are not married!"

Frances could not meet her mistress' eyes.

"Who is the father?" the princess asked.

"I am not certain, Your Grace," and a sob escaped her lady at the realisation that even with this lie, her life as she knew it was likely over.

Mary breathed a humourless laugh, "I can't very well have wanton ladies within my household," she declared hotly, "You do know that don't you, Frances? You took an oath when you came into my service."

Frances nodded, "Forgive me, Princess," she wept.

Mary's mouth pulled into a tight line as she watched Frances cry into her hands.

Having recently discovered the joys of sex – and if Frances' lover was even half as good as Mary's husband – she could hardly blame the lady for having forsaken her oath of chastity.

With a deep exhale, Mary took a step closer to her lady and rested her hands on her shoulders.

"Go home to have your child," Mary said as Frances' shoulders shook.

The lady lifted her head to look at Mary, thinking she had misheard, "What?" she asked, her voice as small as that of a mouse.

"Stay away from court for as long as your family can keep you," Mary continued, "and when you return, we shall inform the court that you were recently widowed."

Frances blinked at Mary, feeling guilt bubble up inside of her. She did not deserve such a kind mistress.

Mary smiled at Frances, hoping to have reassured her, "The child may grow up never knowing its father, but there's no need to lumber it with the title of 'bastard' for the rest of its life."

Part VII

Death comes for us all.
But the ripples we cause in the world are left behind.

Chapter 31

18 months later

September 1535
Greenwich Palace, London

The heaviness in Katherine's chest had never fully disappeared, but she had learned to live with it like she had done with all the rest of her heartache. Although, this, she believed, would likely be the death of her.

Over the past two years, the queen had resorted to visiting Dr Butts and his younger assistant once a month, though they continued as useless to cure her as they would have been had she had the plague. At least then she would not have suffered for quite so long.

"We will leech you next month, Your Highness," Dr Butts' young assistant said, "For now we recommend rest and to drink this tonic each night."

Katherine made a face, "That tonic did naught but turn my stomach," she accused, "I request you concoct another that is less foul."

The assistant looked over his shoulder to Butts, who was shuffling towards them with a candle in one hand and a cane in the other.

"Take the tonic, Your Highness," the older physician said, his voice low and wise, "It will aid you to sleep."

Katherine exhaled in frustration and took the offending vial.

"But next month I expect a new form of treatment," the queen insisted, "One that might actually cure me of this affliction."

Dr Butts nodded his old head as he walked his queen to the door, though he already knew that likely nothing would heal Her Grace now. Not unless prayer and rest could eliminate the malady that had undoubtedly lodged itself deep inside the queen's heart.

November 1535

In honour of the upcoming Christmastide, Katherine had requested that both her children return to court for the festive season, and Mary jumped at the chance to be reunited with her beloved family.

It was Mary's favourite time of year, a time where the court was alive with merriment and celebration, where candles would burn brightly in all the corners of the castle and a delicious, spiced aroma would hang in the air.

Gifts and delectable food aside, it was the atmosphere that Mary enjoyed above all else. And it was exactly what she needed to thaw out from the frosty reception she had received from her lord husband for the past year – ever since she had sent Frances away to have her baby in the country.

The coincidence did not escape her; and it would certainly explain Frances' failure to return to Mary's service following the babe's birth. She often lay awake at night wondering how foolish she must be to have missed the obvious signs that Frances' baby was her own husband's.

But Mary did not dare ask her lord husband for confirmation. For not only would it change nothing, but what good would accusing him do other than highlight the fact that Mary had yet failed to conceive a child by him. And if Frances' child really *was* the Dauphin's, then the blame for Mary's own lack of conception lay only at her feet, her irregular ailment, the strangulation of the womb, no doubt having something to do with it.

Upon hers and the Dauphin's entry into the great hall, the king's usher announced them to the crowd, which led to the hundreds of courtiers to bow and curtsy at them and a fanfare to sound.

Mary searched the crowd for her mother and father with a ready smile on her face, when she spotted a flurry of colour running towards them.

"Mary!" her little sister Princess Alice squealed as she ran at her older sister and held her in a tight embrace.

"Alice," Mary grinned in greeting, cupping the back of her head as she held her close, "How you have grown!"

Alice took a step back and gave Mary a twirl of her dress.

"Do you like it?" the seven-year-old princess asked, her maroon and gold skirts unfurling around her like a blooming flower, "the Lady Bryan says I look as majestic as the Queen of Portugal herself."

Mary smiled at the mention of her childhood governess as well as Alice's successful betrothal to Manuel the Prince of Portugal.

"Where are the king and queen?" Mary asked her sister, looking over people's heads and noticing from the corner of her eye that her uncouth husband had walked off and melted into the crowd, his French grooms following him like poodles on a leash.

Good riddance. Mary didn't want to be around him anyway.

"Come," Alice said, taking Mary by the hand, "Our Lady Mother is by the fire."

They found Katherine standing beside the large stone fireplace looking up at a portrait of Artie, and Mary's chest ached at the sight of her dear brother. The portrait was one of only three in existence – far too few for someone so loved – and Mary thought, not for the first time, what a tragedy it was that Alice had never known him. The two of them had many similar characteristics: Artie and Alice both sharing a more playful and mischievous side, while Mary had always been more practical, a stickler for rules, like their father.

"Mother," Mary said in greeting, announcing their presence. Her mother sighed deeply as she tore her gaze away from Artie's portrait, and Mary noticed a glistening in her eyes.

"Ah, my darling daughters," Queen Katherine exclaimed with a smile as she swiftly wiped at her eyes.

Katherine walked slowly towards them, and Mary thought she detected her mother wincing briefly. But the princess quickly brushed the thought aside. Her mother was no longer a young woman, and at fifty it was only natural for her body to ache from time to time. Her father, too, had been suffering from a stiff knee for some years.

"Let me look at you, Mary," Katherine said now as she held her eldest daughter's face in between her hands.

She gave her a once over, smiling throughout, then sighed deeply and led her back to where she had been sitting.

"Come," the queen said, "Sit with me awhile."

The king's Fool, Will Sommers, must have played a witty prank on someone, for the crowd behind Mary erupted in laughter as she took a seat beside her mother.

Alice was bouncing excitedly on the lounger opposite them with a wriggling puppy on her lap.

"Who's this?" Mary asked, leaning forward to tickle under the puppy's chin, who repaid her with soft licks all over her hand.

"He was mother's gift to me," Alice said, "Isn't he charming?" And she lifted the pup to her face and squeezed it to her.

"Very," Mary replied, smiling.

"I was hoping you would have an early Christmas present for me," Katherine said to Mary then, quietly enough so that only she would hear, a light-hearted smile on her face as she touched her hand to her daughter's tightly corseted belly.

Mary blushed with shame, "Unfortunately not, Lady Mother. Forgive me."

Katherine waved her hand between them, as if to clear a bad smell, "Don't, Mary," she said, "Do not ever seek forgiveness for such a thing. There is nothing to forgive. Children come when they are meant to."

The queen offered her daughter a sympathetic smile and took her hand as it rested on the lounger between them. She squeezed it, a secret endearment meant just for her, and turned her attention back to Alice. Mary never felt closer to her mother than in that fleeting moment, where something that should have been deemed a failure on Mary's part was simply accepted as out of her control.

"What will you name the pooch?" Katherine called to Alice over the noise of the merry chatter and joyful music, and Mary tore her eyes from her mother's face and followed her gaze, feeling grateful beyond measure.

Alice bounced the pup in her arms like a newborn, with its soft pink tummy facing up. She pushed her lower lip out in thought as she looked down at it laying calmly on its back, "Maybe...Yapper?"

Mary frowned, a smile pulling at her lips, "But he is so docile and quiet."

Alice met her sister's gaze, "Well, yes, Mary, it would be in irony."

Mary and Katherine exchanged a glance before erupting in quiet laughter.

"Only you would think in such ways," Katherine said with love, reaching forward and stroking her youngest child's still-chubby cheek.

Mary watched the tender moment in the orange firelight, with laughter and music in the background and the delicious, spiced scent in the air. It was moments like these that made life worth living, Mary thought as she sat back in her seat, hoping to keep this image and this feeling locked away safely in her mind.

For surely, with life being so unpredictable, there would come a time when she might need to seek comfort from these most precious memories.

23rd December 1535

The snow had begun to fall some days ago, thick flakes coming down from the sky in uninterrupted succession, causing the gardens below and the city beyond to be almost entirely covered in a blanket of white.

The fires all over the castle were blazing day and night, the servants having been ordered to keep them roaring until the snow resigned from falling, lest risk the court being frozen to death in their sleep.

King Arthur and his council, bundled up in their furs and blankets, were discussing the growing conflict at the Scottish borders, when Arthur suddenly felt as though the falling snow had somehow snuck into his veins and turned his blood to ice; and he knew that something was terribly wrong.

Hurried footsteps were heard approaching then before the guards threw open the doors to the chambers and his daughter Mary stood before the council, her face as pale as the world outside.

"Father, come quick!" she pleaded, waving a hand so that he would follow, "It is the queen! Mother has fainted!"

Arthur was up from his throne in a flash, the furs on his lap falling to the ground as he raced out the door.

Mary sped ahead, her skirts bundled in her hands before her so that she may lead the way quicker.

"What happened?" her father asked as he caught up to her, his voice thick with worry.

Mary shook her head, trying to regain her thoughts, "We were just playing cards," she said bewilderedly, "She complained of chill and chest pain but insisted she was well. And then she just…collapsed."

"Where is she?" Arthur asked, his voice hitching as he tried to remain calm.

They hurried up the wide staircase, Mary's heels clinking with each hastened step.

"They took her to her chambers, Father," Mary said, "I ordered Dr Butts to be summoned to her there."

They had reached the door to the queen's chambers and stopped in their tracks, Arthur turning to Mary with a sad smile and cupping her cheek in his hand, "You did well, Daughter," he said, before bursting through the door.

Mary knew not to follow her father inside, the king and queen's business being their own for only a short time; and out of respect for them, she would grant them this moment of privacy before the rest of the country found out all the details of their queen's health.

"We can leech her again," Dr Butts' assistant offered the king as he stared at them with pleading eyes, "But it did little to alleviate her pains last time –"

"My king," Dr Butts interrupted his young apprentice's blabbering, turning away from the queen's bed and steering Arthur away, "I have had my suspicions about the queen's health. The tonics we have given her helped to manage some of the pains, the leeching on occasion too, but she has persistently gotten worse. I do believe we have done no more than slow down the inevitable."

Arthur stared at the old man wide-eyed, unwilling to make sense of the physician's words.

He looked back at his wife as she lay shivering under her many blankets, her eyes closed tightly as her teeth chattered and her forehead was beaded with sweat.

"The inevitable," Arthur echoed softly, as though the words were too heavy to say aloud.

Dr Butts followed the king's gaze, "I'm afraid the queen is dying."

30th December 1535

It was a miserable Christmastide, the news of Queen Katherine's ill health having spread like wildfire throughout the court.

There was no joyful music, no plays, no dances, no masquerades. There was just silence and waiting, the only sign of life in the castle being that of the constantly burning fires in the fireplaces to keep the frost at bay.

The blizzard had not yet ceased, though the flakes had finally turned into pitiful drops of half melted slush, causing the thick snow on the ground to dissolve somewhat. But it was little to be celebrated however, for though the world outside was on its path back to normalcy, Arthur's world as he knew it would never be the same again.

"Katherine," he whispered as he knelt beside her bed, one hand holding firmly onto hers while the other gently stroked her forehead.

She had not opened her eyes in thirteen hours, only briefly having woken after the physicians had left that morning, to ask where she was, her chest rising and falling in quick succession as her fear mounted to find herself unaware of her surroundings. Arthur had soothed her with reassuring words, making his presence known by lying down beside her and *shushing* her gently, as he had done so often after their many losses. Katherine's eyelids had fluttered, calmed by her husband's reassuring aura, and she had fallen back asleep in the safety of his arms.

But now, too many hours had passed for comfort, and Arthur needed to know that she was not yet gone forever, for there was still so much left to say.

"Katherine," he whispered again, a little more frantically this time, shaking her gently by the shoulder.

"May I, my lord?" Katherine's lady Jane Seymour said then as she approached holding a damp cloth in her hand.

Arthur nodded and watched as Jane gently dabbed the cloth on Katherine's forehead, cheeks and neck, and Arthur noticed the young woman was holding back tears of her own.

The cold wet feeling stirred the queen awake, just as Jane had hoped it would, and Katherine inhaled deeply as she opened her eyes with effort.

"Arthur?" she mumbled, her voice groggy.

"I am here," he reassured, taking her hand and pressing it to his lips as Jane Seymour stepped back to give them privacy.

Katherine forced a tired smile, "Mm," she muttered, the only response she could muster.

Arthur suddenly did not know what to say, though he'd spent the last thirteen hours holding in an avalanche of things he wanted to tell her.

How she had been his one and only love his entire life.

How life had held meaning not because of his titles and majesty, but because she had been by his side through all of it.

How she brought light into every room she entered.

How she could lift his mood simply with a look.

How he would never be the same without her.

But none of it felt even remotely good enough to explain how he felt, no words being able to express that she had, quite literally, meant *everything* to him.

"If…I…" Katherine breathed then, snapping Arthur out of his tortured mind.

He shuffled closer to her, though he was already pressed against the side of the bed, his elbows resting on the mattress beside her.

"What is it, my love?" he encouraged gently.

"If I die…before you…"

Arthur shook his head, "Don't, Katherine," he begged, "Don't say it."

But Katherine swallowed hard and went on, her tired eyes fixed on her husband, the best man she had ever known.

"If I die…I want you to marry another."

And there it was, the truth that once Katherine was gone, life would inevitably go on without her.

"Alice…needs a mother," she whispered, a single tear falling from the corner of her eye and onto the pillow, "The girls need you…to be happy."

Arthur shook his head, unable to listen to another word, unable to consider life without her, unable to look past his own sorrow.

"I will never again be happy without you," he admitted.

Katherine turned her face away from him, closed her eyes. It was not what she had needed to hear.

"I have...prayed each day that you would...be."

And with that, the Queen of England fell back into a deep sleep.

6th January 1536

"Father, I beg you to let us see her."

Princess Mary and Princess Alice were standing before the king as he sat slumped forward on his throne in the great hall, his head in his hand and his eyes closed in turmoil.

Since their mother's collapse, no one but Arthur and the physicians had seen her – with the exception of her ladies-in-waiting, of course – and Mary was becoming anxious that her mother would slip away before they got a chance to say goodbye.

"You may see her when she is better," Arthur mumbled.

"Father," Mary countered firmly, taking a step towards him, "You know she may not get better."

Arthur did not respond, the only sound in the great hall coming from Alice as she blubbered quietly beside Mary, and Mary's words hung in the air like a poisonous fog.

He looked up at her then, raising his head slowly as though it weighed too much for his neck. Before him stood no longer his little girl but a young woman, tall and elegant in her stance, her hands clasped before her delicately and her gaze firm yet compassionate. She was the image of her mother, the very best parts of her and him, and Arthur realised then that England would be left in capable hands if he were to die of a broken heart alongside Katherine. For it certainly felt like he would.

But, whenever the day would come that Arthur would follow Katherine into the afterlife, he realized he would have been a fool to have denied his children a chance to see their mother one last time. For who knew what kind of trauma that would inflict upon them?

Because no matter how much Arthur refused to accept it, God was calling Katherine to Him, and there wasn't a damn thing he could do about it.

7th January 1536

"Mother?" Mary whispered as she warily entered the queen's chambers, afraid of what she would find.
There was no response, but Mary continued ahead nonetheless, her sister Alice closely behind and Arthur at the tail end.
Mary looked back at her father, a question in her eyes as to whether she should proceed if they had not been invited in, but Arthur nodded his head lightly. He looked like he hadn't slept in months, Mary thought, dark circles having formed under his eyes and his face sallow with grief.
Mary pushed on, steeling herself for what state they would encounter their beloved mother in, and she wondered suddenly if maybe Alice was too young to see her like this. But it was too late now, for Alice was right behind her, clinging onto Mary's sleeve like a lifeline.
"Your Graces," the queen's ladies Jane Seymour and Anne Boleyn curtsied, while Agnes Tilney pressed a damp cloth to Katherine's forehead.
The queen stirred at the feeling of the cold water on her skin, and relief burst through Mary to find they had not come too late.
"The princesses are here, Your Highness," Agnes informed the queen quietly, before backing away to give them privacy.
"*Hijas*," Katherine mumbled, lifting a hand towards them briefly, her gaunt face twitching into a smile.
Her mother looked...no longer like her mother.
At the sight of her, Mary began breathing heavily, unable to stop herself from gasping quietly for air for fear of allowing her sobs to escape instead. And she could *not* break down right now.

"Mama," Alice cried, calling Katherine by an endearment she had not used in years, and laying her head on her mother's chest.

"Carefully, Alice," Arthur urged gently from the archway where he stood, as still as a statue of ice.

Alice sobbed against Katherine, aware suddenly of how real this was, and Mary could do nothing but watch the tragic moment, her chin wobbling as she continued to keep her feelings in check.

"She is...so much like you," Katherine breathed to Arthur though she was looking directly at Mary before her, "Always...in control."

At the remark, Mary could no longer contain her sorrow and she exhaled sharply, fat tears escaping her stinging eyes in a gush. And though it hurt like hell, her chest burning with angst, it felt good to open the floodgates. Even just a little.

"My darling daughters," Katherine mumbled as Mary sat down on the side of the bed and took her mother's hand, "You...have been my greatest...joys in this life. Nothing I ever...did...was as special as having you."

"You will be with Artie soon," Mary whispered, hoping she sounded encouraging.

"Yes," Katherine breathed with a faint smile.

Suddenly, the queen's hand flew to her chest, her face twisting into an ugly grimace as she flinched in agony.

Alice and Mary jumped up in shock, their faces paling.

"Call the priest," Arthur ordered the queen's ladies instinctively as he stared straight ahead at his wife, a lump forming in his throat and his jaw setting tightly. No matter how much his heart was hurting, he had to remain strong for his children.

"Father?" Alice whimpered, and Arthur tore his eyes from his wife and to his young daughter.

"Come now," he said, holding out a hand to her.

Alice stole one last glance at her mother as she lay in bed ashen faced, before taking her father's hand and heading out the door. Mary could already hear the hurried footsteps of the priest approaching in the distance, but as she stood next to her mother, suddenly alone, she could not bring herself to leave her, and she knelt down beside her and took her hands in hers.

"I will make you proud, Mother," Mary whispered ardently to her then, though Katherine's eyes had closed once again, "I will lead by your regal example and make you proud."

Mary bent her head and pressed her hands clasping her mother's against her forehead, praying Katherine had heard her promise, when her mother answered quietly.

"You…have already…made me so very, very proud."

29th January 1536
Westminster Abbey, London

To the king and country's great torment, Katherine of Aragon had died only moments after the priest had raced to her bedside and uttered the prayer of commendation; and the days that followed her passing had been dark and desolate.

"She was so devout," little Princess Alice had cried, "Why would this happen to her?"

Her older sister had held her, allowing Alice to cry into her shoulder, "Our faith does not make us immortal," Mary had soothed Alice quietly as she'd fought back her own tears, "Death comes for us all."

The king had locked himself away in his chambers, allowing entry only to his Lord Chancellor Thomas More when details of the queen's funeral had been necessary.

"Westminster Abbey," was all Arthur had managed to mutter as he'd stared blindly out the window, leaving the rest of the decisions to his council.

And so the king's council, left to organize the grand funeral by themselves, made sure to show their queen all the respects she deserved, choosing to take much inspiration for her interment from the king's late mother, the Dowager Queen Elizabeth of York's, funeral.

Katherine of Aragon, Queen Consort of King Arthur, had lain in state at Greenwich Palace's Chapel Royal for ten days, to allow the people of the English court to pay tribute to their beloved queen. Church bells rang day and night, the nobles and poor folk alike mourning the tragic loss. Thankfully, the snow had ceased to fall just hours after the queen's death, and in the days she lay in state, paths were hastily cleared to allow for an honourable procession to take place for their fallen queen.

Her coffin, topped with an effigy of Katherine wearing her robes of estate and crown, was placed on cushions of black velvet in a carriage. The carriage was escorted by knights bearing banners displaying the royal arms and images of the queen's symbol of the Pomegranate. Five hundred poor people trailed behind bearing torches, followed by members of the royal household and clerics.

Behind the carriage were the queen's ladies-in-waiting Anne Boleyn, Agnes Tilney, and Jane Seymour, all of them accompanying their mistress one last time before their services to her were complete.

Katherine's eldest daughter Princess Mary followed closely behind, acting as Chief Mourner in the king's traditional absence. Clad in black, with a dark veil hanging over her face, twenty-year old Mary walked straight-backed and stony-faced behind her mother's coffin. She had cried what had felt like endless tears in the days following Katherine's passing, at times feeling as though she would never come up for air. But her mother's final words resounding in her mind had aided to drying her tears, the love and pride her mother had felt for her giving Mary the strength she needed to carry on with elegance and poise. Mary would cherish their departing moment for the rest of her days, to remind her of where she had come from, and of where her mother's dedication to her would one day lead.

When the procession reached Westminster Abbey, a thousand candles were lit and placed around the coffin. Two masses and a requiem mass were said before the Bishop of London blessed the grave and the effigy was removed. A lump formed in Mary's throat to watch her mother's coffin be lowered into the grave, and she swallowed it down along with the growing urge to throw herself over it and beg her mother to wake up.

But there was no bringing her back. She knew that.

The queen's officers and guards broke their staves of office then – snapping Mary out of her fog – and threw them into the grave, signalling the end of their service to their queen.

And the symbolic finality of it all made Mary wonder: What would become of her father now?

Chapter 32

February 1536
Esher Place, Surrey

"My palace is a tomb," King Arthur had muttered dejectedly on the day of his wife's funeral, "I need to get away from this place."

And so, as the rest of London attended the grand service, he and his diminished household retired to a solitary residence, where he hoped to remain as he endured his sorrows.

Esher Place was a large country estate owned by the Bishop of Winchester Stephen Gardiner, a statesman and former secretary to the disgraced Thomas Wolsey before Cromwell.

Built of similar brick as Hampton Court Palace, the gatehouse at Esher Place alone was an impressive four-storey building, magnificently built in the typical red brick of the period.

Upon his entrance through the gatehouse, the king was shown to its most grand apartments by Stephen Gardiner himself, who offered his condolences with a heavy heart before retreating from the rooms and leaving Arthur to his own devices.

It was no Greenwich Palace, Arthur thought as he looked around, but it would certainly do for a more secluded residence, and for a much-needed escape from the public eye, Arthur being in absolutely no mind for politics and talk of re-marrying, as he knew his council would soon wish to discuss.

He walked slowly towards the crackling fire in the corner-hearth, rubbing his hands together out of habit though he felt neither cold nor warmth nor hunger since Katherine's death, her loss having numbed him of all his senses.

The world had felt quiet since her passing, a heavy silence following him no matter where he went, as though her demise had sucked all the life out of Arthur too, leaving behind nothing more than a shallow husk of his former self, cursed to walk the Earth without the better part of his soul.

Had he ever told her that? That she had been the blood in his veins and the air in his lungs? How she illuminated every dimly lit room?

He had never been good with words. Expressing how he felt had never come naturally. But he hoped it had been made clear through his actions. Surely, in her final moments, Katherine will have known how much she had been loved.

Loved.

Already he was thinking of her in the past.

Because it was where she now was.

Arthur turned away from the fire and lay down on the bed on the opposite side of the room. The walls were closing in on him, and he squeezed his eyes shut to escape. Curled up on his side with his knees tucked against his chest, Arthur slowly opened his eyes and stared at the empty pillow beside him. Another reminder of where he was; of where she wasn't.

Katherine's death-bed request blared in his mind then, like an ugly reminder of his never-ending duty as the King of England, as well as his duty as a father.

But for now, just this once, Arthur would take some time to himself; allow himself to wallow and grieve without the scrutinous eye of the court watching his every move. It was why he had come here with no more than his necessary household, to be as alone as a king could ever be.

And for now, he would just be Arthur – just Arthur – and grieve the parts of him that he would never again be: a husband who had fiercely loved his wife, a king who had worshipped his queen. And as sleep took him, he wished for nothing more than for God to take him too.

April 1536

The grief of her mother's loss was all consuming, and before long, the burden of it all gave way to Mary's unusual bouts of illness.

For two weeks, Mary had been laying abed with intense cramps in her lower abdomen. The heavy bleeding that usually signified the coming end of her pains had started that morning, and having battled her affliction for several years, Mary was hopeful that the cramping in her belly would soon cease. And yet for some reason, the symptoms were more unwavering than ever before.

"Help me up, Cecily," Mary said as she threw the covers off of herself, pressing one hand against her bloated belly, "I need a new rag."

"Already?" Cecily asked, stunned, "It has been only ten minutes."

Mary did not reply, squeezing her eyes tightly shut as a new wave of agony pierced through her body where she stood. She breathed through the pain as she had been instructed to by the physicians, when suddenly her eyes flew open in shock and she scrambled to lift her nightgown.

"Your Grace?" Cecily said as she watched her mistress from across the room, a fresh rag in her hand.

Mary ignored her and stepped away from the puddle of blood that had pooled around her feet, almost passing out in horror to find a tiny foetus at the centre of it.

"It appears the princess was with child."

The Dauphin of France and his groomsmen were practicing archery in the field behind the palace, the Dauphin having just pulled his bowstring back to take his shot when the messenger brought the tragic news of Mary's miscarriage.

"Was?" one of the groomsmen asked.

The messenger nodded, "Forgive me."

Francis turned suddenly and let the arrow loose at the messenger's feet, missing only by an inch, the arrow embedding itself into the green grass.

The messenger boy jumped back, his eyes wide and wild as he looked at the Prince of France, who was already pulling another arrow from the quiver.

The messenger turned and fled towards the castle, squealing in fright as an arrow flew past him and laughter erupted from the group of French men he'd left behind.

"Looks like your darling wife will accompany us to France after all," one of Francis' groomsmen said in French once they were alone again, "Without an heir for England and France, your late-night rendezvous must go on."

"Don't make me sick," Francis replied with a grimace, pulling his arm back, his muscles clenching before he released his arrow and hitting the straw butt dead centre.

Mary cried day and night for the two weeks that followed, her mother's loss shadowed so closely by that of her baby hitting her extremely hard.

"I didn't even know," she would whimper, as though knowing of the child's existence might have spared it.

Cecily would try to soothe and distract her, bringing Mary her favourite foods and offering to play round after round of her favourite card games. But nothing would stop the misery and guilt, and it was only made worse when her husband finally graced her with his presence. Mary had made sure to inform him of the unfortunate event as soon as it had happened to avoid him finding out through court gossip. Despite their mutual dislike for one another, she *had* expected him to come to her as soon as he'd received the news, but to Mary's surprise she had neither seen nor heard from him.

But now that he finally made an appearance in her chambers two weeks later, his face more sullen than Mary had ever seen it, she wished he'd continued to stay away.

"So," he said, his bored gaze looking her up and down, "You lost a baby?"

Mary was standing by the window with her mother's Bible in her hand, her rosary beads hanging from it like a bookmark. She blinked at him, stunned by his coldness, for though there was no love between them, she would have thought he would show more compassion.

Mary nodded once, a curt jut of her head.

Francis pursed his lips and stuffed his hands in his pockets.

"I depart to France in four months," he reminded her, as though she hadn't been counting down the days since their wedding, "If you are not with child again by then, you will have to accompany me."

"I know," Mary said, a lump forming in her throat. She cleared it, "It is not what I want."

Francis snorted, "You think I do?"

Mary raised her chin at the insult, though she wasn't surprised by his rudeness.

"Are you still bleeding?" he asked suddenly.

Mary flinched, stunned by his crude question. She looked around at Cecily in the corner, and to the guards by the door before returning her gaze to Francis. She shook her head.

"Good," he said, tugging his jackets off his shoulders and jerking his head at the guards and Cecily to leave.

"What are you doing?" Mary asked, frowning as she watched them head for the door. She closed the Bible in her hands with a low thud and held it against her chest like a shield.

"Lift up your skirts," Francis said once the servants had left, tossing his jacket over the back of the lounger and walking towards her.

Mary breathed a nervous laugh, "You cannot be serious," she said, looking at him in disgust.

He grabbed her forcefully by the arm then and pushed her towards the bed, pulling at the string of his hose to open it, "I wish I were jesting, my sweet," he hissed ominously, "Then this would be enjoyable, at least."

May 1536

"I hate him!" Mary whimpered the following month as she thumped her pillow repeatedly, "I *hate* him!"

She pressed her face into the pillow to muffle her next scream, then she rolled over on the bed and cried freely, her tears streaming down the sides of her face.

"Can I get you something, Your Grace?" Cecily asked quietly, aware of Mary's fresh aches.

After their first night together since Mary's miscarriage, Francis had taken it upon himself to visit his wife every night that she did not announce a new conception. And he had become more aggressive with each occurrence.

Mary sported a new red welt somewhere on her body after most occasions, and this time was no different, an angry mark glowing around her neck from where he had held her still when she had protested against his unwanted advances.

Cecily gently touched the mark on her mistress' throat and Mary winced.

"Please, Cecily," Mary said, curling on her side into a foetal position, "Tell the physicians I fell."

Cecily nodded as she got up from the bed and headed towards the door, and she wondered just how much longer the Princess of England would have to endure this kind of vile mistreatment before someone would take notice.

June 1536

Much to the Privy Council's relief, the king had sent word that he would be returning to London within the week, his period of seclusion having aided him in reclaiming some control over his grief.

But after four months away it was time to return, a king's matters never ceasing to accumulate even with a trusty council in place to help lighten the load. And with the impending date of his heir's departure to France, Arthur needed to be back at court to organize the last-minute details of her journey. As well as wanting to spend as much time with his precious daughter as he could before she, too, would be taken away from him.

"Your Grace, there is civil unrest by the borders of Scotland –" Thomas More informed the king as soon as Arthur's feet touched the ground from dismounting his horse.

Arthur raised a gloved hand and strode past his council, stopping More mid-sentence, who looked to Cromwell in shock, and headed straight towards his eldest daughter. Mary was rising from her curtsy when her father approached her and pulled her into his arms, lifting her feet off the ground.

Mary smiled up at him in mild confusion once he put her down, but noticing a sheen of sadness clouding his eyes despite his smile, the princess knew her father to be revelling in what small part he had left from his marriage. The part of his wife that would live on in their daughters though Katherine could not.

"Welcome home, father," Mary said, stepping aside and taking his arm before walking inside together, king and heir, holding each other upright through their troubles.

July 1536

The Dauphin of France was celebrating his concluded time in England with a tennis match the week before he was to set sail back to France with Mary as his reluctant companion.

By now, after four years of an increasingly wretched marriage, Mary had accepted her fate as an unhappy wife to an abusive monster. But she had not yet accepted her need to go with said monster to France, for surely if he felt comfortable to treat her as he did in her own country, there was no knowing what would happen to her once he was back on his own turf.

A shudder coursed through her at the thought of leaving England. And yet, there was nothing she could do to stop it.

But Mary being the regal princess that she was, never let on to the outside world just how much she despised – and equally feared – her husband, and when it was announced that he would partake in the tennis match, Mary made sure to not only show her support through her presence but also through feigned joyful cheers and applause.

The small crowd of courtiers clapped in unison then when the Dauphin hit the dedans, scoring the winning point and grinning arrogantly at his opponent.

"Well done, my lord!" Mary called with a grin, though she secretly wished he would drop dead from exertion.

She was sitting on a blanket in the shade of a nearby tree with several cushions strewn all around her as she observed the match in what appeared to be the utmost of comfort. But underneath the luxuries and her satin gown, the newest bruise on her hip from when Francis had thrown her down on the stone floor the night before was throbbing uncomfortably.

Francis ignored the calls from his wife, turning to his opponent instead, "Again?" the French Prince called, "Or do you accept defeat?"

His opponent shook his head and held up a finger, requesting a moment to regain his breath.

At that, Francis scoffed a laugh and turned towards the servants on the sidelines, clicked his fingers and waved for one to bring him a cup of wine.

Mary watched from the shade of the tree as Cecily approached her husband then, carrying a silver cup of wine and handing it to the prince, who knocked it back in one gulp and handed it back to her without a word of thanks. He wiped his mouth with the back of his hand and waved her away. Cecily curtsied but he had already turned his back on her, and when she turned to exit the tennis court, Mary noticed her lady flash her a brief smile. A smile that, Mary thought, somehow promised that, soon, a secret would be revealed.

That night, Francis did not visit Mary's bedchambers for the first time in weeks, for shortly after the tennis match had concluded, the Dauphin of France had been taken to his chambers complaining of feeling nauseous and light-headed.

Mary could not deny that she felt relieved to have some reprieve from the nightly torture he inflicted upon her of late, but soon her relief morphed into confusion when, just hours later, there was a frantic knock at her door.

"Dead?" Mary said monotonously, unable to believe her ears, a mixture of dread and – most sinfully – delight churning in her stomach.

"Yes, Your Grace," the Imperial ambassador Eustace Chapuys informed her quietly, the castle being almost completely silent in the middle of the night, "The physicians are with the king now. He has requested your presence."

Immediately, Mary nodded and closed the door, ordering for Cecily to help make her presentable.

The lady pinned Mary's long auburn hair up and placed a navy-blue gable hood encrusted with diamonds on her head, before turning to lace the matching sleeves to her dress. The two women worked in silence, both of them unable to voice their thoughts while they knew the ambassador to be waiting behind the door.

But Mary could see the hint of a smile tugging at the corners of Cecily's lips, one which reminded her of that afternoon, when Cecily had offered Mary's husband a cup of wine and looked over at her as though an important mission had been achieved.

As soon as the princess was made ready, she and Cecily hurried through the dark hallways with the ambassador as their chaperon. He led them through the corridors, a candle in his hand to light the way and only stopping once they had arrived at the king's chambers.

The king's guards opened the door, and they hurried inside to find her father, Dr William Butts, Thomas More, and Thomas Cromwell standing tensely around a table.

"Mary," Arthur called, waving a hand for her to join them, "Are you feeling well?" he asked as soon as she approached, taking her by the shoulders and worriedly giving her a once over.

Mary only nodded, her eyes wide as she looked around at the king's Privy Councillors.

Arthur sighed with relief and pressed a kiss to his daughter's forehead.

"What has happened, Father?" Mary managed to ask, forcing herself not to look in Cecily's direction, who had remained in the shadows by the closed door with the Imperial ambassador.

Arthur looked to More, then Dr Butts, before turning his daughter away slightly, "The Dauphin. Dr Butts believes him to have been poisoned."

At the word, Mary's throat began to close up, "Poisoned," she croaked, "By who?" though she thought she already knew.

Arthur shook his head, "Nobody knows. There is no logic to it. You and he were set to depart in less than a week…"

Mary forced herself to swallow the words that were threatening to spill out, her mind reeling to understand the severity of this situation and concluding that, right now, the expected response from her would be fear and sorrow.

"What are we to do?" she asked frantically, "There is a murderer on the loose in the castle!"

The memory of her uncle Harry came to mind then, and Mary felt sick to think of the punishment that would befall Cecily – if it had, in fact, been her who had done this.

Mary risked a quick look to her lady in the shadows and suddenly a crystal-clear realisation came to mind.

If Cecily had indeed murdered the Dauphin of France in order to protect Mary from certain harm, then out of gratitude – if not respect, for suddenly she wished she had had the gall to have done it herself – Mary would do anything in her power to keep Cecily from being found out. She may not have asked for her protection but damn it, Mary was glad for it; and though Cecily may have saved Mary's life by poisoning Francis, now it was Mary's turn to protect her saviour.

August 1536

Arthur's newest member of the Privy Council, the Bishop of Winchester Stephen Gardiner, whose estate Arthur had resided in during his time of mourning, sat looking bewildered at the men around him as they all shouted at once.

"France is outraged, as would be expected!"

"King Francis is demanding an investigation –"

"There is talk of war!"

It had been one month since the Dauphin's dubious demise, five months since Mary's tragic miscarriage and six months since Katherine's death, and Arthur could no longer find the strength to remain composed. His poised exterior was beginning to crack.

"War?" Arthur replied, scoffing and shaking his head, "Francis wants war? As though it was somehow my doing? As though the prince's death somehow benefitted England!?"

"King Francis is beside himself with grief –"

"Yes, well, who isn't these days," Arthur mumbled.

"No doubt he is throwing accusations around," Lord Chancellor More continued, as though Arthur hadn't spoken, "He will want someone's head for this. And if he cannot pinpoint blame onto some*one*, then there is no knowing what he may resort to."

"A devastated king is dangerous business," Cromwell added.

"Isn't it just?" Arthur agreed coldly.

At that very moment, where threats of war were being flung around while Arthur felt more dead than alive, he was starting to care little for what was best and right and good and safe. Right now, as their Anglo-French treaty lay in ruin, as the King of France spoke of suspicion as he had so often done throughout Arthur's reign, Arthur felt suddenly like perhaps he *should* settle the French's distrust in a manner totally unbefitting his tranquil nature.

Someone within his court had done this. That much was clear. But after a month, not one suspect had been identified, no one even coming forth with information as to *why* anyone would have wanted the young prince dead. And Arthur could not very well boil his entire court alive in hopes of catching the one responsible. Without evidence, there was no one to blame.

Except France had England as a whole to blame.

France had been suspicious of England for decades, and Arthur had always chosen to placate their worries with promises and treaties. But what if war had been the solution all along? What if violence was the only language King Francis would understand?

For once, Arthur cared not for placating their hot-headed French king. For once, after everything he had lost and continued to lose despite his best efforts, Good King Arthur was willing and ready to go to war.

Chapter 33

September 1536

Following their mistress' funeral, the late Queen Katherine's ladies had been sent home to their families, their service to the queen having ended with her death.

Anne Boleyn, who had recently given birth to her fourth child with her devoted husband Henry Percy at her family home of Hever Castle, chose to take this time and dedicate herself to her young family. The queen's death had deeply shaken her, Anne having formed a close friendship with Katherine over the years in her service. And, for now at least, Anne preferred not to return to court and to instead stay in the countryside, where she was safer to study the Protestant scriptures that had begun circulating in England.

Agnes Tilney too, at the age of sixty-nine, chose not to serve another noble lady following Katherine's death, her heart not yet having healed from her mistress' tragic loss.

But Jane Seymour, who was yet to find a husband or bear any children, had no good reason to remain at home to waste away at the age of twenty-seven, unwed and useless. And so, after a short break back home at Wolf Hall, Jane Seymour returned to court to serve the late queen's daughter, the Princess Mary.

"It is a dangerous time to return to court, Mistress Seymour," King Arthur warned the pale-faced lady before her readmittance, "The culprit for the poisoning of the Prince of France is not yet found."

Jane had nodded gravely, her doe eyes wide with fear and a hint of excitement.

"I know, Your Grace," she said, hoping she sounded brave before her king, "Pray God he is caught soon. But I wish to serve. Queen Katherine still lives on in my heart, and I know she would wish this of me, to continue serving the crown by attending your daughter, Princess Mary."

Arthur clenched his jaw to suppress his emotion at the mention of Katherine, and the memory of her final days came to mind. He remembered Jane caring for her so tenderly, always quietly knowing what Katherine had needed to make her feel comfortable. He remembered Jane offering him a damp cloth to wake Katherine from her deep slumber, how her gentle voice had sounded like a lifeline in that most terrible moment.

"Katherine would have liked it very much," he finally said, "if you were to join Princess Mary's household. You were a good servant – and a good friend – to the Queen."

"Someone will be executed for this."

"Not if nobody is accused."

"This kind of thing will not come without consequences –"
Mary and Cecily were embroidering by the large window in her chambers, whispering frantically about pretty much the only thing they spoke about of late, when there was a knock at the door and the guards opened them to allow entry to the king.

"Father!" Mary exclaimed, rising from her seat and dropping her embroidery, her eyes so wide and her demeanour so jumpy that Cecily feared Arthur would know immediately that she was hiding something. But to her relief the king hung his head much as he had done for the past six months, his struggles so heavy they were literally weighing him down, and he had failed to see Mary's blunder.

Cecily bent down to pick up the cloth, needle, and thread Mary had dropped. She was going to hand them back to her, but seeing Mary's hands fumbling agitatedly she chose to put them down on the windowsill behind them instead.

"Mistress Jane Seymour," Arthur said then as the lady in question stepped out from behind him, "She will be your new lady-in-waiting."

Mary cast her eyes over Jane and forced a smile, "Very well," she said as Jane curtsied, "Thank you, Father."

Arthur nodded, then glanced briefly at Jane beside him, "It's what your mother would have wanted."

October 1536

"If France persists with the threat of war, England needs new allies to defend herself," Bishop Gardiner said.
With King Arthur having been recently widowed, it would make sense to consider foreign princesses for him to obtain a new alliance in the hope of joining forces with another European nation against France. But instead, he and his Privy Council were deliberating a new betrothal for the Princess Mary, though her period of mourning had not yet passed.
Traditionally, it was expected for a woman to mourn the death of her husband for an entire year, wearing nothing but a shapeless dark dress – widow's weeds – to signify her status as a grieving widow. And while Mary was donning the appropriate attire – projecting a sorrowful exterior while inside she was anything but – her father was already considering who best to marry her off to, to obtain security for England as well as heirs for the continuation of the Tudor line.

"Has Your Grace considered new brides for yourself?" Cromwell asked, raising one black eyebrow, "There are many fine princesses all over Europe if alliances are what we seek. Germany, perhaps? Or Italy?"

"I shan't be taking another wife, Cromwell," Arthur reminded him, though Katherine's plea to him sounded in his ears, "The matter is for Mary."

"The Duchy of Cleves, Your Grace," Cromwell persisted, "Two princesses are available for marriage. Amelia or Anna of Cleves –"

"Goddamn it, man!" Arthur thundered, slamming his fist upon the wood table, "As if I would ever want to unite with the country that spawned the heretic Martin Luther! Are you mad?!"

Thomas Cromwell swallowed and sat back in his chair, shaking his head at himself and his foolhardiness. He must not be so obvious in his attempts to steer England towards the new faith. His life could be in danger if his secret beliefs were to come to light.

"Forgive me, Your Highness. I did not think," he said.

"No, you didn't."

"What of a new alliance with Castille?" Thomas More interjected then, returning the conversation to the matter at hand.

Arthur waved the idea aside, "King Carlos V married my late son's widow, Princess Isabella, not ten years ago. They have no male children old enough to marry, and we need an alliance now."

Gardiner sat forward, eager to add to the discussion, "Princess Alice is to be married to Prince Manuel of Portugal –"

"Not for another six years!" Arthur objected angrily, running a hand through his jaw-length hair, "For God's sake, my lords! Can you come up with nothing of value?"

Gardiner sat back in his seat, rubbing his clean-shaven chin as he thought.

"Scotland, my king," a deep voice added then, a bearded man having entered the King's Council chamber.

"Ambassador Sadler," Arthur said, greeting the Scottish ambassador, "What brings you before me?"

Sadler approached leisurely, holding a rolled-up letter with the Scottish King's seal aloft, "I bring news from my sovereign lord, King James V, that I trust you will be interested to hear."

Arthur held out his hand and Sadler handed him the letter, a self-satisfied smile on his face. He was eager to bear witness to the King of England's reaction.

Arthur broke the wax seal and unrolled the letter, and as he read it to himself, Sadler announced to the room the proposition his monarch had bestowed upon him to pose.

"My lord, King James V, Your Grace's nephew by your sister the Dowager Queen Margaret Tudor, asks for your daughter the Princess Mary's hand in marriage, and to thereby put an end to the animosity between us, to eradicate the borders that divide us, and to unite our two countries under one ruler through any children they may bear."

Thomas More looked to his king in stunned silence, who stared at the letter before him, his eyebrows bunched together.

In the Lord Chancellor's opinion, this proposal could not have come at a better time.

Not only would a union between the neighbouring countries of England and Scotland put an end to the ongoing and increasingly violent raids taking place along the Scottish border, but it would also bring with it the much-needed protection England required against the growing tension with France.

The Auld Alliance was a centuries old peace treaty between Scotland and France made in 1295, which promised protection for the other. This alliance had proven useful for both countries throughout the years and had played a significant role in Scotland's involvement in the dispute between England and France in 1515, which had led to the Battle of Flodden.

But with King James V's proposal of marriage to the future Queen Regnant of England, a union between England and Scotland would mean an umbrellaed protection of England from France through the Auld Alliance, France no longer being able to go to war with England, lest risk the Auld Alliance with Scotland.

It was the perfect solution. And yet the question as to *why* teased in the corners of More's mind.

"It could be the answer to all our problems," Thomas More uttered then when Arthur failed to speak, "As well as something that will no doubt go down in the history books. The union of Scotland and England as one."

Arthur was nodding, though he had yet to voice his thoughts.

"It would quash the border raids," More urged on.

"It would unify the countries under one ruler, your daughter's heir," Gardiner said.

"It would put a stop to the war that is brewing with France," Cromwell added.

At that, Arthur looked up from the letter and stared at Cromwell, his blue-eyed gaze so intense it made Cromwell squirm in his seat.

"What makes you think I would want to put a stop to this war?"

As it turned out, the letter bearing the King of Scotland's seal had not been a written form of Ambassador Sadler's announcement, but a personal letter to Arthur from his sister Margaret Tudor.

In it, she informed Arthur of the Duke of Albany's passing and that this was their time to make an Anglo-Scottish union while she still had some influence over her son. And from the contents of her letter, Arthur got the impression that she had been working on this plan for quite some time.

My dearest brother,

James is eager to join our countries. He has heard of Mary's grace and piety, and I am proud to say he has taken after his English mother more than his Scottish father. I have you to thank for that, Arthur, for without my guidance throughout his minority, he might have fallen into dangerous hands.

I humbly ask you: consider this union carefully. Many others of the Council are pushing for a French match with Marie de Guise to further strengthen Scotland's alliance with France. James is torn between Marie de Guise and your Mary, but I have it under good authority that his English cousin, and to unite with England, has always intrigued him.

Don't let this opportunity pass us by.

Arthur read and re-read the letter by candlelight in his chambers until the early hours of the morning, the passing of time evident only by the diminished fire in the hearth to mere embers, and the delicate change of the sky from black to dark lilac to blushing pink.

The world was waking up.

And Arthur had to make a decision before it was too late.

Would he embark on a new path and lead England into war with France to pursue this new need for self-destruction?

Or would this gift that had been dropped into his lap be enough to light the gloom that had become his entire life?

November 1536

Arthur had taken the question of what he ought to do to God, and after countless hours, days and nights of fasting and prayer, He had granted Arthur the clarity he had needed in the form of a whisper from Katherine herself.

She had guided Arthur back to himself, reminded him of who he was and for what he stood, and suddenly a full-scale war was no longer an option.

But they would have put up a good fight!

A good fight is irrelevant if the end result is total destruction.

His own words from what felt like a lifetime ago had echoed in his mind, solidifying in his heart what he had known all along to be true: Arthur was not the kind of king his father was, or even the kind of king his brother might have been. Arthur was not a king that searched for glory or purpose on the battlefield; and a war fought in anger and grief was a war half lost before it had even begun.

France would not take kindly to England's union with Scotland, of that Arthur was certain.

But it was the safest of all his options, and it was the option he would take to protect his people and his reign. But more importantly, to protect the future he and Katherine had laboured so long and hard for to build.

December 1536

"You will travel to Scotland to wed your cousin, King James V," Arthur announced the decision to his daughter the following month as they walked leisurely through the candlelit palace.
Both countries had accepted the terms of their contract, one of which – specified by England – was that the wedding would take place in the new year despite the princess' year of mourning not yet being concluded.
Mary faltered slightly at the announcement, tripping over her dress, and Arthur instinctively extended a hand to catch her fall, as any father would do, no matter the age of their child.
"Scotland?" she asked once she'd righted herself, slightly stunned at the choice.
Arthur nodded once, "I have faith it is the right thing to do. And King James speaks very highly of you."
Mary narrowed her eyes, pressed her thin lips together as she considered her father's words, "But he does not know me."
Arthur smiled at his daughter, "Word travels far of your grace, Mary. You are your mother's daughter."
Mary tightened her grip on the furs around her shoulders and inhaled deeply to stem the sting in her eyes at the mention of her mother.
"And not only that," Arthur continued as they turned the corner to the snow-covered courtyard, "You are to be England's very first Queen Regnant. That is no small feat."
Mary blushed at her father's compliments, and suddenly, despite – or perhaps because of – her ill luck with husbands, she was curious to know what else King James V had said about her.

*

Princess Alice was overjoyed to return to London for the Christmastide, and the eight-year-old princess brought with her a burst of much-needed energy to the court.

With her puppy Yapper trailing behind wherever she went as she bounded from one games table to another, Princess Alice was the life and soul of any event, her naturally easy charm rubbing off on those who continued to hold on to the gloom of that year.

And yet, despite her external delight to be back at court, her sister Mary would not be fooled, for behind the bright smile and infectious giggle, there was still much suffering within the young princess. But how close beneath the surface, Mary was yet to find out.

"Have you heard about my betrothed, Mary?" Alice asked, giggling from behind her small hand, "He has been officially named his father's heir, replacing his older sister Maria."

"How come?" Mary asked, reaching over to move her rook on the chess table, and then gasping, "Has the *infanta* died!?"

Alice shrugged with indifference, moved her pawn, "But isn't it wonderful? It means I will one day be Queen of Portugal."

Mary raised her eyebrows, surprised at her sister's blasé disregard over the *infanta's* potential outcome.

Alice sensed her sister's disapproval, "She has likely been married off," she said, dismissing the topic.

Later, when the banquet had been served and cleared and the musicians began playing a merry tune, Alice and Mary took to the dancefloor, the sisters spinning around joyfully with the other courtiers when suddenly a high-pitched yelp sounded out.

"Yapper!" Alice squealed, bending down to pick up her puppy, who an oblivious courtier had stepped on while dancing.

"How dare you, sir!" Alice thundered, her round face scrunched up in anger as she glowered at the man she believed to have hurt her pet.

"Forgive me, Your Grace," Edward Seymour stuttered, "I did not see him."

"My father ought to have you hanged for this!" the little princess hissed, pressing her puppy to her chest.

"Alice!" Mary exclaimed in horror, then turned to Seymour, who was stunned into silence, his eyes wide.

"The princess is tired," Mary said, "Excuse us."

"I am not!" Alice screamed, stomping her foot.

By now, the music had slowed and the dancers around them had begun to look their way, a circle having formed around them as though it were a show, and they were the main attraction.

"Come now, Alice," Mary said, taking her sister by the arm. But Alice tore away, "No!" she shouted, her lower lip trembling as she glared at them, "The gentleman should apologise! He should be sorry! Yapper could have been killed."

"I do apologise, Princess –" Edward Seymour began but then the king's voice cut him off.

"What is all this commotion about?"

"He nearly trampled Yapper to death!" Alice accused, pointing a finger at Seymour, her tears finally falling freely.

"I did not mean to, Your Grace," the king's Esquire of the Body explained, "It was an accident."

"Yapper should not be on the dancefloor, Alice," Arthur concluded, before trying to take his daughter's hand.

But she pulled away from him too, shouting and crying loudly when suddenly Mary's lady – and Edward Seymour's sister – Jane, approached. She folded her arms around the princess' shoulders and whispered sweetly into her ear as the others watched, then turned Alice around and walked her off the dancefloor as though nothing had happened.

The music began playing again and the courtiers resumed their dance.

Arthur looked to Mary, "What just happened?" he asked.

Mary took her father's arm in hers and led him off the busy dancefloor, looking over her shoulder at where Alice was being led out of the great hall by Jane Seymour.

"I think my lady Jane just spared us a little princess' tantrum," she said with a light chuckle.

Arthur followed Mary's gaze, caught a glimpse of Jane smiling down at Alice and wiping away her tears, Alice holding Yapper up for Jane to stroke.

"Yes," he said as he watched the lady temper Alice's mood, "It appears she did just that."

January 1537

As agreed upon in the marriage contract, Princess Mary and her household of two hundred servants, guards, and ladies, were to make their journey to Scotland in the new year, King James V being eager to meet his chosen bride as soon as possible.

"His enthusiasm makes me nervous, Cecily," Mary confided in her friend one evening, as the day to depart edged closer and closer, "How can I trust him to treat me any better than Francis did? If I fail to conceive an heir for him swiftly, he might –"

"The Dauphin had no good in him," Cecily interjected causally as she laced the sleeves to Mary's dress, "He was arrogant, spoilt, and cruel. But there are good men out there. Do not let the one who came before sully your second chance at joy."

Mary swallowed, looked at the heavy rain pelting the window, "It is but another political match," she said, "I am no fool to think love is to find me. But," she turned to meet Cecily's gaze then, who had moved to stand before her, "For a time I thought perhaps I had not been born for happiness."

Cecily smiled sadly at her mistress, "You may not find love with this next union either," she admitted, matching Mary's realistic point of view about diplomatic unions, "But happiness. That is once again within reach."

Mary smiled in thanks and watched as Cecily and Jane flitted about packing linens and dresses into travel trunks, the young princess feeling something else besides anxiety at the prospect of marrying a total stranger once again. This time, the young woman felt a flicker of hope.

"I...have an announcement...I wish to make."
King Arthur and his council had just sat down to commence the daily meeting, the matter of Princess Mary's journey and the continued tension with France being at the top of the list of topics to discuss.
But it appeared their king had another matter on his mind.
"Your Grace?" Thomas More asked, his brown eyes curious.
Arthur looked up to meet his councillor's questioning looks, feeling nauseous at the prospect of uttering the words that had been swirling around in his mind of late.
The king swallowed hard, forcing down the acid that was creeping up his throat.
"I have...decided it is time for me to remarry," he announced, though there was no emotion in his voice.
Cromwell, More, and Gardiner exchanged a hopeful look.
"That is excellent news, Your Highness," Cromwell said, shifting excitedly in his seat, "Might you reconsider the princesses Anna or Amelia of Cleves?"
More swiftly shot Cromwell a disgruntled look, "What is it with you suggesting Cleves? The Lutheran faith is rife over there –"
"I only mean to suggest new alliances, their faith does not interest me."
"It should! Our king has made it perfectly clear where he stands on the religious –"
"I have already made my choice!" the king interrupted his advisors' squabbling.

They turned to look at their king as he sat slumped forward in his throne, looking down at his hands resting on the table before him.

He did not appear like a man who was about to announce his choice of bride – showing more signs of anguish than of elation – and More wondered just *who* Arthur was making this decision for, since he clearly wasn't making it for himself.

"England shall not be making a new alliance through my marriage," Arthur explained, "For I have chosen a lady in-house to be my next Queen," his voice broke at the title that was formerly Katherine's, and he closed his eyes and cleared his throat, "A subject of England who I believe will be a model of virtue and goodness for my daughters and the country."

"Who, Your Grace?" Cromwell said, irked to think his final chance to introduce Protestantism to England to be missed.

Arthur inhaled, hoping to sound at least willing to make the announcement.

"The Mistress Jane Seymour."

"Jane?"

The whisper sounded distant to Jane's ears as she stared up at the king, along with the rest of the court.

By now, rumours that King Arthur had decided to make his former Queen's lady-in-waiting his new wife were spreading all over the court; and still Jane could not believe her ears when Arthur officially announced it.

"Jane?"

The whisper called her name again, the voice sounding familiar but still far away.

Jane blinked, then looked around herself as the courtiers surrounding her stared and muttered.

She had heard the rumours. Had even been forewarned by her brother Edward Seymour who, being the king's Esquire of the Body, had known of it before most people. He had raced to inform his sister of the news, as well as alerting the rest of the Seymour family at Wolf Hall, who had travelled to court the very next day to be sure to witness the incredible occasion.

But even with the forewarning, Jane could not make sense of it.

"Jane?"

The whisper again, more harshly this time, followed by a nudge from Mary who stood beside her. Had it been Mary calling her all along?

Jane blinked, waking from her trance. She took a slow step, then another, her feet feeling as though ants had crawled inside her shoes. How could this be happening?

Jane had served the late queen for some time, had tried to do whatever she could to alleviate Queen Katherine's pain in her final days, had wept at her funeral and been devastated to see the king and his daughters mourn her. She had returned to court to serve her daughter as she believed Queen Katherine would have wanted. Had been sure to make time for the little Princess Alice as any decent person would have done.

But never had she and the king shared a private moment or had a conversation beyond pleasantries and business.

Why then would he choose *her* above any other lady, a royal Princess of Europe, or a nobler lady of the court than she?

She was Jane. Just Jane.

What could she have to offer that another woman could not?

"Your Grace?" she mumbled, bobbing a curtsy before the king.

He looked haunted, Jane thought as she looked up at him, as though he too did not know why he had made the announcement. At the age of fifty-one, King Arthur looked tired. His blue eyes held no shine, his hair had gone completely silver following Queen Katherine's death, and he never smiled anymore. But despite all that, Jane could not deny that she had always found his good nature attractive. And king or not, Arthur Tudor was a good catch.

"Will you accept this offer, Mistress Jane?" Arthur asked before the entire court, "To be my next Queen?"

Jane's cheeks reddened; never before had she been asked for her hand in marriage; and though she had never imagined a highborn man to think her good enough to wed, she had always envisioned a slightly more romantic proposal. Alas, she knew what her family was expecting of her in this most pivotal moment, could almost hear their prayers in her mind as though they were screaming them at her back.

She had never looked at the king as a potential husband. Had never for a second imagined this scenario to ever play out.

But here she was, before the entire English court as they awaited with bated breath as her life was about to change before their very eyes. And she gave the king the only answer that would be befitting.

"I humbly accept, Your Grace. If that is indeed your wish."

Chapter 34

14ᵗʰ February 1537
Lamberton, borders of Scotland

Leaving her former lady-in-waiting behind to become the new Queen Consort of England, Mary and her household made the long trip to Scotland by ship to avoid the dangers on the road.

The question as to why King Arthur was suddenly willing to send his heir abroad to marry when it had been outside the realm of possibility for their union with France years ago did not go unspoken. But Arthur, as well as his advisors, were much more relaxed about this marriage than the one that had come before. Not only for the fact that Scotland and England occupied one landmass, but also because they shared a common desire to put their past behind them once and for all – unlike France, whose suspicion of England didn't so much end as dissipate, like a drop of ink in a bowl of water, with a residual taint that lingered.

And so, upon Mary's arrival at Lamberton on the borders of Scotland, the princess was met by the Scottish Ambassador Sadler, her aunt the Dowager Queen Margaret Tudor, and some dozen guards who would escort her to Dalkeith Palace where she would meet her future husband the following day.

"Mary," her aunt said in greeting, a toothy grin splitting her rosy cheeked face. Margaret Tudor had almost doubled in size since Mary had last seen her, her son's court clearly having taken good care of their English Dowager Queen. It gave Mary a glimpse as to how well she would be accepted, the second English princess to be married to their Scottish King in two generations.

"My Lady Aunt," Mary replied cheerfully, glad to be off the ship and back on dry land – though the soggy mud beneath her feet was not much of an improvement, "Thank you for meeting me."

As she and Margaret bundled into the carriage that awaited them, and Cecily got Mary comfortable under two thick fur blankets, Mary flashed her aunt a nervous smile.

"It is…much colder up here than I expected," she admitted timidly, hoping to find comfort from the former Princess of England who too had made this same relocation some thirty years prior.

Margaret Tudor only laughed, a loud and uninhibited sound, which Mary found both staggering and refreshing all at once.

"My dear niece," Margaret replied, wiping the laughter from her eyes as she caught her breath, "Scotland is wet, dark and dreary. But by God, the people know how to brighten the days. Trust me on that."

Dalkeith Castle, Scotland

Mary's party approached Dalkeith Castle at sunset.
Located above a bend in the River North Esk, the beautiful castle was strategically placed in an easily defensible position. Rising to three storeys in the main block, the mansion entrance featured an impressive triangular pediment and lower advanced wings built of grey and white stone.

Mary's nervousness spiked at the sight of it, knowing that on the break of dawn she would come face to face with the next man that would own her.

She sat back in her seat and exhaled slowly.

"Don't fret, Mary," her aunt Margaret said, sensing her anxiety, "The king is just as nervous as you are."

Mary smiled tightly, she doubted that.

Trumpets sounded at their carriage's arrival at Dalkeith Castle, and following Mary's exit from it, she was greeted by dozens of lords and ladies who all bowed and curtsied at her in greeting. They wore garments and cloaks of wool and fur to combat the cold Scottish weather, and Mary made a mental note to update her own wardrobe to accommodate to her new environment.

"Welcome, Princess," the lords and ladies mumbled as she was escorted inside by Ambassador Sadler and her aunt, the Dowager Queen.

Inside, Margaret waved over a guard, "Take the Princess to her chambers," she ordered him before turning to face Mary with an excited smile, "We will feast tonight, to welcome you to Scotland. Then, bright and early, you and my son shall meet."

Mary nodded and Margaret grinned before giving her a once over, "I suggest you freshen up before dinner."

Once in her chambers, Mary waited anxiously for the guard to leave and for Cecily to close the door behind him, her terror suddenly taking shape in rapid breaths and a pounding heart.

"I cannot do this," Mary whispered as she wrung her hands together before the fire in the stone hearth, "He too will hate me."

Cecily shushed her mistress gently as she hurriedly approached, the only one to truly understand Mary's fears.

"He will not hate you," Cecily assured her as she gently took off Mary's gable hood to replace it with a beautiful black and gold one.

"How can you know that?" Mary accused, turning from her and pressing a hand to her forehead, "I possess no beauty nor charm. I am not witty nor –"

"And yet he chose you," Cecily reminded her, "He had his pick, and he selected you. Over a union with France might I add."

"But *why*?" Mary countered, making her point.

Cecily shrugged, "Perhaps it is as simple as wanting to unite the countries."

Mary scoffed, turning to look out the window, at the men hauling her travel trunks inside.

"Can it not be for a noble cause alone?" Cecily asked.

Mary turned round to look at her lady, perhaps the one person left alive who knew her best.

"My guard is up," Mary admitted, "As I am sure you can understand."

Cecily nodded, placed the new hood over Mary's hair, "I do. And you'd be a fool not to have learned to harden yourself from the last time. But until there is cause for concern, try to embrace this for what it appears to be."

"And what is that?" Mary mumbled.

"A chance to be someone's first choice."

The banquet was much the same as a banquet back in London, with musicians playing merry tunes in the corner and jesters performing while the plates were cleared.

Mary sat at the high table with her aunt as they watched the cheerful show, Margaret laughing raucously when a jester dropped one of his wooden rings onto another's foot and he hopped away dramatically, holding his foot in both hands.

But Mary could not muster up any laughter, for the anxiety that plagued her would not settle no matter what she did, and she hoped only for a good night's rest before meeting her betrothed.

Suddenly, trumpets sounded, and the music abruptly stopped. The ladies and gentlemen around the tables all mumbled approvingly, some stealing glances up at Mary as though they had been awaiting this moment the entire time.

"What is happening?" Mary muttered to herself.

But her aunt heard, and she reached over to squeeze her hand.

"Scottish tradition, Mary," she whispered with a sympathetic smile, "Just go with it."

"James V King of Scots!" the usher called, to which everyone quickly rose from their seats and bowed or curtsied as a group of men entered.

Mary's heart beat wildly all of a sudden to think that she was to meet her betrothed in this very moment, a whole day before she was ready to, in the wrong dress and the wrong frame of mind, her belly full of greasy food and her eyes tired from her travels.

She wasn't ready. But there was nothing she could do.

Taking a deep curtsy so low she was practically sitting on the stone floor, her black and gold dress ballooning all around her as the group of men approached, she could do no more than bow her head and quietly pray that King James would – unlike the Dauphin of France – not be disappointed.

At the sound of footsteps stopping before her, Mary looked up to find a tall young man standing before her, with short auburn hair and a trimmed auburn beard. The colour of his eyes was not immediately clear in the dim lighting, but his lids were heavy – similarly to Francis', Mary noted, though not in disinterest, but rather in self-assurance. But most encouragingly of all was the welcoming smile beneath the red beard and the extended hand he now held towards Mary to help her back up.

Mary took it, her hand feeling tiny in his burly grasp, and he pulled her up.

Standing before him, Mary was pleased to see he was indeed smiling fondly at her, his eyes crinkled at the corners with genuine affection; and before even a word had been spoken between them, Mary could sense that this time, her betrothed was a good man.

"Forgive the intrusion," King James said, his voice smooth and his Scottish accent thick, "But we were oot hunting and being in the area, we decided to stop by."

A low chuckle escaped the group of men behind him.

"Hunting?" Mary replied, wincing inwardly at her poor choice of first word to her future husband.

James smiled mischievously, as though he'd been caught out, "No doubt my Lady Mother has informed ye of our little

Scottish tradition, she too having been ambushed, as it were, by my father many years ago on the eve of their official meetin'."

Mary looked back at her aunt who, like the rest of the court, was watching them.

"Your Lady Mother did not," she admitted, turning back to James, "I had no idea."

"Ah!" James called with a laugh, turning to his groomsmen behind him, "We succeeded in maintainin' secrecy, gentlemen. A good start!"

The men behind the king chuckled again. James turned back to Mary and took her hand in his, bringing it to his lips and kissing her knuckles.

His beard tickled Mary's skin and she was surprised to realise that she didn't mind, a genuine smile pulling at her lips.

"Come!" he said then before clapping his hands together for the music to resume, "I do believe dancin' was aboot to commence?"

At that, many lord and ladies rose from their seats and headed towards the dancefloor as the musicians began their song. James bowed at the waist, his hand raised towards Mary.

"Would you do me the 'onour?" he asked with such effortless charm that Mary couldn't help but exhale all the fear she had been holding in.

"Of course, Your Highness," she replied shyly as she took his big hand, feeling suddenly giddy at the prospect of their wedding day.

Part VII

Even in the deepest darkness
comes the dawn

Chapter 35

1 year later

March 1538
Greenwich Palace, London

With England and Scotland having united through the marriage of Arthur's heir, the Princess Mary, to their Scottish King, James V, France was henceforth unable to wage war directly on England without risking the Auld Alliance with Scotland, as well as causing widespread mistrust of France throughout Europe.

With Mary's marriage, England was made safe, and with that safety had come the possibility for King Arthur to marry in-house, having had no immediate need for a new alliance with another European country. What he *had* needed, however, was to keep the promise he had made to Katherine: to remarry a good woman to mother their children. And by choosing a lady his daughters knew and liked, he believed he had done the right thing by Katherine in marrying her former lady-in-waiting Jane Seymour. Her gentleness and devotion to God, country, and his daughters shone through in all that she did, and in truth, she reminded Arthur a little of Katherine.

He and Jane had married just one month after Mary's wedding to James V had taken place the previous year, England having rejoiced much that Spring, two royal weddings taking place so closely together.

England was finally on its way out of the doom and gloom that had possessed it for so long, the people celebrating on the streets for days following the elaborate occasions, both in Forteviot in Scotland, and in London.

Princess Alice loved her new stepmother, who had accepted her little stepdaughter as her own without hesitation. The court and the people had welcomed their new Queen with much warmth and happiness, glad to see the monarchy complete once more. Everything was perfect.

Except when it came to Arthur's heart.

King Arthur could not bring himself to feel something he did not feel, could not force himself to be happy or even at peace with his decision. He had done what he had thought to have been right. He had remarried as Katherine had requested, given Alice and Mary a mother figure to fill the void left behind by Katherine's absence, and provided the country with a new Queen and the possibility of more heirs to strengthen the Tudor dynasty.

But it meant nothing to him deep down, for he had not married out of love or passion or devotion to this woman, and being the gentle angel that Jane was, he knew she deserved better than him.

Still, he could not ever admit to these thoughts and feelings out loud, knowing that it would only lead to spreading his heartache onto others like a disease. And Arthur was not one to unload his pain if he could avoid it, the only one to ever having truly understood him being lost to him forever.

"There is word from our ambassadors in France."

The voice snapped Arthur out of his troubled mind, and he looked up to see a messenger handing his Lord Chancellor Thomas More a letter.

More unrolled the note and read it quickly, his brows furrowing deeply, "France plans to lay siege on Calais."

"Calais?" Bishop Gardiner echoed.

More nodded, looking up from the letter, "They plan to reclaim their city. No doubt to gain the revenge they are so desperate for, for the death of their prince."

"Murder," Gardiner corrected absentmindedly.

More continued as if he hadn't spoken, "Because they cannot wage war on us on English mainland they have turned their attention to Calais."

"But Calais is part of England!" Cromwell added, "Has been for hundreds of years."

More shook his head, handed the letter to Arthur and said, "This way they do not break the Auld Alliance. In France's eyes it is not a direct attack on England. It is a 'reclaiming' of what should rightfully be theirs."

Gardiner was looking from one man to another, his eyes wide and his white eyebrows raised high, "Can they really do this?"

King Arthur looked up from the letter then, his men almost flinching to see the wide grin that had spread across his face, his eyes flashing with excitement for the first time in years.

"My lord?" More asked tentatively.

Arthur inhaled, "I must be frank and admit I am…exhilarated by this turn of events. France has, time and time again, shown their underhandedness, and this time it is no different. I have spent my reign assuaging their suspicions, first of our military and naval increase, then of our supposed involvement in the death of their prince –"

"Murder," Gardiner mumbled again.

"—But perhaps I have been too soft. Perhaps a fight is what is needed to show them not to underestimate us."

"M-my king," More said, tripping over his words as he realised what Arthur was saying, "France won't give in easily. They will not be made to look weak."

Arthur's grin widened. Despite a lifetime of wanting to avoid battle, and his recent reminder from Katherine herself that he was not a fighting man, Arthur could not shake the intense need to *break* something. What better way to let out his persistent anguish and frustration than on the battlefield against England's greatest enemy?

"This is unavoidable now, gentlemen," he said, folding the letter in half, his mind made up, "The French want to reclaim our territory in France. And we shall not let them."

April 1538

Arthur and Queen Jane Seymour were sharing a private dinner in the king's chambers, their usual comfortable silence enveloping them as they ate their roasted pork and pheasant pies, when there was a knock at the door and a messenger entered.

"News from France, Your Grace," the young boy said before bowing his head and leaving once again.

Arthur tore open the letter and inhaled deeply, Jane noticing that he was trying not to smile.

The war with France was all he smiled about these days, Jane thought as she considered her own reason to be happy. Perhaps once she shared her own news, he would have something else besides war to live for.

"France is making preparations for a summer siege," the king told Jane as he folded the letter in half and resumed eating. He scoffed a laugh, "He thinks a swift invasion will drive us out. Francis has no idea the strength England has gathered since the beginning of my reign."

Jane nodded, having nothing of worth to contribute to the talk of battle. But what had he said? A summer invasion?

She touched her hand to her belly. Perhaps she did not have much more time to keep this news to herself.

"My king," Jane said then, her quiet voice sounding loaded, "I have news."

Arthur looked up, wiped his mouth with his handkerchief, "What news? Are you unwell?"

Jane gazed fondly at him. Even in wartime he was able to care for her wellbeing.

"Not in the sense that should cause you concern," Jane replied, smiling meaningfully at him.

Arthur slowly put down his spoon, understanding the implication, "Are you…?"

Jane nodded, touched her belly again, "Yes, Arthur. I do believe I am."

He grinned as he knew he should, got up and walked around the table to plant a kiss to her forehead as he knew would be expected. But inside, a pang of guilt pierced through him as he thought of his life going on without Katherine.

With Queen Jane announcing her condition, the King's Council were frantically urging the king not to lead his troops into battle as he had been planning to do.

"If the Queen produces a son, then the line of succession will need to be revised," Thomas Cromwell argued, to which Edward Seymour – the new queen's brother and newest addition to the King's Privy Council, having recently been made Earl of Hertford – nodded in agreement.

"Why?" More asked from across the table, frowning deeply at the two men, "Princess Mary has been the king's heir for years and the people of England accept her."

"The people of England accepted her because there was no alternative," Cromwell replied in frustration, closing his eyes and pinching the bridge of his nose with his thumb and forefinger, "But if the queen gives birth to a son, then a son is traditionally the next in line."

More scoffed, shook his head, "What would England prefer in this time of war? A strong line of succession with a grown and educated Princess to take over as next heir? Or a weak and easily overthrowable baby who has yet to learn all that Mary already knows?"

Edward Seymour shrank into his seat to hear such strong opposition from the Lord Chancellor, and he thought it best to keep a low profile before outright voicing his own opinions on the matter. For, as the new queen's brother, he would of course wish to see his own nephew on the throne – his young nephew who would need a Lord Protector in place to rule in his stead until he became of age…

Cromwell shrugged indifferently at More's question, "A boy is always preferable," he stated, and Seymour watched carefully to see how the discussion would unfold.

"Is it?" King Arthur chimed in finally, having wanted to hear his council's true thoughts on the matter, and he was disappointed to learn Cromwell held the same beliefs as the traitor Thomas Wolsey had done – that a male candidate for the throne always outshone a female one. And he would have to make it clear that in the event of his death, his daughter's position as his heir would be honoured.

"Whether Queen Jane births a son or a daughter, Princess Mary is my chosen heir," Arthur clarified sternly, staring Cromwell down, "Do I make myself clear?"

The man at least had the decency to apologise and bow his head. And Edward Seymour knew he would have to keep his identical beliefs to himself; at least until he had gained more favour with the king.

1st June 1538

The following month, Queen Jane, dressed in an exquisite green velvet gown and matching gable hood, was standing at the castle gates, her ladies-in-waiting on either side of her as she held one hand up in farewell to her lord husband while the other rested protectively on her swollen belly.

"He will be back soon," one of her ladies reassured their queen, "A king does not engage in fighting. He is going only to boost the troops' morale."

Jane nodded, her light eyebrows bunched together as she tried to hold back her tears.

While she was not in love with Arthur, they had grown fond of one another – as would be expected of two people who respected each other and shared the same values, as well as a bed. But despite not being madly in love with him, Jane cared for his safe return. If not for her own sake, then for that of their unborn child.

King Arthur had explained to Jane, on more than one occasion, that he *had* to do this. And Jane, being a woman and knowing nothing of what men were brought up to believe, fear, and value most in life, accepted his word as final. If he 'had to do this', then she would support him. Besides, Jane was no fool. She knew that, as her lady said, unless it was absolutely necessary Arthur would not see any real fighting.

That was what she held onto now as she watched him leave on his warhorse, wearing his silver and gold armour, leading his men to battle.

He was really going.

France was hell bent on making England pay for the mysterious murder of their prince, and frankly, Jane could not even blame them. She looked down at her growing bump. If anyone dared to hurt the child in her womb, Jane would most likely wish to spill blood too. But Arthur was not to blame for the Dauphin's demise, of that Jane was sure; which was why it felt so utterly ludicrous that he and the entirety of England would have to suffer through a war for the King of France to feel some relief for his loss. It did not make sense to her.

Jane sighed as she turned around to go back inside to put up her feet, the pregnancy causing her all kinds of aches and pains. This was a man's world, and Jane would likely never understand the true workings of a man's mind. If spilling blood in the hope of reclaiming a land long lost to France would set the matter of a lost son straight in France's mind, then that is what would happen.

What could a mere woman's objection to the matter change?

2nd June 1538

In Arthur's absence he had proclaimed his eldest daughter and heir as his Regent, to watch over England in his stead and to send any necessary supplies to their cause in Calais.

It was an honour, one only ever bestowed onto a woman once before, when Katherine of Aragon had been alive.

Back then, of course, Scotland had invaded England on France's behalf to scope out and weaken their military forces due to France's suspicions of England's growth under their new young king. This time, however, there would be no such sly plotting against England, for Mary's marriage to Scotland's King James V brought with it the protection they had formerly lacked.

Mary had arrived in London the day after her father had left for Calais, feeling troubled to have missed him but wondering if he had planned it that way, to avoid a goodbye he knew they did not need. She hoped his certainty for a safe return was the reason, because Mary could think of nothing worse than to lose her only remaining parent while being in the condition she was in.

"Princess Mary!" Queen Jane exclaimed in friendly greeting, her face bright with joy to see her, plump and full of life. Jane waddled towards her eldest stepdaughter – who was more like a dear friend to her since they were so close in age – with her arms open wide.

"I cannot believe you have kept this secret for so long!" Jane squealed excitedly as she embraced Mary awkwardly, both their swollen bellies getting in the way.

Mary grinned at her stepmother, "I wanted to surprise you and my Lord Father," she admitted, "Though I am sorry to see I have missed him."

Jane pressed her lips together in a sad smile, "You know your father. He is a man of few words."

Mary nodded.

"And," Jane continued, taking Mary's arm in hers and walking her inside the castle, "I am certain he will be thrilled to receive such wonderful news while he's away. If anything, it will give him more reason to hurry home."

A beat of silence ensued which Jane quickly filled with an excited squeal, "This is just wonderful, Mary," she said, rubbing a hand over both their bellies, Mary's a lot smaller than Jane's, "A son *and* a grandson for our king. What better news could England ask for?"

Perhaps not to be at war? Mary thought.

But Mary smiled, "I am pleased to be home," she said, the two women walking companionably through the courtyard, neither of them brave enough to express the fear that lingered beneath their friendly exchange.

8th June 1538

Thomas More and Thomas Cromwell had remained in England to aid Princess Mary rule the country in the king's absence, Edward Seymour having accompanied their king to Calais to assist in the defence of the city. And Mary could feel the disdain for her reverberating off lord Cromwell, just as her father had warned her she would.

"We have received reports of safe landing at Calais, Your Grace," Cromwell informed Mary a week after her arrival in London, "The troops are eager and ready to protect the city. They are well aware of its importance to England's profitable export abroad."

He said this as though Mary did not know of Calais' importance to England, and Mary all but rolled her eyes.

"I'd wager their successful return to their families might be more of a cause to fight than our export of wool," she replied drily, "Have we other news from the king?" Mary asked then, turning to More and the ambassadors, "Is he in need of more weapons, armour?"

More shook his head, "Our troops are holding the city, but we should be prepared for anything. Word will arrive often and sporadically in the days to come."

Mary nodded, ran a hand subconsciously over her slight bump, "Do not expect much rest, gentlemen. I have a feeling it will not be an easy victory," and she thought of her former husband's disturbing fate, "France is acting on revenge. I fear it might be stronger than our resolve."

That night, as Mary sat at her desk and wrote a letter to James in Scotland, unable to sleep due to the tension that now lingered in the air, she was pleased to note a smile had crept onto her face at the thought of her husband.

Unlike her first husband, James enjoyed Mary's company greatly and respected her opinions on both domestic and foreign matters. From their very first meeting, Mary had known that James was an honourable man, one who wouldn't dare to mistreat a woman, much less the woman he had pledged his life to. His mother had taught him well.

Princess Mary rested one hand over her round belly as she continued to write home, her heart feeling full to think of her growing family. It was strange, but this political match had, despite her lifelong reservations, turned out to be a happy one. And their happiness had resulted in a beautiful blessing from God – a child Mary had always yearned for, an heir to unite the countries of Scotland and England forever.

The quill in her hand jerked and smudged her letter suddenly when there was an urgent knock at the door, and Mary's chest tightened, knowing it would be pressing news from Calais.

"Enter!" she called, rising from her seat.

Thomas More and a messenger hurried inside, bowing grandly at the waist, "Your Grace, a letter from the king."

Mary took the hastily scribbled note and read it anxiously.

"He requests more troops and weapons," Mary breathed, her eyes wide when she looked up to meet the Lord Chancellor's worried gaze, "He fears France will not rest until Calais is reclaimed."

More inhaled deeply and nodded, "We can round up mercenaries if necessary. London cannot be left defenceless." Mary nodded, swallowed hard, "Do whatever is necessary," she said, "King Arthur must not come into harm's way."

10th June 1538

Two days later, after more troops, armour, weapons and supplies had been sent to aid their king, terrible word arrived from their ambassador in France that Calais had been reclaimed, and that their soldiers had been run out.

"Five hundred have been taken prisoner, Your Grace," the messenger boy informed Mary as she sat on her father's throne, Queen Jane at her side on what had formerly been her mother's, "Two hundred are presumed dead."

"And the king?" Mary asked, "Have we word of the king?!" The boy cleared his throat, wiped his brow with the heel of his hand, "We have word that the king was seen to be pulled from his horse when the French broke into the city," he said, his dark brows furrowed in fear, "There is no other direct news about King Arthur, but some ships were able to set sail back to England. There is still hope."

Mary was stunned into silence, the image of her father being pulled from his warhorse and potentially killed on the spot burning in her mind's eye.

"Pray God our king is on his way home to us," Jane's voice called to the court from beside Mary then, and the princess was grateful to have her stepmother beside her during this time.

Chapter 36

That night, as Mary and Jane prayed side by side in the chapel, news arrived of the English ships' landing at Dover.

"It is good news, Your Graces," Imperial Ambassador Chapuys proclaimed as he approached them, "The king is aboard one of the ships."

Mary and Jane exclaimed with joy, holding onto each other's shaky hands for support.

"*Gracias, embajador,*" Mary replied gratefully, offering him a teary smile.

The older man bowed his head, his thick grey hair flopping over his forehead, he pushed it back, "France may have won the battle, but the King of England is safely returned to you, praise God."

Mary nodded in thanks, turning to embrace Jane who had begun sobbing with relief, her cries echoing through the high ceilings of the candlelit chapel.

11th June 1538

It was the middle of the night, and Princess Mary had not slept a wink, too anxious was she to welcome her father home.

He had been pulled from his horse, if reports were to be believed. Had he been hurt, slashed at, beaten?

More likely than not, her father would be no more than shaken up from the ordeal, in need of a warm bath and rest – he had been defeated in battle, after all – and Mary only hoped that it had been his ego that had taken the most damage.

The baby in her belly lurched then, Mary feeling it for the first time in that very moment. She pressed a hand to where she had felt the little movement, like a bubble popping in her stomach, and grinned from ear to ear.

"No fear, little one," she whispered to her child, "Your grandfather will be home at any moment, no doubt eager to meet you."

Trumpets sounded then, pulling Mary from her thoughts, and she picked up her skirts and hurried out the door.

Cecily met her just outside Mary's chambers, "The king?" she gasped, and Mary nodded in confirmation.

"Open the gates!" Mary called to the guards as she and Cecily made their way down the wide staircase, the servants just ahead of them, lighting torches and stoking the fires to properly receive their monarch.

The courtyard was in near darkness, the torches and candles doing little against the clouded night sky, but Mary could make out the dark outline of several soldiers on horseback and a carriage coming through the gates, which she assumed contained her father.

When the horses came to a halt, she and Jane waited patiently for the carriage door to swing open and for Arthur to emerge with his head low in shame over their loss. They had been prepared to console him, to show their support in whatever means necessary. But when the carriage door did not immediately open, Mary's stomach dropped, and for a brief moment, she wondered if perhaps they had missed some vital piece of information. One of the soldiers swung from his horse then and walked around the carriage to open it, confirming Mary's fear that her father could perhaps not open it by himself.

She swallowed hard to dislodge the lump that had formed in her throat, but it would not budge. And when two more soldiers joined the first and pulled out a long, wooden, coffin-like crate out of the carriage, a raspy *No!* sounded out from somewhere in the crowd.

And it took Mary a moment to realise that the wounded cry had come from her.

*

The wooden gurney was carried in by Edward Seymour and three soldiers who quickly but carefully climbed the staircase to the king's chamber as they had been instructed to do.

"What has happened?!" Mary asked the Earl of Hertford Edward Seymour as they hurried along, trying desperately not to stare at the red-raw gash on his cheek.

"The king was struck down with an arrow and pulled from his horse," Seymour explained, to which Queen Jane called over her shoulder for someone to summon Dr Butts.

"Is he --?" Mary whispered in fear.

"He is alive," another soldier confirmed, "We did what we could, but…"

He did not need to finish the sentence, for Mary could see it in their eyes. The King of England would likely not survive his wounds.

The following morning, after the king's physician Dr Butts had examined the king and treated his wounds, Mary – as Regent – was charged with informing the court and country of the new developments.

Queen Jane, who had been due to enter her confinement, would not be by her side to make the announcement, for the stress of her husband's frightful return had caused her to feel the first pains of labour, and the midwives had ordered for their queen to retire to bed, in the hopes of stopping the early arrival of her babe.

Mary was alone.

As she sat on the king's throne in the great hall, the many faces of the lords of the Houses of Parliament and the court looking up at her with wide, questioning eyes, Mary gripped her rosary beads tightly in her hand.

"My lords," she said, addressing them all and taking a moment to compose her thoughts, "Our king is returned home, and for that we must thank God!"

A murmur of agreement ensued, many heads nodded.

Mary continued, "He fought valiantly against the French, and stood his ground when they sought to take what was rightfully ours. Our king did all that he could to defend the city of Calais but…I regret to inform you all that it has been lost. Calais has been reclaimed by the French."

Many shook their heads, others exhaled angrily. The loss of Calais was both a devastating embarrassment as well as a blow to the country's trade. And the people would not take this news well.

"Good King Arthur stood his ground," Mary said, tripping over her words when she realised she had already said that. But she quickly regained her train of thought, "But in doing so, he almost gave up his own life! The enemy struck him down and beat him savagely. There was no honour. But our king is strong! And though he was severely wounded, be assured that the king's physician expects a full recovery. And until then, my lords, I beseech you all to pray for his speedy improvement, so that we may show France that though we have lost Calais, we have not lost our faith!"

The crowd called loudly in agreement then – albeit half-heartedly – and pumped their fists in the air.

And though Mary had known that such comforting words had been necessary to settle the concerned crowd, as their future Queen Regnant, she hated herself for having so blatantly lied to their faces.

11th July 1538

Queen Jane of England had been labouring for two days and two nights, her water having broken shortly after entering her confinement. And throughout the entire ordeal, King Arthur had not yet roused from his coma.

"The wound on his leg has festered," Dr Butts informed Princess Mary a month after the king's return from France,

"It has caused a fever, and I'm afraid it's taken hold of our king."

Mary swallowed, disturbed by the increasingly negative news she was receiving of late, her father's condition having gotten worse and worse since his return.

"Can nothing more be done?" she asked the old man.

He pulled at his white beard in thought and glanced to his younger apprentice beside him who looked just as lost, "We will continue to debride the wound with maggots," the old man said, "The wound to the king's shoulder responded nicely to the treatment and is now in the stages of healing. Pray God we can soon say the same for the wound on His Highness' leg."

Then he bowed and hobbled back into the king's chambers, his cane clinking rhythmically on the stone floor.

Mary's mouth twitched as she watched them go, the babe in her belly kicking violently. She placed a hand over her bump, and desperately yearned for her mother.

On the third day of Queen Jane's labour, news swiftly broke that she had given birth to a healthy baby boy, and Mary decided to make the most of the good news, and to lead the court out of its despair with a merry celebration of life. A banquet was hastily planned following the birth of the new royal prince, as well as a Robin Hood inspired masquerade. Mary also organised for cannons to be fired from the Tower of London and for free wine to be made available for the people of London. And she was relieved to notice it lightening the people's mood.

Queen Jane would need to rest well to recover from the difficult ordeal, her labour having taken longer than the midwives had been comfortable with. But after being rolled back and forth in a sheet to dislodge the child – as recommended by the male physician in attendance – the babe had quickly been born thereafter. And by a miracle of God, both mother and child had emerged in good health. The midwives deemed the babe strong enough to delay the christening until in four days' time, giving Mary some hope that her father would yet wake in time to give his son a name.

"A boy, sister," Edward Seymour said as soon as he entered the queen's chambers, an arrogant stride in his step, "Well done."

The way he grinned at her – like a wolf who had just spotted its prey – made the hairs on Jane's neck rise to attention, the new red scar on his cheek adding to his already menacing aura. She knew of her brother's lust for power, of his belief that the crown should be worn by a man.

"It does not matter," Jane whispered angrily, hoping she sounded stern, "His claim is no greater than Mary's simply because he is male. Leave my son out of your plotting!"

Edward reached for his sister's cheek then, intimidating her though he brushed it lightly, "Leave the thinking to the men, dear sister. You have done your part."

"Will Queen Jane allow me an audience?" Princess Mary's voice sounded then from the other room.

Edward and Jane looked towards the sound, then at each other before the Earl of Hertford bowed theatrically to his sister and turned on his heel. Jane narrowed her eyes at him, and he flashed her a smug grin.

"She has been waiting for you," Jane heard one of her ladies say as she watched her brother quit the room through the archway, crossing paths with Mary; and Jane was relieved to see that Edward bowed his head at Mary in greeting, at least.

"Mary," Jane breathed, plastering on a smile as she gingerly sat up in her four-poster bed, "I am so happy to see you. How is the king?"

Mary sat down on the edge of the bed, none the wiser as to what had just been discussed in that very room, "Do not fret," she said, "He will get better."

She hated that the lie was getting easier to tell the more she said it.

Jane nodded lightly, her brows furrowed as though she didn't quite believe her. Mary forced a smile.

"So," she said, "Where is he? May I meet him?"

Just then, a plump wet nurse came in through the archway to the adjacent rooms holding a squealing bundle in her arms.

"He has fed but is quite sleepy, Your Grace," the wet nurse muttered as she handed Mary the newborn.

Mary gasped at the child's adorable button nose and pouty lips, his mouth open in a gummy protest.

"He is perfect, Jane," Mary whispered, gently running a hand over the baby's wispy blond hair, "He has your hair," she grinned.

Jane watched her stepdaughter and son, a tired smile on her face, "And to think he will be an uncle in just a few months," Jane mentioned quietly, noticing her son's eyelids growing heavy in Mary's arms.

Mary chuckled lightly, "They will be best of friends," she added, amicably looking over to her dear stepmother.

Jane nodded, love blooming in her chest for both the child she had created and the one she had embraced as her own. And she hoped only that her brother's greed for power would not ever come between the Tudor children.

August 1538

The prince's christening came and went and still the king did not stir from his sleep, the physicians having had to spoon feed him warm small ale to keep him from starving to death. But then, when almost all hope had been lost – and certain members of the Privy Council had begun to slyly ascertain if any of the noble lords would support the young prince over the Princess Mary – King Arthur awoke as suddenly as a crack of thunder.

"Katherine!" he called into the darkness, his throat feeling raw from weeks of silence.

Footsteps hurried towards him then, the light of a candle growing brighter with their approach.

"My king..." someone muttered, then louder, "Someone call the physician!"

And before long, Arthur was surrounded by half a dozen worried faces, none of which were that of his beloved wife.

"Where is Katherine?" Arthur mumbled, to which the many voices talking over one another stilled.

"Your Grace?" Dr Butts asked, leaning over his king to hear him better.

Arthur licked his dry lips and tried to sit up but to no avail, "Where is Queen Katherine?"

In his late wife's stead, Thomas More hastily summoned Princess Mary from her bedchambers, outvoting Edward Seymour who had wanted his sister, the new queen, to come to King Arthur's bedside instead.

"He has clearly forgotten, however momentarily," More had argued quietly before sending for the Princess, "To thrust Queen Jane in his face now would only confuse and frighten him. And we need to keep the king in good spirits for now. Let the man remember in his own time."

Seymour had not been able to argue with reason, fearing his scheming would be found out that much sooner if he did not at least feign caring for the king's recovery.

Moments later, Mary entered the king's chambers, her haste to be by her father's side breaking the silence with a loud rustle of fabric.

"Father!" Mary called frantically, grabbing hold of his hand and holding it to her cheek, "You're awake!"

"Where...is your mother?" Arthur asked, his voice labouring to be heard, the short burst of lucidity having ebbed his energy.

Mary's face crumpled and she opened her mouth to speak before closing it again. Could she really inflict such heartache upon him again?

"Mother is…" Mary began, then stopped to clear her throat, "You will be with Mother soon," she said, realising with a heavy heart that what had been meant as a white lie to spare him distress, may very well turn out to be the truth.

Arthur nodded, a smile pulling at his lips, "Ah, my Katherine," he whispered slowly, his eyes closing again, "I've missed her so much."

And then, with one shuddered breath, King Arthur fell back asleep.

King Arthur awoke the next morning with the sun, his eyes snapping open as its light poured over him, and his mind suddenly released all the recent tragedies that he had been spared the night before.

And it was like he had escaped from one nightmare and awoken in another.

Katherine's illness. Her death. The Dauphin's poisoning. France's rage. The loss of Calais.

It all came rushing back to him, like a dam bursting, allowing way for a flood. And the weight of it all made him struggle to breathe.

"Mary…" Arthur croaked, remembering he had left her as Regent, "Someone fetch me the Princess Mary!"

By the time his eldest daughter had arrived, Arthur had been propped up against his pillows with the help of two servants, and a tray of warm, soft bread and broth had been placed on his bedside. He was just about to pop a small piece of bread in his mouth, when the sight of his daughter – heavy with child – caused him to freeze.

"Mary," he breathed, in awe at her appearance, "You look radiant."

Mary blinked, forced a smile, "I haven't slept in days," she said, subconsciously running her fingers over the dark circles under her eyes, "I'm sure I look terrible."

Arthur shook his head and reached to take her hand as she sat down beside him on the bed.

"You don't know how happy I am for you," Arthur said with a smile, before turning away sharply and coughing into his closed fist.

Dr Butts' young physician jumped forward then and mopped the king's brow. Arthur waved him away.

Mary leant over then, picked the broth up from the tray on the bedside table and began to spoon feed her father, his strength quite clearly failing him already after just an hour of wakefulness.

"I sent you letters," Mary said, "I wrote to you of my news." Arthur swallowed the broth, wincing as the warmth of it burned his throat, "There was not much time to pour over letters."

Mary nodded in understanding, feeding him another spoonful.

"Do you recall the time before you left for Calais?" Mary asked tentatively then, unsure how to tell the king that his new wife had given him a son if he could not remember the death of his former one.

Arthur exhaled and leaned his head against the cushions, his shoulder-length silver hair falling back to give Mary her first full view of a healing wound on his hairline above his ear. She flinched to think what kind of blow he had suffered to obtain it. A boot, a sword hilt, an armoured fist –

"I remember, Mary," he said, interrupting her thoughts, "There's no need to walk on eggshells around me. I've relived it all."

"Jane," Mary carefully went on, the corners of her mouth curling up, "She has had a successful birth while you were unconscious. You have a son, Father."

Mary's smile radiated warmth, and Arthur was pleased to note that it must mean the child was in good health.

"A son," he echoed, closing his eyes with joy, "Does he have a name?"

Mary nodded, "He was christened. After your royal grandfather."

In Arthur's exhausted state it took him a moment to recall of whom his daughter spoke, but then he raised his eyebrows, "Ah! Edward. A strong name!"

"Yes," Mary replied encouragingly, feeding him another spoonful.

Arthur nodded as he carefully watched Mary for any hint of mistrust but found she seemed to have no objection to her brother's chosen name, believing it simply to be what it appeared on the surface.

But Arthur was not so easily fooled, having been witness to dozens more underhanded actions by people over the years than his less experienced heir. And it made him realise that, in order for Mary to inherit the throne without issue upon his death, it would no longer be enough to simply trust those he left in charge to respect his wishes. Arthur would have to leave behind an irreputable, air-tight decree that would name Mary his successor above his newborn son, for some people within the court clearly had ideas of their own for the crown in the inevitable event of his death.

For, the connection to Arthur's grandfather aside, why else would *his* son share a name with his new queen's own brother?

Chapter 37

September 1538

Following his realisation that some members of the court and his council were likely already acting against Mary, Arthur petitioned Parliament to pass an Act of Succession, to legally and indisputably declare Princess Mary as his heir.

This act would require all his subjects to accept his eldest daughter as his rightful successor over any other of his children, male or otherwise. And he was glad when Parliament passed the act without much ado, for perhaps now he could finally give in to the infection that was slowly killing him.

Arthur knew his time was running out – his body being unable to shake the fever that coursed through him – but he had owed it to his children to leave the country in a state of peace before he breathed his last. He would not allow his death to cause England to fall back into civil unrest, especially given that his very birth decades earlier had put an end to the last civil dispute, the Cousin's War.

With this clear Act of Succession, and its addition to King Arthur's will, Edward Seymour – or any other who wished to seek power at his children's expense – would not stand a chance to gain support.

Arthur sighed heavily then as a pain shot through his leg, and he fought to shift his weight, his eyes scrunched up in agony at the movement.

In truth, Arthur was ready to leave this world behind. He had had enough of people's greed, treachery, and hatefulness. The crown, Arthur had learned in his twenty-nine-year reign, was a poison; one which promised glory and honour but for which men would just as quickly become dishonourable. Its very contradiction did not escape Arthur, and he hoped only that when the time came for Mary to wear it – the first woman in

England to do so in her own right – perhaps the world would become that little bit more progressive.

But for Arthur, none of it was worth it any longer without Katherine by his side.

He had tried to go on. Had done as she had asked on her deathbed: to find a good, stable mother figure for their children. And as Katherine had hoped it would, it had given him some joy in his last couple of years, at least; Jane Seymour having been a wonderful companion and sweet-natured wife. She would most certainly go on to make another man very happy; one who would be so much more deserving of her affection than him. They had shared some special moments together, had produced a son who Arthur loved as much as all his other children, dead or alive. But he would not watch this son grow up, of that he was certain, and though it hurt his soul, Arthur was accepting of it, knowing that baby Edward would be loved and cared for by his gentle mother and his two loving half-sisters.

"He is clammy," Arthur heard a voice say then, realising suddenly that he must have fallen asleep.

He opened his eyes with effort.

"Jane…" he mumbled as his blurry vision focused on the woman standing before him, and Dr Butts shuffled out of the room.

"My lord," she whispered, her voice cracking. He must look terrible, "I have come with Edward. I thought you would like to hold him?"

"Ah, yes," Arthur replied, his thin lips curling up into a smile, "Yes I would like that…very much."

It occurred to him then, as Jane moved closer and placed little Edward in the crook of his thin arm, that he had not yet held his son since waking three weeks earlier, and the thought of leaving his children behind felt suddenly like a punch to the gut. It seemed not even rationalising his demise took away the sorrow of it.

"He is beautiful, Jane," Arthur admired, looking up at his wife as she wiped her eyes with her handkerchief.

She sniffed loudly, forced a smile, "Do you wish me to fetch Mary and Alice to you?"

Arthur shook his head and looked back down at his newborn son sleeping soundly in his arms and regarded his chubby cheeks, "I have given them everything I had while I was alive. Let my son have me to himself for what little time I have left."

Jane nodded sadly and sat down at the edge of the bed, leaning over to dab a damp cloth on her husband's forehead.

"You did the same for…Katherine…when she lay dying," Arthur reminisced fondly, "Your gentleness was how I knew –"

He coughed then, his frail body convulsing. Baby Edward frowned in his sleep at the disruption but did not wake.

"Shh," Jane soothed, patting Arthur gently on his bony back, "Do not exhaust yourself with words. I will look out for all three of them," she said, knowing what he would have asked her if he could, "You have my word. And Mary has my loyalty."

Arthur inhaled raggedly and leaned back against his cushions. He observed her with tired eyes as he caught his breath, then nodded, believing her promise to be true.

With a heavy heart, Arthur took one last look at the sleeping infant in his arms, "What colour eyes does he have?" he asked then, desperate to know.

"The same as yours, my lord," Jane whispered lovingly, "Blue with a ring of gold."

Jane stood then, holding out her arms for her son, "Rest now, my king," she urged, taking the swaddled bundle from Arthur and pressing a kiss to his damp forehead, forcing herself not to flinch at how hot his skin felt.

"I will pray to God that tomorrow you will be better."

Arthur nodded tiredly as he watched her go, his mind telling him that there would be no tomorrow for him, and his heart –

though saddened to leave his children behind – soared at the prospect of reuniting with his Katherine in the afterlife.

When news broke the following morning that the King of England had succumbed to his fever and injuries, the entire court and country felt the pain of his loss.

Good King Arthur was dead, his reign of peace and tranquillity having come to an end due to a fight he had tried to avoid for years. But France had prevailed, and England had lost Calais and their king.

The silence that spread all over London was like a plague, the people of England mourning the passing of their most gracious monarch.

But none felt more burdened with grief than his eldest daughter who, though she wanted for nothing more than to break down and cry, no longer had that privilege as the first Queen Regnant of England

"Shh, Alice," Mary soothed as her little sister sobbed in her arms, her own tears stinging her eyes. She rubbed Alice's small back in gentle circular motions, "He is with Mother now."

As a woman, Mary knew she would not be given the same respects as her male counterparts, and to begin her reign with weeping would only end up being used against her, for *nothing* said weakness like the tearful blubbering of a woman.

"We will give him a splendid funeral," Mary said, forcing a smile when Alice looked up at her, her own face crumpled and red from crying, "And we will lay him to rest beside our Lady Mother."

Alice nodded eagerly then before a fresh wave of misery engulfed her.

"Promise me you will never leave me, Mary," ten-year-old Alice sobbed into her older sister's shoulder.

A lump formed in Mary's throat as Alice's sorrow threatened to ooze into her, and she swallowed hard to force it down.

"I promise," she whispered as she tightened her grip around Alice, "Of course I promise."

And though she meant every word, Mary couldn't help but think of the child in her belly and its inevitable birth in the weeks to come. She should not have promised such a thing to her sister in this moment of weakness, for it was a promise she may not be able to keep.

Due to Mary's condition, there was much to be achieved in very little time.

"I strongly advise Your Grace to be crowned before you enter your confinement," Thomas More informed his queen one morning on her way to chapel, "Your father may have passed the Act of Succession, but there are still those within the court who would sooner see the late king's newborn son on the throne."

Mary stared at More, her hand resting subconsciously over her heavy belly where the babe inside kicked. At eight months pregnant, Mary should have already entered her confinement. But with her ascension to the throne as the first female ruler, all usual customs were temporarily misplaced.

"After my father's funeral," Mary replied, hoping to gain some time to think.

"There is little time, my queen," More reminded her, as though she was unaware of her condition, "Those who would seek to supplant you will strike when you are out of sight."

She raised her chin, anger suddenly burning within her.

"Do we know of *who* these people may be?" she asked, suspiciously looking over at a small group of courtiers as they walked past.

More raised one greying eyebrow, "Your Grace, the whole court knows of whom I mean."

She ran her tongue over her teeth in frustration, "Speak then, More! As you yourself have said, I have little time!"

More took a step towards his queen, lowered his voice, "The council you have inherited from your father is rife with pests," he said, "Traitors are among us and, I believe, *heretics*."

27th September 1538

As the new monarch, Mary was not able to attend her father's funeral. Her stepmother, the newly styled Dowager Queen Jane Seymour, therefore acted as Chief Mourner in Mary's stead as she and the rest of the court left Greenwich Palace on procession to Westminster Abbey.
And Mary, having the castle much to herself for the first time since her father's passing – except for her ladies, guards and servants – took this opportunity to seek solace from God, in the hope of relieving herself of the growing angst in her soul. As the church bells tolled glumly in the distance and the procession for the salvation of King Arthur's soul took place in the streets below, Mary and her lady Cecily headed for the castle's chapel.
Too much had happened in a short space of time, and Mary *needed* to get some of her emotions off her chest if she wished to begin her reign with clarity. And what better way to do so than under the watchful gaze of the Good Lord.
With plump cushions beneath her knees, Mary remained at prayer for the following three hours, rocking back and forth and whispering to God as the tears she had been holding in were finally allowed to fall freely. In His presence, Mary was able to truly feel her grief, God being the only one who would not judge her for her sorrow. And when her knees could no longer take her weight, Mary wiped her cheeks and inhaled deeply before rising to her feet with Cecily's help.
The following week, Mary would be crowned before her people – as recommended by her Lord Chancellor Thomas More – before entering her confinement the very next day.

She would become the very first Queen of England in her own right. And now that she had purged some of the pain from inside her, Mary exited the chapel feeling that much lighter, though the baby in her womb weighed more and more each day.

30th September 1538

On the eve of her coronation, Mary found herself in the midst of a screaming match with her Privy Council.

"England will not be ruled by some savage Scottish King!"

"It shall be ruled by our queen, you imbecile!"

"And are we to believe that her *husband* shall have no say?"

"MY LORDS!" the queen bellowed then, her brows furrowed so deeply and her cheeks so warm she had no doubt her face was bright red, "You dare to insult my lord husband – your future king – thusly!?"

At that, Edward Seymour raised one eyebrow and turned to Thomas More, "You see, she admits it herself. That savage will be our king!"

"*'She'* is YOUR QUEEN!" More thundered, spittle flying through the air in his rage, "The disrespect in this council is outrageous!"

Mary exhaled in shock, "Indeed," she agreed before rising from her seat at the head of the table and standing as straight as her aching back would allow.

"I cannot help but note disdain in your tone, my lord Earl of Hertford," she said, her voice eerily calm, "And in yours, my lord Cromwell."

Cromwell shook his head bewilderedly, as though he were battling with himself on how to reply. He settled for no reply at all, and Mary began walking slowly around the council table.

"Upon my coronation on the morrow," she said slowly, "I shall become your reigning monarch. My husband is to be crowned as my consort. Just as I was crowned *his* consort in Scotland. We are our own country's rulers, with our respective titles of 'consort' in the other's," she shrugged and stopped behind Cromwell's seat, placing her hands on either of his shoulders, "It is quite simple, really. Or do you continue to misunderstand?"

There was a beat of silence within the council chambers, a silence Mary could feel was vibrating with contempt and disregard. And she did not like the idea of simply *hoping* that these men's minds would change.

There was too much at stake.

"You are dismissed, Cromwell," she said then, breaking the silence, "You, too, Seymour."

The two men bowed their heads, rose from their seats with unnecessarily loud scrapes, and began to quit the chambers.

"Do not think to show your faces in my court again, gentlemen," the queen called after them, and the two men turned back around, their eyes narrowed in confusion.

"Oh," Mary said, "Did you fail to understand? *Again?*" she tutted mockingly, "My lords, your dismissal is permanent. You are no longer a part of my Privy Council or my court. And if I hear so much as a *whisper* of a plan to usurp me, I will have your rotting heads decorating the Tower of London quicker than you can say '*savage king*'."

1st October 1538

It was the morning of her coronation, and Mary felt jittery with excitement.

This day would mark a glorious change in the history of England, where women would henceforth be deemed as able as any man, and she had her forward-thinking mother and father to thank for it.

Cecily and her two new ladies, Kathryn Howard and Catherine Parr, rushed around their Queen in a flurry of fabrics and shoes as the servants brought in water of lavender and rose.

Due to her heavy belly, Mary was seated before her looking glass as Kathryn Howard – a young girl brought to court by her uncle Thomas Howard the Duke of Norfolk – dabbed the sweet-scented water along Mary's neck and jawline.

"Your Grace, your husband the King of Scots has arrived," Catherine Parr informed her as she held two pairs of shoes in her hands for Mary to choose from.

Mary pointed to the comfier looking of the two, her feet being too swollen to even attempt the other pair.

Mary sighed with delight.

She and James had been in constant correspondence about her coronation, Mary even having suggested that they be crowned together as her parent's had been almost thirty years ago. But James had been adamant that this day should not be shared, for nothing should deflect even slightly from the momentous event that it was.

And Mary had loved him all the more for it.

"Never has a King of Scotland travelled so far south before," Mary said as she observed her smiling reflection in the mirror, "It truly is a day for firsts."

Westminster Abbey, London

Mary's ascension was such a grand occasion that Italian ambassadors later compared it to their annual celebration in Venice where 'the city wed the sea'.

The streets had been covered in flowers, and men, women and children alike filled the streets, some standing on walls and barrels, craning their necks to catch a glimpse of the first Queen Regnant in England's history as she was carried along in an open litter, a thousand riders escorting her through London and the cheering crowds.

Mary entered Westminster Abbey wearing a rich dress of purple velvet stitched with cloth of gold, her auburn hair hanging like a red river down her back, and an elegant gold circlet placed upon her head like a halo.

Her heart pounded hard as she entered the beautiful abbey, tears pricking her eyes as she thought of her mother and father, and the path of great loss that had led her here. She breathed in the rich scent of the incense that filled the air to calm her nerves.

All around and before her were thousands of onlookers, noble men and ladies, ambassadors to all the countries of Europe, princes and princesses of foreign lands – and among them she spotted the only one who mattered, her loyal husband.

Seeing his smiling face was enough to calm her, and with each step she took towards the altar where the bishop stood beside her throne, Mary could feel her nervousness fading away.

The coronation went by in a blur, the babe in her big belly kicking furiously throughout, and Mary smiled to think her son was dancing in her womb.

"If any man," Stephen Gardiner the Bishop of Winchester called when she was finally presented to her people in full majesty with her sceptre and orb, "will, or can, allege any cause why Mary should not be crowned, let them speak now!"

And before she could even take a breath, the people before her, as well as outside the abbey, called in unison, "Queen Mary! Queen Mary!" followed by the thunderous sound of trumpets, drums and bells ringing loudly.

The Arthurian era of peace and prosperity had come to an end, but Mary wished only to follow in her father's footsteps. She would do all in her power to make her parents proud, and to lead England into a golden age. It was time to look ahead, to the future of England with Mary as its Queen, and all that she would achieve because Arthur Tudor had been her father.

Epilogue:

5th October 1538

Queen Mary had been in confinement for just three days when her water suddenly broke.

"Something is wrong," Mary muttered wide eyed as she lifted her skirts to reveal a bloodied puddle at her feet.

"Fetch the midwives!" her lady-in-waiting Catherine Parr called before turning back to Mary, "Be calm, my queen. All will be well," and she took her stunned mistress gently by the arms and led her to the bed.

Just moments later, the darkened rooms of the birthing chamber were alive with movement and sounds, the many midwives fluttering to-and-fro boiling water, dabbing at Mary's brow, fetching linens, and preparing ointments.

"What is that?" Mary asked, her lip curled up in disgust, "It stinks!"

"It is for the pain, Your Grace," the midwife applying the offensive salve to Mary's belly said, "In a moment you will be glad for it."

And the midwife had been right, for not long thereafter, her body was convulsing with contractions.

"Cecily!" Mary called in agony as she pushed with all her might.

"I am here, Mary," Cecily said, stepping forward from the corner where all three of Mary's ladies had been praying in silence, "I am here. Do not worry."

Mary breathed a shaky laugh as the contraction abated for a moment, "Worrying is all I have done for so long," she admitted, "I fear it is in my bones."

Cecily shook her head and firmly took Mary's hand in hers, "You are surrounded by people who love you, who would do *anything* for you."

The two women looked into each other's eyes, both of them knowing how true it was for Cecily.

"Thomas More appears to be a good man," Mary said, deviating from the subject they knew they could never again broach for as long as they lived, "With his guidance I will not falter."

Cecily smiled, "I believe you are right," she agreed.

Another contraction ripped through Mary then, and as she pushed, the midwife at the foot of the bed let out an excited chuckle.

"I see the head!"

At that, Mary's chest burst with relief. It had been real. It had all been real. And soon she would get to meet her very own heir, the one who would one day reign over a unified England and Scotland.

"One last push, Your Highness," the midwife said as two others stepped closer to catch the first glimpse of their future monarch.

Knowing the end was near gave Mary a burst of strength, and with one deep inhale she pushed with all her might. And just seconds later her baby was born.

"It's a girl!" the midwife called, Mary falling back against the cushions, dizzy with exhaustion.

Her babe squealed then, an angry little cry which filled Mary's heart with a love that was unmatched.

She reached out her hands for her, "Let me hold her," Mary whispered, her cheeks wet with tears of joy and her voice cracking with emotion. And as her bloodied, wailing little newborn was cradled against her chest, the gloom that still clung onto the edges of Mary's world suddenly fell away, the inexplicable joy of holding her child in her arms proving that even in the deepest darkness comes the dawn.

10th October 1538

Three hours before his daughter's christening, James King of Scots knocked at the doors of his wife's birthing chambers, caring little for ancient traditions deeming a woman unclean to be seen by their own husband after having given birth. What utter nonsense!

"You cannot enter, Your Grace," one of the queen's ladies – Catherine, was it? – tried to tell him. And he was about to tell her where to shove it when Mary's voice called out from behind her to let him in.

James refrained from smiling at her smugly, knowing it would gain him no favour in this court, where it appeared humour was lacking.

Catherine Parr stepped aside and allowed him entrance, and James headed straight towards the four-poster bed where Mary sat propped up against her many cushion, looking exhausted but as beautiful as on the day they met.

"My queen," he said, "I wanted t' come sooner but thought it best to let ye rest."

He leant over her and kissed her firmly on the lips, and Mary heard the young Kathryn Howard gasping with delight at the display of affection.

"I hear we have a wee girl?" James whispered as he broke away, an excited grin on his face beneath the red beard.

Mary nodded, her cheeks flushed at her husband's delight, "She is strong."

"Of course she is!" James called, turning to search the room for a crib, "Strong like her mother. Where is she?"

Just then, Mary's wetnurse entered from the adjoining room with their little daughter bundled up in fresh swaddling.

Mary watched from the bed as the wetnurse handed James their infant, a look of pure amazement on his face.

"She is tiny," he whispered, not wanting to wake her up, "And her eyelashes, so white!"

Mary grinned and nodded.

"What shall we call her?" James asked as he moved closer to the bed and sat down on the edge of it.

Mary leaned forward and gently stroked the perfect dome of her daughter's fuzzy red head, "I was thinking after my mother. Or yours, perhaps."

James nodded as he considered the two names, "Both strong names," he agreed, then looked over at his wife, "But would naming her after *her* mother not be better suited?"

"Mary?" she replied with a slight frown.

"Aye," James said with a smile pulling at the corners of his mouth, "Mary, Queen of Scots."

Mary breathed a chuckle then as she rested her head on her husband's shoulder and they both looked down at what their love had created.

"You forget yourself, James. This child will grow up to become Mary, Queen of Great Britain."

Author's notes & acknowledgements

This alternative version of Tudor history has been in my heart for quite some time, and I am so very glad to have been able to bring it to life.

Of course, this is a work of fiction. However, I wanted to give credit to some real-life events that really did occur, such as Katherine of Aragon's struggles with child loss and infertility, Mary I's title as first Queen Regnant of England, the passing of the Act of Poisoning, among other things.

I am happy to say that most characters in this story really did live through the Tudor era, some of which had very similar fates even with Arthur Tudor as their king; while others such as Anne Boleyn, were able to pursue a different path. Prince Artie and Princess Alice, however, were completely fictionalised.

I hope you enjoyed my take on what would have become of Harry had he not been King of England, his devotion for Catholicism and his original wish to pursue priesthood being completely true. His demise was something I believe we all perhaps hoped for a little, though I did feel some sadness in writing it, this version of Harry Tudor having been just that little bit less awful than the Henry VIII we know him as today.

As ever, I want to thank my husband for brainstorming with me despite having little to no interest in the Tudor era. I want to thank my best friend for reminding me that 'I can do this' when I felt defeated, and for telling me when a character I created is hot, and when one is not. I want to thank my mum for always being so supportive and for reading the first draft, chapter by chapter, in email format. I also want to thank everyone who has been telling me how very excited they have been for this book – I sincerely hope the wait was worth it.

www.ingramcontent.com/pod-product-compliance
Lightning Source LLC
Chambersburg PA
CBHW030541080526
44585CB00012B/217